B-29 Superfo
Combat Chronicles

Written by Bob Hilton

Stories of the men of the 40th Bomb Group
of the 58th Bomb Wing

Squadron Signal Publications

Cover Art by Don Greer

(Front Cover) The lead aircraft's bombardier releases his payload and calls "Bombs away!" Following aircraft loose their bombs when they see the leader has dropped his ordnance.

(Back Cover) Flying from India and China, Major Dan Roberts's crew and, above him, Major Woodrow Swancutt's men are at bombing altitude and inbound to target.

About the Combat Chronicle Series

Volumes in the *Combat Chronicles* series bring you action-packed, eye-witness war stories, interviews, and first-hand reminiscences from the front lines. The wartime history of a particular type of aircraft, vehicle, or vessel is recounted systematically from the factory to the field of battle, through the reports and recollections of the former crewmen.

Hard cover ISBN 978-0-89747-673-7
Soft cover ISBN 978-0-89747-672-0

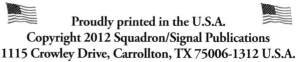 **Proudly printed in the U.S.A.**
Copyright 2012 Squadron/Signal Publications
1115 Crowley Drive, Carrollton, TX 75006-1312 U.S.A.

Military/Combat Photographs and Snapshots

If you have any photos of aircraft, armor, soldiers, or ships of any nation, particularly wartime snapshots, why not share them with us and help make Squadron/Signal's books all the more interesting and complete in the future? Any photograph sent to us will be copied and returned. Electronic images are preferred. The donor will be fully credited for any photos used. Please send them to:

Squadron/Signal Publications
1115 Crowley Drive
Carrollton, TX 75006-1312 U.S.A.
www.SquadronSignalPublications.com

(Title Page) B-29s fly supplies to POWs in Japan after the end of hostilities in August 1945. (40th Bomb Group Collection)

Acknowledgments

Grateful thanks to the 40th Bomb Group Association for providing copies of the *Memories* publication, in which Group personnel recounted their experiences. Very, very special thanks go to William A. (Bill) Rooney, who edited the entire *Memories* series for the 40th Bomb Group Association. Bill was G2 officer in the 40th and briefed every photo mission flown during the Group's tour in India and China. A very good, personal friend of the author, Bill has been enthusiastic in support of writing this book He urged the use of any or all of the Memories chapters that would help "tell the story of the brave men of the 40th." Sadly, Bill died during the writing of this book in late 2011. We are also grateful for the support and assistance provided by the staffs of the New England Air Museum (NEAM) and the Admiral Nimitz Museum. Thanks are also due to daughter-in-law Joan Hilton, who did much of the typing and grunt work during the initial stages of preparation.

Dedication

The book is also dedicated to the memory of all those who served with the 40th, 444th, 462nd, and 468th Bomb Groups, as well as those with Boeing, other companies, and the AAF personnel who participated in the development of the B-29.

B-29-1-BW serial number 42-6242 was delivered to the Army on 2 November 1943 and assigned to the 468th Bomb Group, 794th Bomb Squadron, at Smoky Hill Army Air Field, Salina, Kansas. The aircraft departed with its squadron for the China-Burma-India (CBI) Theater in April 1944. (National Museum of the United States Air Force)

Prologue

In the late 1930s, events were unfolding in Europe and Asia that compelled U.S. political and military leaders to begin preparations for an imminent, large-scale war.

In Asia, Japan was expanding its empire with increasing aggressiveness. It had occupied China's island of Taiwan (formerly known as "Formosa") and the entirety of Korea before the First World War. Then in 1931, the Japanese invaded and occupied the northeastern provinces of China, collectively known as Manchuria

In 1932 Japan attacked China's largest city, Shanghai, and forced the Chinese military to withdraw from the city, in which they then installed Japanese garrisons.

In the summer of 1937 Japan launched an all-out invasion of China south of the Great Wall, occupying many major cities and great swaths of territory and forcing the Chinese central government under Chiang Kai-shek to evacuate Nanjing, the country's capital, and relocate to Chongqing far to the west.

When Germany under Adolf Hitler invaded Poland in 1939, a major European conflict erupted that would soon engulf virtually the entire globe, including the United States.

As the world slid inexorably to war, the United States began planning for needs of updated military equipment required to wage a modern conflict. Much of the armed services equipment at that time was vintage materiel related to World War I. Many of the Army Air Corps (AAC) aircraft were still of the "open cockpit" type, although two modern bombers – the B-15 and B-17 – had been built and were being tested. AAC commanders, led by Gen. Henry H. (Hap) Arnold, believed that a more advanced bomber was needed to counter the new, technically advanced equipment being fielded by potential U.S. adversaries. At Gen. Arnold's instruction the AAC began planning a new type of bomber that was to incorporate the following minimum capabilities:

1. A combat range of 5,000 miles,
2. An airspeed of 400 miles per hour,
3. High-altitude capability,
4. At least a 2,000-pound bomb carrying capacity.

At the same time changes were also being made in the overall military structure, as respects the development and use of aircraft. The Army Air Corps, which had been a part of the Army Signal Corps, was made an independent branch of the Army and was redesignated The Army Air Force (AAF).

The Boeing Aircraft Company was the manufacturer of several types of prewar commercial aircraft as well as some AAF aircraft including an early 1930s fighter plane. (Fighter planes were then called "pursuits" rather than "fighters" hence the "P" designation as in P-38, P-40, etc.) Boeing also developed the B-17 Flying Fortress which was subsequently used extensively in the European theatre of war. Boeing was invited by the AAF to begin the design and testing of an aircraft to the new bomber type specifications. The new bomber was dubbed the Superfortress but was officially designated the B-29. AAF personnel selected for the B-29 program would be receiving an elite assignment. In April 1941 the AAF placed an order with Boeing to build 150 of the new aircraft. Subsequently, the original order was increased to 250. With a firm order for 250 aircraft in hand, Boeing began the manufacture and testing process.

When Japan attacked Pearl Harbor, the order for the B-29 was doubled. Early models were designated XB-29 and then YB-29 (the latter referencing aircraft to be tested by AAF personnel rather than

Robert Hilton, the author of this volume, entered the U.S. Army Air Force (USAAF) Aviation Cadet Program in 1943, following graduation from high school. At boot camp a classification officer became aware of the author's interest in photography and determined that he be sent to the AAF's Photo School in Denver, Colorado. Following graduation from Photo School, Hilton was assigned to the 40th Bombardment Group at the Pratt, Kansas, Army Air Base. Unknown to the author at that time, Pratt was one of the four original training bases selected for training in the newly developed B-29 program. Although theoretically the B-29 was still "secret," everyone in the Air Force was aware of the aircraft and considered it to be an elite assignment.

Boeing employees).

During the design and testing phase the new aircraft incorporated, in addition to the original specifications, newly designed more powerful engines, new electronics, i.e., first airborne radar, electronic gun controls, and aircraft pressurization. Pressurization allowed crews to operate free from the heavy, fur-lined flight suits and oxygen masks that were needed for high-altitude flying until that time. Each of the newly designed engines provided power equal to that of a railroad locomotive. The new engines were, however, to become the source of many of the B-29's operational problems, some of which continued to plague the aircraft throughout the war.

Early in the Boeing test period (February 1943) one of the test aircraft suffered engine failure, crashed, and killed Boeing's most experienced test pilot (Eddie Allen) and his crew. To meet

With its sleek fuselage, large bomb capacity, impressive performance, turbo-supercharged engines, and long-range capability, the B-29 Superfortress epitomized American air power in World War II. Boeing's Renton, Washington, plant turned out this example, B-29A-30-BN serial number 42-94106.

AAF production demands, Boeing established two manufacturing facilities at Renton, Washington, and one each at Wichita, Kansas; Marietta, Georgia; and Omaha, Nebraska.

The 40th Bombardment Group came into existence in early April 1941. The new Group was formed, and subsequently stationed, in Puerto Rico. The Group was then flying B-17- and B-18-type-aircraft, patrolling and protecting the Panama Canal. Subsequently, the Group was stationed in Panama and the Galápagos Islands. In 1943, the 40th was reassigned to the U.S. to begin training to fly a new aircraft still under secret development. New AAF Bases to provide aircraft and equipment testing, as well as personnel training for the new aircraft, were established in Kansas at Salina, Pratt (where the 40th was assigned), Great Bend, and Hayes.

The story begins as a combination of the development and operation of the B-29 by Boeing and the 40th Bombardment Group, Very Heavy (VH). No snub is intended with respect to the other B-29 Groups or the other Kansas locations. Those Groups participated in the same pattern of development and operation as the 40th. It is simply that this writer was an active member of the 40th, after having been assigned to the 40th at Pratt in August 1943. I remained with the Group until October 1945 and my own personal experiences, not only at Pratt but also throughout operations in India, China, and on Tinian in the Mariana Islands, form the basis of this book. A considerable amount of the writer's personal outlook and activities inevitably comes through and hopefully will be forgiven by the reader. It is also the intent of this book to reflect as much as possible the personal feelings and outlook of the people involved. To that end, many sections, some of them fairly extensive, are derived from the first-hand, personal accounts that members of the 40th Bomb Group contributed over the years to the unit's newsletter *Memories* and from a few book-length memoirs, all of which have been made fully available to me.

My own time in the military was almost entirely involved with the B-29 and I became a part of that program just as it was getting started.

At the conclusion of my training at the AAF's Photo Training facility at Lowry AAF Base in Denver, Colorado, I received travel orders to report to the AAF Base in Pratt, Kansas. I was to proceed to Pratt on my own initiative but in the quickest manner possible. Approximately 75 miles west of Wichita, Kansas, the city of Pratt was a wheat farming community of some 2,500 people. After the war began, the AAF built a huge air field at Pratt to be used for training personnel. I was elated when I arrived at the Pratt base and found that it was one of the B-29 training bases.

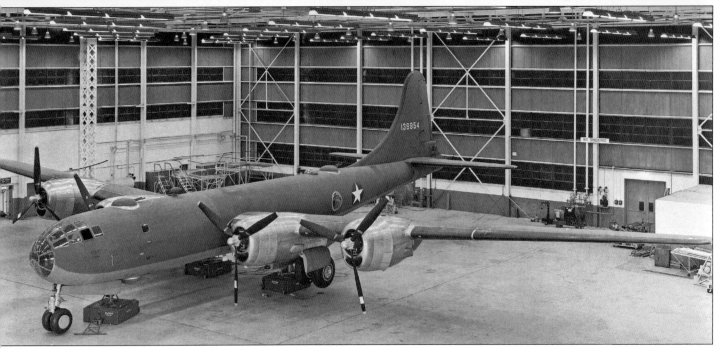

The first XB-29 on the portable scales at Boeing during June of 1943. The General Electric remote gun turrets have been installed, as well as new engine cowlings for the Wright R3350-13 engines. (Peter Bowers)

Many of the 40th's pilots and air crews were checked out in the YB models of the B-29. In early production, not enough '29s were available for full training and some war weary B-17s and B-26s were substituted for training purposes. Although the B-26 was a twin-engine aircraft, it did have the B-29's tricycle landing gear configuration as well as similar engine power and wing loading characteristics. The B-17s were four-engined heavy bomber aircraft and were deeply involved in the European Theater of War.

As WW II expanded to include both the USA and Japan it became obvious the longer flight distances demonstrated the B-29 to be the ideal aircraft for the war against Japan. Political ramifications grew to include China and other Southeast Asian nations. As a result, the USA, led by President Franklin D. Roosevelt, committed to the Chinese leader, Chiang Kai-shek to bring as much military action and damage as possible to the Japanese homeland. Such actions were to be staged, to the extent possible, from China. Training for these purposes accelerated with a goal of having the B-29s in action against Japan by early 1944. Thus, intensified training of personnel and increased production facilities for B-29 operations in China were established in mid-1943.

The increased pressure to begin combat operations, as indicated above, led to what later came to be termed by B-29 personnel as "the Battle of Kansas." The intent of that "Battle" was to have both trained personnel and adequate numbers of aircraft available to meet the operational target date. The result was 24/7 hours and days for trainers, trainees, and equipment suppliers. The target date was met but at greatly increased cost of future combat operational efficiency, including losses of both aircraft and personnel.

Victor Agather and M.E. "Red" Carmichael provided a detailed description of the "Battle of Kansas" in all its complexity in the 40th Bomb Group Association's newsletter in September 1986.

"The origin of the problem and the sequence of events which resulted in the Battle of Kansas are manifold but can be summarized," Agather wrote. "The loss of the prototype B-29 in February 1943 redoubled the necessity of freezing production design on both airframe and engines with the knowledge that modifications would have to be made after production of each B-29 was completed. Therefore, the system of modification centers, to be supplied by modification kits, was instituted.

"After the complete airplanes came off the production lines, they were taken to modification centers where they were matched with modification kits, and installed systems were removed from the aircraft and replaced with modification kits. The whole purpose of this system was not to stop the production line of the B-29's, but whenever a modification could be scheduled in the production line without stopping the line, it was so programmed by serial number of aircraft, and the kit was dropped from the modification center as the production line picked up the modifications.

"Col. Carl Cover, who had been a vice-president of Douglas, was placed in charge of modification centers. This theoretical approach of both production and modification made sense, but in practice it broke down rather rapidly because there was a substantial time lag between the training of people at the modification centers, the matching of the kits with the aircraft and the return of the completed aircraft to the four bases in Kansas for the staging of the aircraft for the combat crews. As the modification centers dropped behind schedule and the combat crews did not have B-29 aircraft for training purposes, the decision was made to switch the modification from the modification centers to the four bases in Kansas; that is: Salina, Pratt, Great Bend, and Walker, and in so doing, the crews could become familiar with the aircraft and its modifications as well as assist in the test flying of the aircraft

The Boeing XB-29 experimental heavy bomber evolved from a progression of Boeing designs of the late 1930s that had culminated in the Model 345, which was that company's response to a January 1940 Army requirement for a very-long-range heavy bomber capable of meeting the demands of any foreseeable war. Already on the fast track for a deal with the Army because of its design work and experiments on heavy bombers in the 1930s, Boeing received an order on 24 August 1940 for two prototypes (serial numbers 41-002 and 41-003) and a static test model of the Model 345, redesignated the XB-29. The army ordered a third prototype on 14 December 1940, serial number 41-18335, shown here. All three prototypes were built at Boeing's Seattle, Washington, plant. (Stan Piet Collection)

after modification. Once again the flaw in this thinking resulted in the 'Kansas Blitz,' as within a short period of time, there was not a flyable B-29 in Kansas and utter confusion reigned. In the transfer of the aircraft and modification kits from the modification center to Kansas bases the continuity of modification was lost. The kits became separated from the aircraft to which they belonged, the modification logs were incomplete, and in the end nobody knew exactly what modifications were to be accomplished. Furthermore, the B-29 ground crews had already left for India and there were no adequate ground crews at the Kansas bases to accomplish the modifications, provided anybody knew what modifications had to be made on any given aircraft. As you can easily see, these were the basic ingredients for an explosion which took place, which involved General Arnold, General Myers, the B-29 Group Commanders and the Base Commanders, as well as everybody either directly or indirectly involved in the B-29 program.

"If you will pardon the personal references, maybe I can tell the story in a little more lucid form. Whereas I had been working on the engine fire program at a very early stage in the development

of the B-29, the 'B-29 Project Office' at Wright Field was the central clearing agency for the requests by the various organizations demanding modifications, such as Air Corps Flight Test, 58th Bomber Command, Electrical Laboratory, Boeing Engineers, Armament Section, Power Plant Section, etc. Thus, all of us identified with the B-29 Project Office were somewhat familiar with all the requests for modifications as well as those finally approved to be incorporated in the B-29. We all knew that an explosion was about to take place, but that was somebody else's problem.

"Early in February 1944, I received a call from Col. Erik Nelson at about 2:00 o'clock in the morning, telling me to get my tail in the saddle and get out to Salina immediately with a list of all serial numbers of B-29s as well as modifications required by serial number, and that General Bradshaw's airplane was standing by at operations to bring me to Salina immediately. Upon arrival in Salina early that morning, we were informed of the ungodly confusion that existed at the four bases and that nobody knew just exactly what modifications had to be made in any given aircraft. In the meantime, all the airplanes were grounded. We split the four bases between several

The third prototype XB-29, serial number 41-18335, speeds above the clouds over the Pacific Northwest. Unlike the first two prototypes, this aircraft had the semi-spherical gunner's sighting blisters that would appear on production B-29s, but at the same time it retained the teardrop-shaped aircraft commander's blister aft of the cockpit canopy. (National Museum of the United States Air Force)

groups of us and four of us immediately flew to Pratt, Kansas, where the 40th Group was stationed, and I started to check each aircraft personally to make a complete list of modifications that had to be made to put each aircraft in flight condition. I went five days and five nights without going to sleep. By the end of that time, we knew exactly what had to be done on each aircraft. In the meantime, the group of four of us had to identify the kits for each aircraft and then locate the kits. After having completed the list we flew to Boeing, Wichita, one night and walked down the production line and as we saw an individual who might be doing the sort of work that Pratt required, we merely pointed to that individual and he was immediately taken off the production line and driven to the airport where a C-47 flew him to Pratt. In the meantime, the name and address of the individual was taken, a car was driven to his home to pick up his clothes and advise his family, and these were also sent to Pratt. In all, we took almost 400 individuals from Boeing, Wichita.

"The additional problems at Pratt, as well as in the other bases were that we had basically only two hangars; therefore, the bulk of the work had to be done in the open on the ramps. It was mid-Winter with dust and snow flying and bitter cold. These crews could

only work on the airplanes for approximately 20 minutes. Then they went into the hangars to warm up while other crews came from the hangars to do the work. Thus, we worked 24 hours a day. We had all the additional problems which are inherent with such an emergency operation, housing, food, clothing, tools, disgruntled laborers, etc. However, General Arnold had told General Myers and Col. Nelson and anybody within earshot that we had priority for anything we wanted in the form of tools, materials, personnel, etc., which priority we used judiciously. For example, at Pratt we had almost 100 engines that had to be changed as the airplanes had the old type engines. One night, we located engine slings in Erie, Pennsylvania. An American Airliner was ordered to unload its passengers. The engine slings were cut with torches, and loaded over the seats of the DC-3. The next morning the pilot, copilot, and stewardess, red-eyed from all-night flying, arrived at Pratt. We welded together the engine slings and proceeded to start out the engine change program. Engines were flown in cargo planes together with many of the other accessories and tools which were needed.

"As the Kansas Blitz developed, it became only natural that many swivel chair generals and other authorities wanted to get in on the

Two Olive Drab and Neutral Gray-camouflaged YB-29s fly in formation during the flight-test phase. The YB-29 was the service-test version, built to production standards and equipped with the General Electric central fire-control (CFC) system, including four remotely controlled machine gun turrets. Also present was a tail turret with two .50-caliber machine guns and a 20mm M2 Type B cannon. Fourteen YB-29s, incorporating serial numbers 41-36954 to 41-36967, were built under U.S. Army contract AC-19673 at Boeing's Wichita Plant Two. The YB-29s' Wright R-3350-21 engines initially powered Hamilton Standard three-bladed propellers, but these were later replaced by four-bladed propellers. The first flight was on 2 June 1943, and flight testing was conducted jointly by Boeing and the U.S. Army Air Forces. (National Archives)

act and make 'Brownie points' with their superiors, as they would be the ones to try and take the credit for solving the problem. Within a three-week period of time, more than 60 generals arrived at Pratt alone, offering their services, but really they were a menace because they knew nothing of what had to be done. One particular incident may be of interest to you. As I was in the bowels of a B-29, I was informed that General 'so and so' wanted to talk to me. I merely sent word back that if he wanted to speak to me he could climb into the B-29 and he could have a conversation with me. I could see him through the Plexiglas. A beautiful pressed uniform and all the characteristics of a 'dandy,' with the exception of perhaps a swagger stick. Just from his appearance I knew that he did not know how to climb into the nose section of the B-29 without a ladder and there was no way he was about to, but very shortly thereafter, I was informed that I was being cited for insubordination with a possible court martial. When I reported this to Col. Nelson, he immediately took up the matter and the last I heard was that the General was relieved of duty and sent to Greenland to cool off.

"By some miracle, we completed the work on time and the 40th Group left for Newfoundland on Easter Sunday in April 1944. There were four of us performing this task at Pratt – Lt. Col. Harry Hubbard, Lt. Col. Mark Maidei, Captain Arthur Borden, and myself, I believe I was a Major at that time. The four of us shifted from Pratt to Great Bend, Walker, and finally Salina to see the last B-29s. Shortly after the B-29s arrived in India, operational problems began to multiply themselves, principally over the engine heating problem, and we went to India with additional kits to set up pilot operations for modifications at the four bases there. We did work with the R-3350 engine overhaul plant in Calcutta (today spelled Kolkata) and the Hindustani Aircraft Company in Bangalore. I must say that the cooperation we had with the India B-29 crews was fantastic. Subsequently we moved to the Marianas – Saipan, Tinian, and Guam – and performed the same function.

"In summary, you must remember that normally a prototype aircraft is basically built to test the flight characteristics of the plane, that is, performance in the air, speed, altitude capability, load-carrying capacity and range, as well as these general flight characteristics under different types of operational conditions. Thus with the loss of the prototype and the basic freezing of design, the combat crews became a test bed to the B-29 in actual combat operations. Generally speaking, a prototype is always re-designed after flight testing to accomplish two basic factors: one, ease of production and two, ease of maintenance. Just as one example, the original cowling in the prototype was called an envelope cowling, whereby in order

B-29A-5-BN serial number 42-93865, in the foreground, has received its inner wing assemblies, with the outer wing assemblies yet to be installed. On the next B-29A in line, the gap between the wing and the fuselage has been closed with aluminum skin. In the background are stocks of tail and fuselage sections, awaiting their turn to be installed.

to remove the cowling to get at the maintenance of the engine it was necessary to remove the propeller and then remove the cowling. Thus, it was almost easier to change an engine than it was to change spark plugs. If you want to have poor maintenance, make it difficult for the mechanic to get to the accessories to be maintained. This cowling was subsequently changed to split cowling and thus maintenance was much easier. Probably an interesting sequel to the above is that when the Russians got their hands on the four B-29s that went into Siberia they copied the prototype with all the problems that we had incorporated into the prototype aircraft. After the war, an Air Attaché from Russia came to my office in New York and showed me pictures of the Russian version of the B-29. My only remark was: 'I am sure that the Russian mechanics cursed and swore at their aircraft as our mechanics had cursed and sworn at our B-29s at the difficulty of getting to the accessories to be maintained.'"

In February 1986, M. E. "Red" Carmichael, a crew chief, recalled:

"Much has been said, and I'm sure much will be written about the Battle of Kansas. To me as one of the original crew chiefs on the B-29 at Pratt, it didn't seem to be that great a hardship. We crew chiefs were used to the many hours in the cold, trying to get the 'Big Bird' ready for flight.

"It was quite a change for the flight crews, who, up until that time, had only to climb into the aircraft when we finally decided it was ready for flight. The following episodes are not intended to throw aspersions at the flight crews who had taken over the chore of trying to get the "Big Birds" ready for flight. They did remarkably well under the conditions they had to work in.

"Capt. William Hunter and Capt. Robert Tisserat and their combat crews were assigned to No. 250. No one on Hunter's crew had worked as a maintenance mechanic, but Hunter was an ex-engineering officer, and I thought he would be an asset. Tisserat had one man who had worked on B-17s and B-24s and was also a good maintenance man. Tisserat said he had worked as a maintenance man when he was a Corporal.

"So, we started. One combat crew was assigned to day and one to night shift. The first task I assigned to Tisserat was the removal of all four carburetor air scoops, I cautioned him to take a good look at all the control cables going to the carburetor, as he would have to disconnect them to remove the air scoop. He assured me that he would have no trouble, and he started working on No. 2 engine while I assigned various chores to the rest of his crew. Some time later, he came over to me and said, 'Let's check this one first to be sure everything is correct.' He dutifully informed me that everything

A scene that would terrify the Axis leaders – American productivity. Boeing built a total of 3,960 B-29s between September of 1942 and May of 1946, including these Renton-built B-29As with the four-tun top turret. (David Menard)

was O.K., but I checked everything in the nacelle and said, 'You watch the throttle arm and mixture controls, while I move them from the cockpit.'

"I went to the engineer's station to work the controls. The throttle was O.K., but I couldn't move the mixture control. I climbed down from the engineer's position and up the maintenance stand at No. 2 engine. I had to tell the Captain that he had crossed the mixture control cables. He didn't argue with me; just asked me how to correct the error. I told him and Bob: 'You did great on the other three engines.'

"We were changing all the brakes, inspecting the wheels, and repacking all the wheel bearings. Capt. Hunter and his crew were furnishing the muscle. We worked the right side, and I explained how to change brakes, pack the bearings, inspect the wheels, etc. Then we went to the left side, removed wheels and brakes, and installed new brakes. Then Hunter said, 'Go home, Sergeant, and get some rest.' I agreed to this suggestion, but I asked, 'Can you manage to finish this without any problems?' In his superior, captain's manner, he informed me it would be no problem. So, I left. This should be the end of the tale, but when Hunter and crew took the aircraft out for a taxi test, the left-hand outboard brake started to leak fluid. After pulling the aircraft back to the maintenance stand, jacking it up, and removing the wheel, I found the inner and outer bearings had been interchanged. Lesson No. 1: Bill, it can't be done!

"During the modification program, all engines on No. 250 were replaced. All we had were problems with engines overheating and failing due to inadequate lubrication. Our Squadron Commander,

Lt. Col. Cornett, decided we should remove all engine rocker box covers, fill the cavity around the rocker arms and push rod housings with oil. So, we dragged the aircraft into the hangar, removed all the rocker box covers, and started filling the upper cylinder cavities and push rod housings with engine oil. Col. Cornett decided this wasn't enough: we also had to get oil into the lower cylinder cavities. How? We froze engine oil in a bucket, using CO_2 fire extinguishers, then pushed the tarry, gooey mess into the cavities and slapped on the rocker box covers!? You should have seen that combat crew with crap all over their hands, face and clothing. Col. Cornett, that was a good idea for the upper cylinders; but when the oil thinned out and we pulled the props, we lost most of that lower cylinder oil.

"Another crew was assigned to service all fuel tanks for the entire Squadron. When they came over to No. 250, they proceeded to drag the fuel hose and nozzle from the rear side of the aircraft over the aileron. (This was at night.) I immediately started yelling at the guy up on the wing, questioning his ancestors, etc., for pulling that hose over the aileron. Clarence Bradley, a flight engineer, started trying to quiet me down, saying, 'Sarge, that's Major White. You don't yell at majors.' I informed him that I yelled at anyone that dragged fuel hoses over an aileron.

"When we were getting ready for our first 'after mod' flight, the putt-putt (auxiliary power plant) went haywire. So we had to order another one, which, after some time, was delivered to the aircraft. Capt. Vic Agather came with it. A. C. Denny and I uncrated the new putt-putt. I removed the spark plug and poured some oil into the spark plug hole to lubricate the cylinder walls. Vic immediately

The B-29, without a letter suffix following that designation, was in essence characterized by a feature that was not visible on the exterior of the aircraft: a joint between the left and right wings inside the fuselage. The B-29s were assembled by Boeing-Wichita, Bell-Marietta, and Martin-Omaha, but not by Boeing-Renton: those aircraft were designated B-29As. Here, B-29-25-BW serial number 42-24464 appears with only the national insignia and tail number for markings. The -BW suffix stands for Boeing-Wichita; B-29s from Bell-Marietta carried the -BA suffix, while those from Martin-Omaha had the -MO suffix. Preceding the manufacturer's suffix was the production block number: on the aircraft shown here, it was from the 25th production block. Production blocks were typically numbered 1 or multiples of 5, but there was an exception: a production block suffix numbered 26, for example, represented the 25th production block with a design revision. (Stan Piet collection)

The seventh YB-29 was experimentally fitted with an ERCO ball turret in the nose, and twin gun turrets on the fuselage sides that had been developed for the Convair PB4Y-2 Privateer and B-32A Dominator (Peter Bowers)

informed me that the putt-putt would never run. I bet him a dollar it would, and I'd even let Denny start it. He agreed. So, Denny and I installed the putt-putt in the aircraft. I told Denny he was going to be the operator and to turn the engine over several times before starting it. I climbed out of the tail section, and Vic told me again that it won't start. We exchanged a few opinions as to why it would and why it wouldn't. About this time Denny turned the putt-putt over electrically and it started immediately. Vic, Denny, and I sure enjoyed that beer we bought with your dollar!

"We are now getting the aircraft ready for our overseas travel. The bomb-bay rack is installed; all gear is aboard. I've serviced the aircraft, and I have started a preflight inspection with the help of Art Denny. Jerry Noble, the flight engineer, is up on the wings (which are icy), dipsticking the fuel tanks. Denny and I hear the clatter of the dipstick as it hits the concrete, and Denny yells, 'I'll get it for you, Lieutenant.' Noble yells back, 'Never mind; I'm down here with it.'"

Waiting for their next mission, B-29s rest in the parking and maintenance area of the Chakulia air base in India. (40th Bomb Group Collection)

From the beginning of the War, and continuing through 1943 and 1944, there were no facilities or bases of operation, even with the increased range of operation provided by the B-29, from which to reach Japanese homeland targets. Consequently, B-29 operations were to be conducted from primary bases in India and China. From the forward bases combat operations could be conducted over Japanese-held areas in Southeastern Asia. Indian bases provided access to bases in China from which combat operations could be taken to Japan proper as well as to Japanese-occupied Manchuria, Taiwan, and Japanese occupied areas in eastern China.

India Base

Inasmuch as no land road or railway was available to access China from India, all equipment, materiel, and personnel used or required in China had to be flown over the "Hump." The "Hump" consisted of the Himalaya Mountains that separated India and Burma from China. The "fly in" requirement resulted in combat operations from China being much less frequent than was desired as well as limiting target selection to the southern geographical area of Japan. It also required the B-29s to be loaded in India with bombs and other operational necessities, to fly over the "Hump" to the forward bases, and then to refuel and proceed to the selected target. The B-29s would then return to the China bases, again refuel, and return to India. In late 1944 and early 1945 the acquisition of the Mariana

Islands in the western Pacific allowed for B-29 combat operations to be conducted not only over all of the Japanese homeland but also to operate much more efficiently and with greater damage effect on the southern islands of Japan.

The route from the training bases in Kansas to India ran from Kansas to Gander Bay, Newfoundland; to Marrakech, Morocco; to Cairo, Egypt; and thence to India. In addition to normal crew needs, each B-29 carried in a bomb bay, a spare engine in event a change of engine became necessary. Some aircraft were two weeks or more *en route* because of necessary engine changes. Bases were established for each of the Groups near the eastern city of Kolkata ("Calcutta"), near the northern reaches of the Bay of Bengal. These Groups and locations were:

40th Group – Chakulia
444th Group – Dudkundi
462nd Group – Piardoba
468th Group – Kharagpur

The combined four Groups were, for operational purposes, designated the 20th Bomber Command. Direct command of the B-29 operations was retained by AAF Headquarters in Washington, D.C., much to the chagrin and disappointment of existing operational Commands already located in the Asia and Pacific area.

A forward base for each Group was established in China near the southwestern city of Chengdu (formerly spelled Chengtu).

Local commercial traffic would pass through the air base at Chakulia. (40th Bomb Group Collection)

As indicated previously, there was, at that time, no land route to reach China, although the Burma Road and Ledo Road were under construction. Chakulia was a small village some 70 miles or so west of Kolkata (formerly "Calcutta"), India. More to the point, Chakulia was almost exactly on the opposite side of the world (12,500 miles, 50 hours flying time) from Kansas and much closer to the Equator. Chakulia was surrounded by flat land and was encased by jungle. The jungle consisted primarily of bamboo rather than the rainforest flora normally thought of as "jungle." Prior to our arrival, the Chakulia Base had been home to a P-40 Fighter Group and, prior to that, a B-25 Light Bomb group. Burma (today Myanmar), just across the Bay of Bengal to the east, was largely occupied by the Japanese.

Having just arrived in Chakulia from the USA and *en route,* where secrecy about the B-29 and our movement was paramount, We were astounded that Chakulia town was virtually a part of the air base and that the native population could wander through the base at will. Much local labor was used for both construction and base services. We were later to learn our advance base in China was

to be much the same. In any event, Tokyo Rose, the temptress voice of Japanese propaganda radio, announced our arrival, the date, the name of our commanding officer, the number of B-29s, etc. Later in the war, Rose would announce the arrival of individual replacement B-29s and crew names. So much for the secrecy and security! It was said (rumored) that the jungle contained elephants and tigers as well as other colorful wildlife. Some China-Burma-India veterans also said that the CBI was the only theatre of war where you could be shot by a Japanese infiltrator, bitten by a cobra, or eaten by a tiger; all just while walking to and from the latrine. I don't vouch for the accuracy of the vets' statement, but I was then at a very impressionable age and I thereafter attempted to limit my visits to the latrine to daylight excursions.

Our base at Chakulia was within the range of Japanese bombers located in Burma and we were protected by British anti-aircraft batteries. The Japanese only made one excursion to hit our base (Christmas night of 1944) but hit nothing of any consequence. The Brits' AA crew seemed to enjoy nighttime target practice, making it an almost nightly affair that didn't lend to sound sleep on our part.

The local town was virtually a part of the Chakulia air base and native commercial traffic and residents could freely wander through. (40th Bomb Group Collection)

Soon after the 40th's arrival in India we were delivered a new B-29 with the name *Eddie Allen* painted on the nose. Allen of course was the Boeing test pilot killed in a crash of one of the prototype B-29s as mentioned earlier in these pages. The story accompanying the new B-29 was that the plane had been paid for by deductions from the salary of Boeing's employees in Allen's honor and they wished his name to remain on the plane. The plane was assigned to Capt. Ira Matthews and his crew and the name was retained as requested.

Subsequently the *Eddie Allen* was sufficiently damaged by Japanese fighters and ack-ack that it was retired to the salvage yard. A second B-29 was again christened "Eddie Allen" and it was severely damaged over Tokyo and was retired from combat operations. Both crews survived.

The Hump

Flying "the Hump" was such a distinct feature of operations in India and China that I have elected to treat it separately, drawing on a chapter included in the book *Remembrance of War,* which J. Ivan Potts wrote and published in 1995.

Shortly after joining the 40th in India, Potts was assigned his first trip to the 40th forward base in China. He described the event: "It was a trip that I certainly didn't look forward to but knew it was coming. I'd already talked to other pilots who had previously flown the Hump, and had learned a good deal about the Hump. I learned that no two trips were ever the same.

"Only those who flew the Hump realized what an accomplishment it was to fly from India, across northern Burma, into China above the most rugged terrain in the world. There was so much danger involved that B-29 crews were later given combat credit for the flight."

Potts continues: "I knew the accident rate was appalling and that we were losing almost as many planes over the Hump as in combat. There were no weather stations. The maps were sketchy at best about where the mountains were and what their elevation was. There were only some non-directional radio beacons and only two low-frequency radio ranges between Chakulia and Chengdu, China. The maps had vast areas that were completely blank. One of our jobs would be to try to map these areas as we traveled back and forth to China over the highest mountains in the world.

The original B-29 named *Eddie Allen* sits on the field at the base in Chakulia, India. The "M" on the vertical stabilizer reflects the aircraft's assignment to Capt. Ira Matthews and his crew. (40th Bomb Group Collection)

"The weather was the worst in the world. Clouds came in from the Indian Ocean, turned into thunderheads that towered over the highest peaks. One hundred mile an hour winds and severe up and down drafts buffeted the airplanes till the rivets sometimes popped. Ice getting thicker and thicker on the wings slowed the airplanes and limited their ability to climb out of the turbulent weather.

"The weather over the Hump changed from minute to minute. The trip was begun in the hot steamy jungles of India and ended on the cold snowy mile-high plateaus of northwestern China and between lay the deadly mountains. When you entered the clouds there was no way to climb over them. They reached well over 30,000 feet. Planes caught in the drafts up and down could rise and fall over 3,000 feet a minute. Looking at the clouds, there was no way to measure the turbulence inside. In addition to the severe icing, there was terrible sleet and hail in the storms.

"On a sunshiny day the emerald green jungles looked extremely peaceful. The prospects, however, were that most all crews that bailed out were never heard from again. To the south in Burma were the Japanese. To the north lived headhunters who made slaves of some prisoners and ate others. Flyers were afraid to ask themselves what the chances were if they had to bail out in the Hump area. They already knew the answer: poor.

"We departed Chakulia in the morning, very heavy and loaded with gasoline. We took off at dawn because of engine overheating and the cool air would give us better lift. Our flight plan called for 5,000 feet to Cooch Behar in East Bengal and thence to Jorhat in Assam at the same altitude. There was a Range Station at Cooch Behar and a radio beacon at Jorhat.

"Our flight took us over eastern India which later became East Pakistan and Bangladesh. The land below was brown and dusty, with an occasional brown pond and a few trees and shrubs. The thatched roofs of the huts blended in with the countryside. Soon we crossed the muddy and polluted Ganges, the sacred river of India, less than 300 miles north of Calcutta.

"Soon also we passed over Manir Hat, 30 miles south of Cooch Behar, in eastern Bengal. Cooch Behar was one of our check points with a landing strip. At Manir Hat we took up a heading of 74 degrees toward Tezpur and Jorhat, our next check point.

"The land below us gradually changed as we moved into the Assam valley and along the Brahmaputra River. The valley was a beautiful green. The Bengal and Assam Railroad ran along to our left and there were cultivated fields of rice everywhere. To our north lay Tibet and mountains over 25, 000 feet, including Mount Everest and a myriad of snow capped peaks.

"As we crossed Jorhat radio beacon, we began our climb to 21,000 feet. We were now turning to an almost due easterly direction. We were running into scattered buildups of cumulus clouds and we couldn't always see the ground. We were heading for Lijiang (formerly called "Likiang") and the highest point of the Hump.

"Just east of Jordat were the Naga Hills, named for the headhunters who lived in this uncharted area. Further east, an abrupt wall of mountains rose to over 12,000 feet. Further on we crossed the Upper Chindwin River. Below us was a thick, lush jungle. Crews lost in this area were never heard from again. They could wander forever in the dense undergrowth, till they died, or if they were found by the natives they would be enslaved or turned over to the Japanese.

"Now we had to be certain of our position. Fifty miles to the

A B-29 takes off on the first mission out of the Chakulia base in India. (40th Bomb Group Collection)

north were mountains 25,000 feet high. We were flying a narrow roadway 500 miles long and 50 miles wide. We and the Air Transport Command had lost over 400 planes on this stretch over the Hump.

"Soon we would cross the Kumon mountain range. We were between Fort Hertz in the north and Myitkyina (pronounced, Mish-in-naw) to our south. A while later we crossed the Mali and Nmai Rivers which form the Irawaddy and flow south all the way to the Andaman Sea.

"In looking down through the scattered clouds we were amazed with the land we saw. Every bit of tillable soil in these mountains and canyons is in use. Every bit of every mountain is covered with terraces from the bottom up to 10,000 or 11,000 feet. They are emerald green in beautiful patterns. Not much exists above 16,000 feet. Above that life line the mountains are brown and ugly with patches of snow in the shadows. As we look the north, the mountains disappear in a blue velvet haze. Even the snow is blue in the shadows.

"Ahead of us is one after another mountain range running in a northern and southern direction. Between each range are awesome canyons, thousands and thousands of feet deep. In each gorge flows a yellowish brown river.

"Approaching the highest ranges of these mountains, we cross the Salween River. Its gorge is something like 14,000 feet deep. We wonder how the myriads of people exist in this area. This is the area named by the transport pilots, 'the Rockpile.'

"We cross the gorge of the Mekong and cross the radio beacon at Lijiang (formerly spelled "Likiang," in Yunnan Province, China). There is no room for error here. The mountains tower above us just to the north of Lijiang. We sure are glad there some visibility today.

"There is a landing strip at Lijiang. It was very short and at 8,100 feet elevation, a B-29 might get in there but would never get out again."

"Here we turned to our heading for Yibin (then spelled "Ipin," in China's Sichuan Province.). We were maintaining 21,000 feet because there were 19,000-foot mountains below us. Shortly toward Yibin we ran into a solid wall of clouds, extending from the ground to infinity above us. We hoped there wouldn't be too much icing although there was extreme turbulence.

"After about two hours of the turbulence in the clouds, the air smoothed out. We crossed the Yibin beacon at 21,000 feet. The peaks around Yibin ranged from 14,000 to 15,000 feet but they were not supposed to be. At Yibin we took up a heading for Leshan ("Loshan") and began a let-down to 17,000 feet. As we crossed the Leshan radio beacon we called Chengdu ("Chengtu") and came under their control.

"With all the traffic going into Chengdu we were held in the instrument pattern along with other B-29s, C-46s, B-24s, and C-47s. It was nerve wracking,, being up there in the clouds with four different kinds of airplane, each with a different airspeed and two pilots with all kinds of varying experience and judgment."

"We were now being worked down with all the other airplanes. 500 feet at a time, using the Xinjin ("Hsin-Ching") radio range. When we got down to 1,000 feet, Chengdu control advised us to start our instrument approach and we broke out of the overcast at less than 500 feet. After landing we saw wrecked airplanes everywhere. We taxied to the turn-around on the runway. It looked like the largest airplane junkyard in the world.

"On top of that, the runway was covered with hundreds of Chinese coolies. I thought we could have to land on top of them but miraculously they parted and all moved to the side as we touched down.

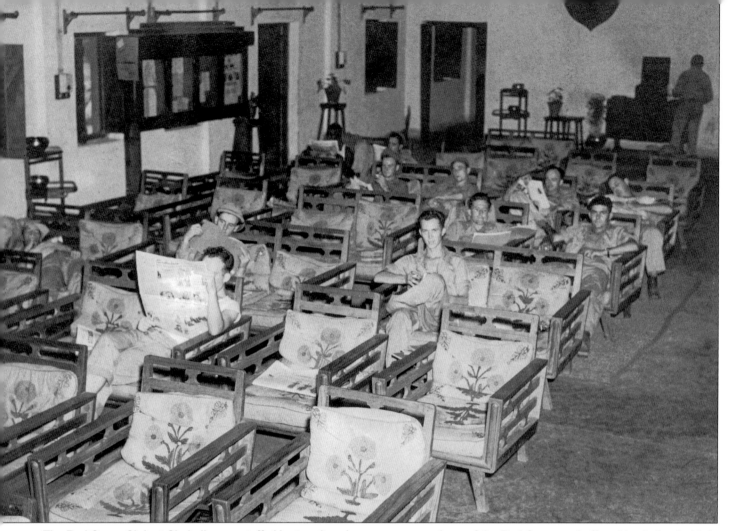

The Red Cross Club at Chakulia was staffed by two American women members of the Red Cross and offered basic food, drink, and books and magazines to servicemen. The menu featured hamburger made from ox meat and the available soft drinks were mostly local Indian varieties. (40th Bomb Group Collection)

"After landing we taxied to the turn-around at the end of the runway, turned left into the revetment area for B-29s, parked and our ground crews began pumping our precious gasoline into 55 gallon drums.

"We had landed at Xinjin, which was one of four B-29 bases clustered around Chengdu, China. Our field was 22 miles southwest and was code-named A-1.

"On this flight our flying time had been five hours and 50 minutes. We had beaten the average flying time of six hours but not by much."

There is little to add to Ivan's description, it is quite typical of the Hump flights but as Ivan noted "no two trips were ever the same" The writer can attest to the fierce up and down drafts.

There were occasions when a 500-pound bomb would snap loose at the bottom of a down draft and fall through the bomb bay door. There was one occasion when I was snoozing peacefully, stretched out on the floor of the rear compartment. Beside me was a heavy equipment part (an engine supercharger, being brought to A-1) we were taking to China. Suddenly I awakened plastered to the top of the compartment, the supercharger still beside me. The next instant I was thrown to the floor as the plane hit the bottom of the down draft and was immediately thrown upward again on an updraft.

Then there is one other intimate detail of service aboard the B-29 that deserves recounting. Because of the pressurization system of the B-29, the traditional military aircraft urination system (a tube extending outside the plane from a funnel-like device inside the plane) wouldn't work and was not installed on B-29s.

Instead, each aircraft carried a portable metal toilet about the size of a 10-gallon can in each of the pressurized compartments. It was a "rule" of the Air Force that the first crewman to use the john was responsible for emptying and cleaning it at the end of the flight. You can imagine that there was a tremendous effort to control the need "to go" and, if no one had use the portable facility in-flight, there was a very quick departure from the aircraft on landing. It couldn't have been done quicker even with evacuation slides – and then there might have been a danger of exploding on thumping into the ground, too!

China Base

As indicated previously, with the 40th's main Base at Chakulia, India, the B-29, bomb laden, could only reach Japanese-occupied areas in Southeast Asia from Chakulia. To reach the Japanese home islands the 40th Bomb Group established a forward base in Western China. Even with forward base in China the bomb-laden B-29 could only reach Okinawa and Kyushu, the southernmost of the Japanese home islands as well as Manchuria and Taiwan ("Formosa"). For reconnaissance, without bombs the B-29 could reach the Philippines and most Japanese home islands. The advance Base was designated A-1 in Air Force parlance and was also the 20th Bomber Command headquarters in China. A-1 was located near the village of Xinjin ("Hsin-Ching"). The nearest large city was Chengdu, some 20 miles

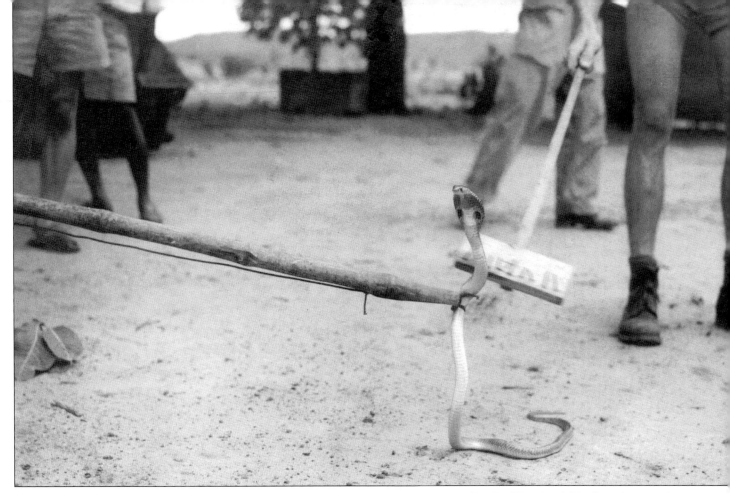

When unwelcome intruder appeared outside the mess hall on the Chakulia air base, Charles Kissel quickly rigged up a cobra-catching device out of a long pole and some string. (40th Bomb Group Collection)

away. Chongqing ("Chungking"), the wartime capital of China, was some 90 miles to the southeast. The upper reaches of the Yangtse River curved around A-1. The eastern area of China was occupied by Japan, as was China's northeast ("Manchuria"), in addition to Korea (to the north) and Indo-China (to the south).

Unoccupied, or free, western China, was totally cut off from its western Allies by the "Hump" (the Himalaya Mountains) on the west and by Japanese occupied territories to the north, east and south. The Burma Road was under construction from Assam in northern India through the mountains to Kunming in China but, during the time that the 20th Bomber Command operated in China and India, construction had not been completed. No railroad line existed either. As also previously indicated, the result was that every drop of fuel and every needed supply of any kind had to be flown over the Hump. Only agricultural crops grown in China (food) and hand labor were available "on the ground" in China. Some 20th Bomber Command personnel were permanently detached for service at A-1, but many personnel were transients, flying into China for missions and then returning to India between missions.

The 14th U. S. Air Force, commanded by Gen. Claire Chennault, was permanently based in China, though not at any of the B-29 Bases. The 14th was an outgrowth of the famous Flying Tigers. It consisted primarily of fighter aircraft (P-40s) and B-25 medium bombers. The 20th did depend on the 14th's fighter aircraft for Base protection from Japanese bombers. Also at the bases were U.S. Army anti-aircraft units. As with the 20th Bomber Command all the permanent units in China were totally dependent on air supply delivered by the Air Transport Command (ATC).

Construction of the forward bases, each with a single 8,000-foot runway, was accomplished by Chinese manual labor. There was no mechanical equipment, no cement or construction materials available. All labor and such local materials as were available were provided by the Chinese Nationalist Government headed by Chiang Kai-shek. The labor force consisted of 150,000 Chinese laborers. The runway was constructed of packed rock; each rock was hand selected and hand carried from the riverbed to the runways. The hand-carried rocks, between the river and the Base, were in two baskets suspended at each end of a pole carried across the shoulders of a Chinese laborer. Once delivered to the runway site, the rocks were hand fitted together and pounded into a hard, relatively smooth surface. Eventually, enough cement was flown in to build a couple of concrete rollers to be used to smooth the surfaces of the runways. Each roller measured some eight feet in diameter and 12 feet long and was pulled and pushed by about 200 Chinese laborers.

It was about this time the writer received a box of cookies from his girlfriend back home, which he had been hounding her for since arriving in India. Naturally, the cookies were shared with buddies, who came to the unanimous opinion that she should immediately forward her recipe to the Air Force for surfacing of the Chinese runways. Her nose became somewhat out of joint when informed of the recommendation. She blamed the concrete-like consistency of the cookies on the long trip they had made from Kansas to India.

Because of the construction methods and materials, runway maintenance was a daily, ongoing affair, requiring what appeared to be thousands of laborers to be constantly on the runway and taxiways. It was always a concern on approach for landing whether the laborers would clear the runway ahead of the landing plane (same on takeoff). Generally the laborers did clear the runway,

A sight every B-29 crew member welcomed – Iwo Jima-based P-51 Mustangs appearing in the scanner's bubble as everybody heads for home. Mustangs and Lightnings with drop tanks were the only fighters with long enough legs to fly escort for the Superfortress. (USAAF)

dividing to the runway sides in front of the plane as it rolled along, and then reuniting after the plane had passed.

Pilots were particularly nettled by one particular activity of the laborers. Apparently many local Chinese believed they were born with a personal dragon that followed them throughout their life causing no end of trouble. They were therefore always seeking some method of ridding themselves of their dragon. One of the methods was to dash across the runway right in front of the landing or departing B-29, just clearing the plane but leaving the invisible dragon to be fileted by the B-29's props. This dragon slayer method may have had some credence if you were a dragon believer. Those who were successful in losing their dragon were highly regarded by their buddies.

In China the home away from home for 20th personnel was called a hostel. Indigenous to the area, the hostels were made of a stucco mud type material over bamboo with a thatched roof. Windows did have coverings and doorways actually had doors. Floors were dirt. Each hostel would sleep 40 or so men. The toilets were similar to the old four-holers of pioneer days but were emptied each morning by area farmers for farm field fertilization. Each hostel did have a shower room for which water would be heated over an open fire in 55-gallon drums in which aviation gas had been brought over the Hump (normally the empty drums would be taken back across the Hump to be filled for another trip). The

hot water would be mixed with cool water in a wooden bucket. The bucket had a shower head in its bottom which was opened after the hostel attendant had hoisted it over the showeree's head with a rope and pulley. One bucket per shower for each man! The hostels were not heated. Weather and daily temperatures in China were much, much cooler than India and in winter months were quite cold. Personnel were issued kapok filled sleeping bags to carry to China. The bags were mummy shaped and after slipping into the bag, it was zipped up, leaving only a nose opening. The bags were really quite toasty and, when tossed on a straw mattress, were quite comfortable. Getting out of the bags into the cold morning was another matter and many airmen slept in their flight suits. Both the hostels and mess hall were very, very clean and well scrubbed.

Food in China was wonderful compared to that in India. Since it was all locally produced, all the food was fresh. Pork, chicken, eggs and all kinds of vegetables and fruits were available. The mess hall was staffed with Chinese cooks and waiters. Eggs could be ordered cooked to individual tastes.

Gasoline was primarily brought up from India by the ATC flying C-47s, the military version of the DC-3s, C-46s, and cargo versions of the B-24. A few B-29s were converted into tankers, using 600-gallon bomb bay tanks. On arrival at A-1, the tankers would taxi to a large, metal, above-ground tank at the end of the runway and the gas would be hand pumped into the tank.

An early-model B-29, converted for transportation of cargo and personnel between India and China, prepares to leave Chakulia. (40th Bomb Group Collection)

Arriving for a mission, the B-29s would taxi to the tank for fueling then to a hardstand (a hard-surface parking area) to await the mission. Bombs would have been loaded into the bomb bays in India. There always had to be sufficient fuel for the mission and for the return to India. The dollar cost of transporting full support for missions was not the total cost by any means. On one occasion the writer observed a B-24 tanker on approach. The aircraft failed to make the end of the runway and crashed into the river. With several hundred gallons of gasoline aboard, a huge fireball erupted and there were, obviously, no survivors.

Security was a problem in China and our planes would be circled at all times by armed guards provided by the Nationalist Chinese Army. The Bases were visited by Japanese bombers on a number of occasions; the Japanese always seemed to know when B-29s were in residence. Available information indicated there was a substantial number of Japanese paid subversives in the area and when the Japanese bombers came in (always at night) there would be signal fires ignited leading them directly to the runway. After dropping his bombs, the Japanese bomber would often turn on his bomb bay lights, apparently to be sure all his bombs had dropped. Some damage was done to B-29s, buildings, runways and taxiways but there was never a known fatality. The damage to planes and property never seriously hampered actions.

Generally our personnel thought very highly of the attitude of the Chinese people. No matter their situation or condition they always seemed to have a smile and a thumbs up: "Ding hao!" ("the very best!").

They also had a great sense of humor – all the while picking your pockets. The American dollar, specially marked for use in China, was the unit of currency we used. Flight personnel were issued a "pointee talkee" (Chinese/English phrase book) for use in the event of a bailout of the plane. It was of little use for conversation with the Chinese about the base, since it contained phrases such as "I am an American flyer, 100 American dollars for you to hide me from the Japanese and take me to your nearest China soldier."

Time spent in China accomplishing or supporting missions never allowed us to stray from A-1 and public transportation in China was zilch. On the Base there was a very limited number of jeeps and small trucks but nothing for off-base use. There were trains in some parts of China but they served mainly as targets for fighter planes (Japanese or U.S., depending on location).

There were few buses (always occupied by 100 or so Chinese it

Sgt. Raleigh Johnson encounters Lord Louis Mountbatten, Supreme Allied Commander of the Southeast Asia Theater, who is visiting the 40th Bomber Group to bid the unit farewell prior to its departure from India. Mountbatten asked the 40th Bomb Group about where the British should send the bill for the destruction of the British-built dry dock in Singapore. The 40th had destroyed the dock, which at the time was being used by Japanese occupation forces.

seemed, each one carrying a pig, chicken, etc.). Also available were ox carts, wheel barrows (for both cargo and passengers), rickshaws and sampans (if you happened to be going the same direction as the river). Ever thought of being wheel barrowed 22 miles to Chengdu? The small village of Xinjin did have a few shops and restaurants, but few bought anything and especially did not sample local cuisine. A local type of orange wine was available but was also little sampled.

In our last days in India we were visited by the CBI Theater of War Commanding Officer, Lord Louis Mounbatten of the British Forces. He came to express the gratitude of the British Forces for the work we had done, particularly in Southeast Asia, which they felt greatly assisted the British recapture of Singapore from the Japanese. The British were grateful, but they were also anxious to know where to mail the bill for one of their dry docks we had sunk in Singapore Harbor. It seems it was a prewar dry dock built and used by the British but used by the Japanese after they captured Singapore early in the war. A factual story! Lord Mountbatten did award numerous decorations to personnel of the Group.

First Mission

After all the various 40th Group personnel and equipment were assembled in Chakulia in early April 1944, it took roughly 60 days to prepare for the initial mission and for the combat induced loss of our innocence to begin.

The first combat mission flown by B-29s was flown from bases in India on 5 June 1944. The initial mission was to be a "milk run," – in reality a training mission. As with any "milk run," if the milk isn't handled quickly, with efficiency and hand-in-glove coordination with other parts of the process, the milk can sour very quickly. And "sour" was the results of the first mission. The mission was a daylight bombing mission to the Makason Rail Yards in Bangkok, Thailand. I was not scheduled for the first mission. Initially I was very disappointed not to have been scheduled, but I was able to rationalize that feeling as the mission developed.

Departure takeoff was scheduled for early daylight on 5 June.

Bob Gaughan looks out the copilot's window prior to flying the war-weary No. 254 back to the United States in 1945. One of the very first aircraft completed and delivered to the AAF, this B-29 arrived in an olive drab paint scheme and was used for crew training at Pratt. It was then flown to India and converted into a tanker for delivery of fuel to the China base. Numerous crews served aboard the No. 254, which never took part in combat but flew many vital gas hauling missions over the Himalayas. (40th Bomb Group Collection)

Very early, in the procession of takeoffs, one of our B-29s crashed just after liftoff. I was awakened to the sound of the crashing B-29's impact and subsequent explosion of the fuel tanks. Except for the bombardier, who was thrown from the aircraft and severely injured, both the aircraft and crew were a total loss.

(A sidelight: the bombardier was evacuated to the States immediately for medical treatment and rehab. He was "lost" as far as address or location in the Group's records was concerned. Years later, at a Group reunion in Anaheim, California, he read in a newspaper about the upcoming reunion and walked into the meeting festivities unannounced – a reunion indeed with his disbelieving old buddies).

Back to the mission. The outbound trip was uneventful. At the mission's target, the bombs hit everything but the target. As far as the mission being meaningful to the war effort, it wasn't. Almost immediately after leaving the target area, the planes began encountering a developing typhoon, which became worse and worse as they flew back towards India. Weather reports and weather stations on which to base forecasts in that area were non-existent and it was a problem that was to plague us throughout the Group's time in India and China. Ultimately a few planes did return to Chakulia that day, but many sought emergency fields in unoccupied Burma and India. It was several days before all the aircraft had returned. Hello combat!

A total of three of the Group's aircraft were lost. One of those that failed to return was forced to ditch in the Andaman Sea. Wayne

Wiseman chronicled the 5 June 1944 incident later: "We were notified one morning to report to a certain place that afternoon for briefing. Of course, there was lots of speculation as to what the briefing was about, and as to where the target might be if it were a bombing mission. We reported to briefing and found out, much to our surprise, the mission would be the next day and the target wouldn't be disclosed until just before our departure next morning. They told us we would be doing most of our flying over water and what interception and anti-aircraft fire we could expect to and from the target.

"After briefing, everyone went to their planes and began preparing and getting the planes in the best of shape, for it was here-what we had been waiting on for a long time. I remember while I was working on a turret late that afternoon our pilot, Major Alex Zamry, came up and said, 'Wiseman, are you going to get one tomorrow?.'" (Meaning a Japanese Zero.) I told him, 'Yes sir, think I'll get two just to make sure.' He smiled and went on over to the tent to get his personal things together for the flight.

"All our regular crew was to be on the flight except our bombardier, Lt. Greenfield, who was in the hospital, and in his place we were to have Lt. Wotipka. In addition to the crew, we were to have one observer, Capt. Drislane. There were 12 men to go on the mission: Pilot Major Alex N. Zamry, Copilot Lt. Ashley Briggs, Navigator Lt. Jim W. Evans, Bombardier Lt. Barney Wotipka, Engineer Lt. Joseph Phalon, Radio Operator Joseph Harvey, Radarman Lt. Jesse C. Beal, Right Gunner Sgt. Gilbert Bleyl, Rear Gunner Sgt. William

"Bring your own stool or sit on the ground" was how seating was arranged at the movie theater on the Chakulia air base near Calcutta, India. (40th Bomb Group Collection)

F. O'Connel, and myself as Left Gunner.

"That night I guess we were all rather restless but we got some sleep and were awakened early next morning, about 2 o'clock to be exact, some to go to the final briefing and others to give the last minute check of everything. The pilot returned from the final briefing and we all lay down on our cots for a last minute rest and to discuss the target and what we expected. We found out the target was to be a big Japanese supply base. I remember our pilot commenting that he didn't sleep much for he had fought flak and fighters all night long. This tickled all of us and we had a good laugh over it.

"We all lined up in front of our plane for a final crew inspection and last minute orders from the pilot. Major Zamry then said, 'Gather around' and we all went into a huddle like a football team with our arms around each others' shoulders. The pilot said, 'Well boys, this is it and I know everyone of you are ready so lets go and give them hell, good luck!' Of course we all had a little tingle in our blood, or at least I did. We all are close to each other on our crew, but I ran around with the radio operator, Joe Harvey, and I suppose we thought the most of each other. We were always kidding each other about different things and I remember now how we were hitting each other that last morning and saying, 'Oh man, I'll live to .... on your grave.' That was just the way we were and we had lots of fun telling each other such things. (I would have given my right arm for that boy.)

"We took off and I won't say much about the target etc. I will say we gave them hell and we didn't run into much flak or interruption.

"After we had left the target a few minutes, I felt someone tap me on the shoulder and I turned around to see who it was. I was keeping my eyes peeled for enemy planes, but I turned around, and it was Joe. He asked me what I wanted to eat, a spam or peanut butter sandwich and I told him spam. He laughed and went away to get me one. He soon brought it back and I remember him saying, "Boy, I'll get your – if you let a Zero get in here on us!" and laughed. Little did I realize that was the last time I was to see him, for he left and went back to the radio compartment.

"In a few minutes, the pilot called up on the inter-phone to our tail gunner, O'Connel, who is a very good mechanic and said, 'O'Connel, the transfer system is out and we haven't enough gas to get home. Come up and see what you can do.' All of us were confident that if anything could be done O'Connel could do it. We had enough gas for about an hour or more of flight we knew and with the pilot changing R.P.M. and mixture control maybe longer. We worked on the transfer system for over an hour, all the time sweating out having to land the ship in water. After we saw it was useless and that we were going down, we prepared. All the time the pilot was doing everything he could to get us as close to land as possible which he did beautifully as long as we had any power at all.

"I won't go into detail about what we did preparing for a water landing such as getting our water ready and the position we all got in etc., for that will mean nothing to you.

"Anyway, the pilot brought the plane down and made a beautiful landing considering the high waves, etc. The copilot later told me Major Zamry was smiling up to the last. (Truly a great pilot in my estimation, and the reason the others of us are here now.) The radio

The Yibin ("Ibin") turn mountain, rising some 21,000 feet into the sky, marks the east end of the Hump. After passing to the left of the peak, aircraft turned almost due north to begin their descent towards the base named "A-1" located near Xinjin, China. Marking the turn was the first radio beacon on the China side of the Hump. (40th Bomb Group Collection)

operator was continually sending out SOS and when we started to hit the water he braced himself, for it was his job to pull the life rafts. On the contact with the water, some object hit the radio operator and that was the end of him and I presume the pilot hit his head against something, for he had no time to put a pillow or anything in front to protect himself.

"Upon hitting the water, we were blown out of the ship, all except Lt. Briggs and Lt. Phalon who escaped through a window, and it seemed it shot me under the water like a bullet for I could feel the water pressure on my chest. To be perfectly truthful, I could see the gates of hell opening up to receive me. After coming up and going down for the third or fourth time, I finally got my Mae West to inflate and could see some of the other fellows around. It seemed as if Lt. Beal and I were further away from the ship than the others and I saw Lt. Briggs and Lt. Phalon finally get the rubber life rafts out of the top of the ship.

"They began to pick up everyone which was a bad job, trying to paddle those little light rubber rafts in such waves. It seemed I was being carried further away by the waves. I saw Lt. Beal float by one time perfectly still and I thought he was gone. I kept hollering for the waves were so high I couldn't see anything and I know the boys on the raft couldn't see me. I heard Lt. Beal hollering too in a few minutes and recognized his voice, but I still didn't hear the boys in the life rafts. They (all the rafts) later told us they all paddled until they were given out, for some were throwing up blood from the salt water and some had broken bones etc. They were forced to give up getting to Lt. Beal and me and left us there to die.

"I floated around and kept hollering until nearly night for it was four thirty in the afternoon when we hit the water. I kept thinking I might hear the boys on the raft but I heard no one, not even Lt. Beal. When it became dark or just at dark, I heard some one holler and I recognized it as Lt. Beal. I yelled back and he answered. I told him to keep calling and that I would try to get to him, so we both kept hollering and I kept trying to get to him. Finally, it seemed the waves changed and brought us right together. He grabbed hold of me for he was nearly gone and he had an oxygen bottle under one arm.

"I took that and put it under his head. This brought him out of the water enough to get air. He told me he didn't think he could make it any longer for his leg was broken and so was his arm. After getting his head up on the bottle and getting a little air, he felt some better and I told him to keep holding on to my arm. I put my head up on the bottle beside his and he held on to my left arm while I held the bottle under our head with my other arm and the string in my left hand. We floated around with the waves rolling over us and kept drinking the salt water and throwing up blood. We would go as long as we could and Lt. Beal would say he had to have some air so I would tell him to hold on, and with my legs I would turn us around so our heads would be into the waves. The bottle would break part of the wave and I would push Lt. Beal up as high as I could and jump myself until we got some air. After going this way awhile, a squall came up and we thought sure that would be our end for the waves began to get higher and the sky was the blackest I have ever seen, with lightning flashing and pounding rain. We tried opening our mouths to get some rain water but every time a big wave would roll over and fill us full of salt water. Lt. Beal and I prayed that night and now as I sit here writing this I can look back and see those prayers were answered. I have thanked the Lord many times since

Xinjin village residents meet with US Army Air Force personnel. (40th Bomb Group Collection)

then and I will continue to thank him by trying to live the kind of life I think he wants me to. After this first squall, it cleared up and got fairly calm but of course we were still getting waves to cover us up. We kept on floating and wondering just when we would run into one of those sharks, for we knew they were there.

"We kept fighting the waves and the crabs that would pinch us with a terrific pinch, I had more trouble with them for my clothes were torn and Lt. Beal was weaker and so was I. It seemed now he was even delirious at times. We weathered that squall much the same as we did the other, by going as long as we could and then turning us around to get a little air. That was the longest and most dreadful night I have ever spent or hope to spend in my life.

"After we could faintly see day breaking, we decided to try to go in a certain direction for we knew land was that way somewhere but had no idea how far. We could see another squall coming up but we were on the edge of it and only got some high waves from it. We could paddle until we couldn't and then rest, and paddle some more. Lt. Beal would say he couldn't help much and then rest, and paddle some more. He had one good arm and he had to use his good leg to hold the broken one up, but I had two good legs and the cuts on me didn't bother me for the salt water seemed to have helped them so we kept paddling on and on.

"The next day about noon we sighted land and it looked like the waves were going to help us reach it, but all of a sudden the wind and the waves changed and we just couldn't get any closer. We tried and tried but couldn't do any good. It was some feeling being so close but yet so far from land. We kept on trying and about two o'clock we saw a small boat of some kind so we started toward that.

"We couldn't tell what kind of boat for the saltwater and sun, also the blows we had in our eyes, had them nearly closed so we couldn't see very well. After seeing the boat, we both were encouraged and I started paddling as much as I could. When we got close to the boat, we could see it was our own men on the two life rafts and they had them tied together. When we first saw the boat we thought it was a Japanese boat for we had no idea which way we had been washed during the night.

"We were very relieved when we got to the boat and found it was the rest of our crew. They put me in one raft and Lt. Beal in the other. They had just a little fresh water for they weren't able to find our big water can out of the wreckage. All they had was a few little half pint cans that were in the life raft, four to be exact and most of those were empty. We were in sight of land and we thought we could get water when we hit land so they gave Lt. Beal and me all the water we had and boy it was good. My tongue was swollen so much from the salt water I could hardly close my mouth. They had salvaged a kit or at least Lt. Phalon had gotten out with a jacket that contained some sulfanilimic powder and they sprinkled our cuts and wounds with that. They covered us up with the boat sail and

Despite its lack of running water, the forward base of the 40th Bomb Group in China boasted a shower room. (40th Bomb Group Collection)

kept sea water on that to keep us cool for the heat from the sun was almost unbearable, I didn't realize I was so weak or that Lt. Beal was in such a bad shape until they got us in the boat.

"We found out we couldn't get into land trying to paddle with both rafts tied together so we decided to cut loose and both try for land. The one to get there first would try to get help and come for the other. On my raft were Capt. Drislane, Lt. Evans, Lt. Wotipka, Belcher and I. They started paddling, at least Capt. Drislane, Lt. Wotipka, and Belcher did for Lt. Evans had a bad arm and I was even too weak to sit up. They paddled until they gave out and we still weren't doing any good for the tide was terrific. Right after dark, the wind started blowing and we put up our little sail and started for an island we could barely see in the distance. The raft started going off the edge of the island and nothing we could do would make it hit the island; however, in a few minutes with the wind blowing strong, we sighted another so we headed for the top tip of this island hoping to at least hit the lower tip for we were drifting terrifically and we didn't want to miss it as we had the other island.

"We hit that island but when we got close to it we could see high rocks with the waves beating against them and we knew the waves would end us if they caught and smashed us against the rock, but it was a chance we had to take. Just as we got close to the island, it

seemed a big wave just caught our little raft and put it down gently on the rocks.

"On the island, we thought we would be o.k., and could build a fire and find water. Everyone got out of the boat. Belcher had to crawl everywhere on his all fours for he had a bad leg. I tried to walk but was so weak I fell. Lt. Evans found a little open place and we all got to that. They tried to build a fire, but all the matches were wet. Lt. Wotipka tried digging to find some water that wasn't salty but that was useless. They all finally lay down to try to get some rest in order to get up early next morning and start looking for some fresh water, streams or something. We couldn't sleep for we were all wet and cold and the mosquitoes were terrible. All that night I was still passing blood from being in the salt water so long.

"At the first sign of day next morning, Lt. Evans and Lt. Wotipka started out to see what they could find and try to find some water and food. In a few minutes they came back and said there was a river not too far from us so we all got the raft back in the edge of the water and they pulled Belcher and me to the mouth of the river. The tide was just coming in and it would take us up the river a long way, maybe to a native village or up where there was fresh water. We went up the river as far as we could go and the sun was awful, but we found nothing at all and that afternoon we started back down the

Typical of the friendliness of the Chinese people to the U.S. fliers was this "Dĭng hăo!" salute by a Chinese toddler in Xinjin, the small town enveloping the 40th Bomb Group's A-1 base in China. (40th Bomb Group Collection)

river to the shore where we had stayed the night before. That was an awful day with no water. I can't explain how awful it really was.

"When we got back to the mouth of the river or whatever it was, we went back to the place we had stayed the previous night and prepared the sail etc., to catch rain water for we were hoping and praying it would rain that night. I had only my shorts on and didn't have the sail to cover in that night for we had to have it ready if it did rain. Lt. Wotipka dug me a big hole in the sand and covered me up with sand to help keep me warm. No rain that night and no sleep for any of us for you can imagine our condition.

"The rest of the time on the island was much the same, no water and we were all too weak to attempt to get in the life raft to try to paddle to another island or anywhere. We just had to hope for rain but none came. That is really a miserable feeling to want water so badly and not be able to get any. All this time we didn't know where the other fellows in the other raft had landed.

"Late that afternoon we saw a little sail boat and two natives in

it away off shore, so Lt. Wotipka took a mirror and flashed them and waved etc. They waved back and took their sail like they were going to paddle towards us but later put up their sail and went on off. This was very disappointing but we had hope they had gone back for help.

"Next morning after a bad night with no rain, we heard a whistle and some one hollering for Lt. Wotipka. We were all about done for with no water and no luck fishing. Lt. Wotipka answered and started down to the water and found Lt. Briggs and Lt. Phalon who had contacted some natives. The native chief had found an interpreter and gotten a boat and had come after us for the little native boys had told them about seeing us that afternoon before on the island. The native men and the chief had with him on the boat water and coconuts, which they would open and give us the juice. They wouldn't let me drink but a little at a time, but when I first got water I couldn't help but cry like a baby with joy.

"It seemed the other raft had landed on another island. They had been having much the same trouble as we had about finding nothing but salt water, and Lt. Beal was in the worst shape of any with pain and wanting water. They had sent out different ones to try to find water or some natives or something. They finally contacted the natives. Lt. Briggs and Lt. Phalon did as I have mentioned and they came for us and carried us over to their island by the natives to pick up the others, but when we got there some native doctors had been there for O'Connel had contacted them at a district dispensary. They then made a stretcher and started through the jungle with Lt. Beal to the dispensary for they thought that would be faster than by boat. O'Connel was already at the dispensary for they had kept him there when the natives took him there to get help.

"The natives took all the rest of us in their boat and the chief said he was taking us to his village for food and water. The natives rowed the big boat and the chief seemed to like me for he kept a piece of cloth over me to keep the sun off. We got to his village and they took us to the chief's house to give us water and make us some hot tea. The chief had me a bed fixed and they put me to bed. They asked Lt. Briggs if he wanted some fish and he said yes, so they went out in the channel and in a few minutes they brought back two great big fish and put them on the floor in front of Lt Briggs. The fish were still flapping. He said they were very nice so the natives took them and prepared us some stuff to go with it. All ate much, but I drank tea and water for I was afraid to start putting much hard food in my stomach yet. I ate only a small piece of the fish but it was certainly delicious. The natives put some of the prettiest green banana leaves I have ever seen over the table for a table cloth and the food was really clean. They were certainly wonderful to us and you should have seen them gather around me and talk to one another and point to my cuts. I will never forget those people for they did everything they could for us.

"Late that afternoon we heard a plane flying low and Lt. Wotipka ran out with the mirror to signal it, but it didn't see his signal. Later it came back and saw our signal and let us know that he had seen us. It was an amphibious plane so he landed in the channel behind the chief's hut. After finding out the plane was looking for us and was to take us to a hospital, the natives got the boat to carry us out to the plane. From the chief's house to the boat, Lt. Briggs started helping me and the old chief was white headed he was so old, but he held on to me and went right along until they put me in the plane.

"The other natives lined the shore and waved and shouted for if there was one there were hundreds out there. The natives all seemed to be enjoying the whole show and had a good time watching us take off. Guess we owe our lives to them for it seemed they came just in time, and did all they could."

Wayne Wiseman sustained a head injury in the ditching that would ultimately be the cause of his death. Shortly fter the ditching, he was returned to the U.S. and in December 1944 was given a medical discharge at Maxwell AFB.

The Group's second mission was scheduled for 10 days later, 15 June 1944. It was to be the public relations piece of the year for the Air Force and for the B-29s: it was to be the first attack on the Japanese homeland (with the exception of Jimmy Doolittle's 1942 raid) since the war began. The mission was to Yawata, Japan, and was to be launched from our base in China. The target in Yawata was an iron and steel plant and it would be a nighttime raid. Virtually every general officer and admiral in the Far East, as well as a large contingent of news reporters, were on hand. Some of the reporters

Kickapoo-II, a 468th BG B-29 tanker with 41 missions over the Hump, is pulled to its parking spot by an Army M3 halftrack. B-29 tankers were devoid of all armament except tail guns.

were allowed to ride along on the mission. Target-wise it again was not too effective. But as a PR coup, it was quite effective.

Following those initial missions, with each successive mission everyone became more proficient, both air crews and ground crews. At Tinian, 90% to 95% of the aircraft scheduled would actually complete the mission and the same percentages, 90% to 95% of the bombs would be in the target area. Between those two points there was much blood, sweat and tears – literally!

One statistical note heard years later was that the average mission life for flying personnel was 17½ missions – much worse initially, much better later. Much of the problem was related directly to the airplane and specifically to the engines. The engines were untested prior to use in the B-29 and they had a horrible tendency to overheat, gobble valves and fail on takeoff. I never knew the exact mission life statistic but my own estimate is that 50% of our losses of aircraft and personnel were the result of engine failure on takeoff, when the planes were loaded to absolute capacity with fuel and bombs.

One of my closest friends, Art Jordan, who had gone home with me for Christmas in 1943, was forced to bail out of the B-29 in China, along with all the crew, after a night takeoff and engine failure. They were a lucky crew that day, they had gained sufficient altitude to allow the opportunity to bail out. (At that time, if you bailed out and were in position to retain the chute, it was yours to keep. I helped Art fold and store his chute and later sent it to his parents.) Unfortunately, Art would later be killed in action.

In my own experience, one of my most hazardous flights occurred on takeoff from China. We were departing for a long, long mission fully loaded with fuel; including both bomb bay tanks. On takeoff (night takeoff for a day recon mission) engine No. 4 (far right) blew an exhaust collector ring, the prelude to an engine fire. Unable to shut the engine down immediately, because of the plane's weight, the pilot salvoed (dropped) the bomb bay fuel tanks. Meantime, the No. 4 engine was emitting a trail of sparks from the blown collector ring. It was hairy for a few minutes bur thankfully, there was no contact between the sparks and the salvoed tanks. The pilot was able to shut down the No. 4 engine and return for a landing. No mission whiskey when you need it; only if you successfully complete the mission! We hadn't! Sometime later (22 October 1944), we lost two aerial photographers (Jacob Bruzos, killed; Bob Dickens, permanently disabled and evacuated to the States) in the takeoff crash of another recon B-29. So many of the engines were a problem that the Air Force established an overhaul facility in India

A Chinese guard stands by B-29-10-BW 42-6340 of the 444th Bomb Group, 677th Bomb Squadron. A protective sleeve is secured over the 20mm gun barrel. The retractable tail guard is lowered; this protected the bottom of the fuselage from hitting the runway on nose-high takeoffs and landings. The rudder and elevators were covered with fabric. (Stan Piet collection)

Chinese laborers who helped construct the base at Qionglai (formerly spelled Kiunglai), west of Chengdu in Sichuan Province, China, watch as mechanics work on the *Princess Eileen,* a 462nd BG B-29-10. Bases such as Qionglai were constructed by Chinese laborers using mostly hand tools. (Dave Lucabaugh)

employing Indian mechanics. The overhauled engines were termed Bengal Engines by the air crews. No one wanted to fly on an aircraft equipped with the Bengals.

Another problem with the B-29, which began immediately upon delivery to the training Bases in Kansas and persisted throughout the war, was the nasty tendency of the Plexiglas blisters in the gunner's pressurized compartment to blow out – as in an auto tire blowout. When a blister blowout occurred the plane depressurized immediately and everything loose in the compartment was sucked out of the aircraft, including the gunner on the side of the blowout. In flight, using the guns, the gunners would unfasten their safety belts in order to maneuver the gun sights and, while doing so, they would pretty well up in the blisters. We lost a number of gunners that way during training.

The 'fix' was to attach a single long strap to the back of the belt worn by the gunner and anchor the other end firmly to the aircraft floor. The 'fix' worked fairly well but there were occasions when the blister would blow, the gunner would be dangling at the end of the strap outside the aircraft and his crewmates would have to haul him back into the aircraft. It was Rube Goldberg at large with respect to the 'fix,' although the engineers preferred to call it American ingenuity!

Takao Mission

The tragic loss of gunner Edward Hornyia on the mission to Takao on 17 October 1944 provides one example of the severity of the blister blowout problem. The special circumstances of Ed Hornyia's loss and the events surrounding this mission by *Monsoon Minnie* warrant telling, and copilot Carter McGregor did just that in his 1981 book: *The Scourge of the Fire God: the Kagu-Tsuchi Bomb Group.*

On that mission, the crew of *Monsoon Minnie* comprised:
AC: Robert Moss
Copilot: Carter McGregor
Bombardier: Fritz Kulicka
Navigator: Ralph Weinberg
Flight Engineer: Edward Haggerty
Radio Operator: Royal Klaver
CFC Gunner: Not known
Right Gunner: Edward Hornyia
Left Gunner: Not Known
Tail Gunner: Joseph Dueming
In his book, Carter McGregor relates the story: "On 17 October

Chinese officers present visiting U.S. Vice President Henry A. Wallace with a bouquet of flowers upon his arrival in Xinjin for an awards ceremony in the summer of 1944. (40th Bomb Group Collection)

1944, briefing was at 05:00, so after a decent breakfast of fresh eggs, we headed for the briefing hut, curious to know where we were going this time. When the Intelligence Officer pulled the covering off the big wall map, there was the island of Taiwan (Formosa) with the harbor installation at Takao (today known as Kaohsiung or Gaoxiong) outlined in red. The briefing officer said that we were to bomb the harbor and dock facilities in order to assist in the Philippine invasion.

"I was daydreaming about how much better off we were than the GIs and the Marines until the briefing officer got my attention, saying that the Japanese were very proud of Formosa, so there would be heavy anti-aircraft fire, and near Takao was a major base for fighters. This trip might prove to be more interesting than I wanted it to be, but I didn't know what to do about it except go and sweat.

"The takeoff went smoothly, with the usual goose bumps that were a part of a heavy takeoff. I didn't know whether I said it or one of the other crew members did, but someone muttered over the intercom, 'Come on *Minnie*,' as the four big engines were turning out 8,800 horses to get Minnie off the ground – the moment of truth when everything had to go just right to get enough flying speed to lift 70 tons of metal, bombs, gas, and men into the air. I couldn't help but think what a mess that would make, not only of

us but of the coolies still lining the runway, if our big plane were to fail to make it off.

"The bombs still had the pins in the fuses, but there had been cases when pinned bombs had been known to explode from a crash or a fire, and ten tons of high explosives and 6,700 gallons of high octane would make one giant firecracker.

"Our route was east to the China Coast, each airplane going individually. The section of China over which we were to fly was occupied by the Japanese, so our gunners had to stay on the alert for China-based Japanese fighters who might want to come up and say "hello." As usual, we did not climb to our bombing altitude right after takeoff but stayed at a lower altitude to save gasoline. We avoided the coastal installations and larger cities where there were known anti-aircraft batteries. There was no use asking for more flak than we knew we were going to get anyhow.

"Later, some of the other ships reported fighter passes over China, but even though our gunners had test fired their guns and were ready to greet any visitors, we didn't have any come to us. On this trip, we had a replacement gunner in the right blister, Sgt. Edward Hornyia, since our regular right gunner was too sick to make the mission. Sgt. Hornyia had never flown with us before, but our men knew him and said that he was a good man.

The Japanese controlled industrial area in Anshan, northeastern China comes under U.S. aerial attack on 29 July 1944. (40th Bomb Group Collection)

"We cruised on over the Yellow Sea, climbing to altitude, and the navigator was busy with position and winds aloft to get us to the assembly point right on time. We were to assemble off the coast of Taiwan, and then go over the island in formation, drop our bombs on the harbor installations, break off back over the water and head for home. With that plan, we would be over the anti-aircraft fire for a minimum of exposure.

"When we arrived at the assembly, the leader was already circling, with some other ships joining on his wing. It was to be a ten-ship formation, and we were to be on the right wing of the right element leader. The lead element was a four-ship formation, and each of the others had three ships apiece, a very good defensive formation. While we were circling, but before we completed the formation, was a very vulnerable time for us to be hit by fighters. I didn't need to call the gunners and tell them to be on the alert; they were ready. As was our habit, everyone had strapped on his chute when we started to climb and had checked all his survival gear. It was miserably uncomfortable to wear a Mae West, parachute, survival vest, canteen, and pistol, but if we needed any of that, it would be better to be uncomfortable and still have it than suddenly realize it was somewhere in the airplane. One of the two pilots and

one gunner in the rear compartment were to wear oxygen masks anytime we were pressurized and nearing the target. The tail gunner, alone in his cubbyhole, was always to wear his mask at altitude. If we had a sudden decompression, then at least one would be available to help the others, if they needed it.

"Since we were on the right side of the formation, Moss, the pilot in the left seat, would have to do most of the formation flying. He hooked up his oxygen mask, but mine was just hanging where it would be handy.

"The formation headed out, right on time, and everyone had "tucked" in real tight, but still we had not seen any fighters. As we turned from the Initial Point, we could see flak ahead, aimed at the formation already close to the target. The briefing officer had been right. The Japanese were proud of Taiwan, and the flak gunners were doing their thing. The flak bursts were black so they were too far off to do any damage, but if the bursts started turning orange and we could hear the "thump, thump," it was hard on our nervous systems.

"Still no fighters, and we couldn't understand why, but we were grateful for small favors. The flak was thick and accurate as we approached the target, and at least now we knew the fighters might

33

Reconnaissance shortly after the raid on Anshan revealed the extent of the damage done to the industrial hub. (40th Bomb Group Collection)

not hit for a few minutes since they generally stayed out of their own anti-aircraft areas.

"Our bombardier was watching for fighters and at the same time following the target in his bombsight. We were all to drop on the leader, but each bombardier was also supposed to follow through on the aiming just in case something happened to the lead ship. Fritz said, "Something is wrong-we are way off target." Just then the radio operator, Sgt. Klaver, said he picked up a message from the lead airplane that it was a bad run so the formation would stay together, go out and make a big circle, and come back in from the other direction. I wondered if we could put in for double combat pay for having to do this twice.

"Sgt. Hornyia, the right gunner, reported that he could see the airfield in the distance, and there were a good many fighters taking off and climbing to our altitude. I knew that they would get there just about the same time we returned, for it takes time and a lot of space to turn a ten-ship formation of B-29s, so our greeting committee would be on hand.

"It seemed like an eternity before we made the 180-degree turn and headed back for the target. We could see that the other formations had already hit the target and headed for home. I was ready for us to do the same.

"The lead ship started to open the bomb bay doors, so Kulicka hit his switch to open ours. I could hear the rush of the air as the doors were coming open. Fritz had already given to me the toggle switch extension to salvo the load on the leader and had set all his switches and had everything cranked into the bombsight, so now he was watching for fighters but also had one hand on his drop switch. All I had to do was watch the lead airplane, and as soon as I saw the first bomb come out, I would hit my toggle switch to salvo our load at the same time. With the formation on the other side and Moss having to do all the flying, all I could do was sit and watch.

"'Bombs away,' and *Monsoon Minnie* jumped from the released weight of our load. The flak was thick and heavy, and I heard myself muttering to the lead airplane, 'Make your turn and let's get the hell out of here.' At the same time I saw Fritz reach for the switch to close our own doors.

"The leader had just started his turn when the Nipponese greeters arrived on the scene, and every gunner started calling fighter positions. Moss was still busy, flying the formation, but I could see those nasty little Zekes coming from all directions. The best way to spot them at a distance was by their vapor trails, and then when they would get a little closer you could see the leading edges start blinking, and you knew their calling cards were on the way.

The Imperial Iron and Steel Works in Yawata, which produced a quarter of Japan's steel, had been bombed in June 1944 but with little effect. Yawata was targeted again on 20 August 1944 but this time the Japanese, aware that Yawata was a target, had prepared their defenses well. (40th Bomb Group Collection)

"Suddenly, there was an explosion, and the interior of the plane filled with fog. I didn't know what the noise was, but I knew that we had taken some kind of hit and had depressurized, causing the warm air inside the airplane to vaporize. For a few seconds, the fog was too thick to see anything, but I yelled for everyone to get on a mask at the same time I was grabbing for mine and hooking it to my helmet. We knew from past experience that if the hole in the plane was not too big, we could put something over it-a magazine, a cushion, anything that would cover the space and then the pressure would build back quickly, so I wanted everyone to look for holes.

"At the same instant, Weinberg said, 'I'm hit,' and Sgt. Klaver said, 'I'm hit too, but I can't tell how bad.'

"Right at that moment, there was nothing I could do for either of them until we got out of that hornet's nest, for the fighters were still pouring it on, and every turret on our ship was in action. I looked around me to see if we had any holes in the front end, and I just happened to look up, right over my seat, and saw blue sky through a hole about four inches in diameter, just above my head. I turned to see where the shell had hit, and there was a big scar on the armor plate behind my seat, about six inches behind me. Later, we surmised that when the 20mm shell hit the armor plate, the bullet shattered, and the fragments ricocheted back and hit the navigator and radio operator. I could not believe I was not hit too, but I couldn't feel anything hurting, although there was no way some of that shrapnel could have missed hitting me, somewhere.

"One of the lower turrets was firing a steady stream, and I yelled at the gunners, "Fire bursts. Get off the trigger of those guns."

"The left gunner came back, 'Captain, Hornyia had that turret.'

"'Well, tell him to quit firing it in steady-fire bursts.'

"'Captain, I can't. He's gone.'

"'What do you mean, he's gone?'

"'His blister must have blown, and he went out and took the sight with him, and he still had control of the turret.'

"The turret was still firing in a steady blast, so I said, 'Hit his switch and take control of the turret and then see what has happened.'

"The tail gunner, Sgt. Joe Duemig, spoke up, 'I saw him go out and watched his chute open, but some of the fighters left us and started making passes at him. I can still see him floating down.'

"We soon discovered that when Sgt. Hornyia was sucked out the opening, he knocked the gun sight off the pedestal, but the heavy

The 40th Bomb Group targets Yawata, Japan, on 20 August 1944. (40th Bomb Group Collection)

electric cable that connected with the gun computers did not break, and the slip stream of the airplane was holding the sight against the side of the airplane, depressing the trigger. Obviously, the gunner did not have his seat belt fastened or he would never have been pulled out of the plane. In his excitement about the fighters, he had unfastened his belt so that he could turn and fire more easily without being hindered.

"The left gunner took control of the runaway turret, but we were still under heavy fighter attack. Bob Moss was getting pretty tired flying formation, so I took the controls to give him some relief. The formation was still in good shape, maybe even tucked in closer than before because when the fighters appeared, it just seemed a natural tendency to edge in closer to the next guy for mutual protection.

"When we were pretty well out over the Yellow Sea, the fighters dropped off, deciding they were getting too far from home base. This gave us a chance to take stock of our injured and to determine the extent of damage to the plane. Weinberg and Klaver had both sustained wounds from the fragments, and while the injuries were painful and bleeding, they did not appear to be too serious.

"Each had been giving first aid to the other. We were not quite ready to let Kulicka go back and help them since we still might need him for nose gunner. It seemed as though the two wounded men could take care of each other for the time being. Shorty Haggerty was checking all the systems on Minnie and found that there had been other damage, primarily electrical, to the airplane, but the engines were running fine. There was a bundle of cable that had been severed, and it was impossible to determine where all the wires were leading from that bundle, so we just had to hope that they were not vital to getting Minnie back to free China.

"Moss and I decided that it would not be feasible to try to go all the way back to Xinjin, so we elected to try for an alternate field, a fighter base inside the Chinese lines. There we could better determine our damage as well as get our wounded to a doctor, so we notified the lead airplane that we were going to break off and head for Luichow (modern day Liulang).

"Even though there was still the danger of China-based Zekes coming to intercept, Kulicka went back to the navigator's station and gave directions to us as to course and distance. Klaver was able to operate his radio key, so he told our base what we were doing and where we were going, as well as alerting the fighter base that we were on the way.

"When we were ready to land, we had to sweat a little more, still wondering what all those wires were that had been cut. However, the gear and flaps came right on down just like they were supposed

When B-29s returned to Yawata in August 1944, the Japanese were already aware that it was a target and had concentrated fighters and anti-aircraft batteries around the city. Combat over Yawata was fierce.

to, with no problem, and the landing was normal.

"The ambulance met us to take our wounded, and an intelligence officer for that base was also on hand to get a full account of all that had happened. There was never any report on the fate of Sgt. Edward Hornyia; the last any of our crew had seen of him, he was floating down in his chute with the fighters making passes. We did not know whether he opened his chute or whether the force of being sucked out of the plane opened it, but in any event, his chances for survival were nonexistent.

"We were about halfway between Formosa and the Chinese mainland over the Yellow Sea when the incident occurred; and although he was wearing a Mae West, to survive the initial attack, the fighter target shooting, and then land in the Yellow Sea would have been a miracle. He was simply listed as missing in action, one among thousands during the war who disappeared with no trace, who gave their all, their lives.

"While it is impossible to minimize the tragedy of the loss of even one life, of far greater magnitude concerning the entire war effort was the evaluation of the strike photos on the Takao harbor and dock installations. Pictures taken at time of impact of the bombs showed that the entire formation dropped their bombs in the water,

with no damage to harbor facilities. Some of the other formations had done a better job, hitting the target and thus materially assisting the forthcoming invasion of the Philippines; but as far as our ten ships were concerned, the entire mission was a fiasco. In war you expect losses, but you must anticipate results, and for this trip against the Japanese, the only accomplishment for our crew was tragedy for a young man whom I did not even know. Certainly this same circumstance happened on other missions, but we cannot forget that this man died a hero as much as did anyone, although his death will not be recorded in historical archives nor in the annals of war records and deeds.

"Ralph Weinberg records his memories of the mission: On the return home, we were at least a mile behind on the left side of the formation. As a result, two Japanese planes didn't have to worry about anything but our own guns. I looked out my window and saw one airplane flying level with us and parallel, just out of the range of our guns.

"Just as I figured out he must be transmitting information to an airplane above us, the shell came through the top of the plane and hit behind Carter McGregor. The concussion knocked Carter's helmet off and blew out the right gunner's blister. Royal Klaver was

The 40th Bomb Group lost several aircraft during the Yawata raid. Major Richard McGlinn's *Cait Paomat II* was damaged and had to divert towards Vladivostok. Off course due to a variation in compass readings, the crew bailed out and began a grueling odyssey of wandering the Siberian Taiga, being interned, and finally "escaping" to Iran. (40th Bomb Group Collection)

standing slightly behind the pilot's position, trying to see what was going on since, at his radio position, there was no outside view. As a result, he picked up quite a few shell fragments on his legs.

"I was knocked off my seat by the concussion, and I picked up a shell fragment in my right foot and right calf. After a few minutes of recuperation from the shock, it was determined that we couldn't make it back to Chengdu with the oxygen and gas supply we had on board, so we were going ahead for the nearest American air base in unoccupied China.

"I checked with the lead navigator of the formation to make sure that I had the right position before giving a heading for the base. About ten minutes before my ETA was up, Moss started circling. I asked what he thought he was doing; he said he was trying to do some dead reckoning or to pick up some checkpoints. Just about that time, two Black Widows from the base came up and escorted us back to the base.

"After first aid from the flight surgeon at the base, Royal Klaver and I were lying under the wing of the plane while they were refueling it, and this jeep pulls up. A sharp-looking young lieutenant jumps out. He looks at me, says, 'You're Weinberg, aren't you?' I said, 'that's right.' He said, 'You don't remember me, but I have to salute you

now.' And he threw me a highball. He said, 'I was in the first class of bombardiers sent to navigation school, and you were our head instructor. We thought you were the most iron-assed SOB that God ever sent to this earth. We all hated your guts, but I want to tell you, I thank you for what you did because you made it possible for me to perform my duties and stay alive up to this time.' You know, that helped ease the discomfort quite a bit.

"We then proceeded to Chengdu without any problems. Royal Klaver and I were taken to the base hospital where the shell fragments were removed from us. They kept me there for two months, the main reason being that the shell fragment that they took out of my foot had lodged in a particularly sensitive place, and if I had to bail out going back to India over the Hump, I wouldn't have been able to walk out. And as a result of favoring that foot (I used a crutch for quite a while), I threw my back out, so even when I got back to India, I spent 10 days flat on my back.

"Bob Moss recalls the explosion in the plane and the events that followed: Fighters attacked us as we turned back over the Straits of Formosa heading toward China. A tremendous "swoosh" scattered papers and other items as the aircraft, at that instant, lost cabin pressure. The crew in the back reported the side blister was gone

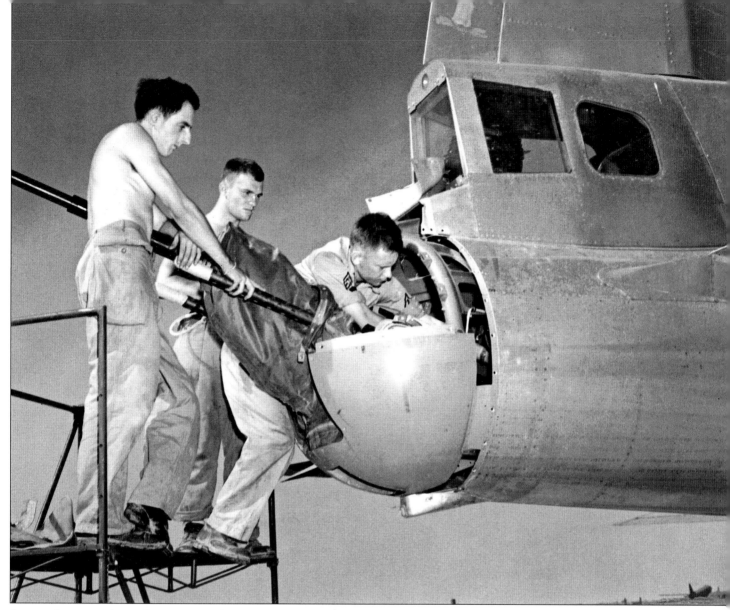

A ground crew works on the gun suite of the tail turret of a B-29 based in India. To access to the weapons, they have removed the fairing on the fuselage and the top half of the semi-spherical housing. The 20mm cannon proved ineffective and was discontinued. (National Archives)

and so was Sgt. Hornyia. A shell exploded over the copilot's position injuring Lt. Weinberg and Sgt. Klaver. Other damage to the plane involved the wiring in the bomb bay, the oxygen system, etc.

"Because of the injured crew members and the damage to the aircraft, we decided to seek a suitable place for assistance. The Japanese had taken control of the eastern part of China so, after some consultation via radio, we decided to land at Luichow.

"After landing we were told that the enemy was very close and that they would probably attack after seeing our aircraft. Hasty efforts were made to camouflage the plane and make repairs to both it and the injured crew members. This was done overnight, allowing us to depart the next morning and return to A-1."

Fritz Kulicka has vivid memories of the mission: "There was that fighter about two o'clock high. He was looking us over when I gave him a short burst from our twin fifties. The tracers bounded off his aircraft, and he must have been displeased because he dipped his wings and came at us. I could see bright flashes coming from his guns. So, apparently, we were shooting at each other. After a brief moment there was a loud explosion in our cockpit. Bob Moss sensed an explosive decompression and called on the intercom for us to immediately put on our oxygen masks.

"We were still in formation," Kulicka recalled. "After all the hell broke loose, we settled down to survey the damage. It appeared that we were hit with a 20mm explosive shell just inches above Carter's head and right in Ed Haggerty's flight engineer's position. Ralph Weinberg was sprayed with shrapnel as was Royal Klaver. Joe Duemig informed us on the intercom that our right side blister had blown away, and Sgt. Hornyia was parachuting down. Royal Klaver radioed life guard submarines of our predicament, but Hornyia was never found.

"We continued our flight to Luichow (today Liulang) and landed there. About sunset, we were called for a meeting with an Associated Press news reporter named White. In retrospect, I think it was Teddy White, the China correspondent for *Time* magazine. We were briefed not to mention our names because Tokyo Rose would pick it up and make an issue of it in her broadcasts. This did not concern us so we gave names anyway. The story was filed, and our names made all the newspapers the following day. My hometown newspaper – the *Delta Democrat Times* – in Greenville, Mississippi, carried the story.

"We departed Luichow the next day. I remember seeing trains evacuating the area with hundreds, maybe thousands of Chinese

General Curtis LeMay arrives to take over the XX Bomber Command in September 1944.

aboard. The Japanese captured the base a few weeks later."

Ed "Shorty" Haggerty remembers some hairy moments on the mission: "After leaving the target area, Mac and I had removed our helmets and were kind of leaning over to put them on the floor. Mac would have been leaning to his left and I to my right when the fighter hit us. He must have come in about one o'clock high because as we were leaning over, a shell came bursting into the cockpit right over Mac's head, hitting the armor plate between Mac and me. I believe if Mac hadn't been leaning over, he would not be with us today. As the shell hit the armor plate, portions of the shell started flying around. I think some parts hit the large rheostat for flying suits just to the right of my instrument panel. The shrapnel and parts of the rheostat all contributed to the cockpit damage and the injuries to Ralph and Fritz. After things calmed down somewhat, we began checking the systems. I found we couldn't change prop or turbo settings. With wounded on board and a sick airplane, it was decided to head for the nearest friendly base.

"After getting Weinberg and Klaver to the hospital we worked on the plane and found that the wire bundle along the front space on the left side was damaged. We managed to run down and make temporary repairs. As for the blown blister, there were, of course, no spares in China, so we found a piece of metal and by removing some blister mounting screws, we secured the metal over the forward edge of the blister hole. We hoped the air stream passing over the deflection would cause a venturi action and relieve some of the air blast into the aircraft. Back in India, repairs were made, and the aircraft was ready for the next mission.

"Just for information, my mother's name was Minnie and along with the monsoons we experienced in India, this is how our aircraft No. 6295 got its name, *Monsoon Minnie.*"

Meanwhile, back home

Meanwhile, back in the States, the author's girlfriend, CC, was having her own problems with the military. In one of her letters she described a visit to Ft.. Riley, an Infantry training base in Kansas. CC and a girlfriend whose husband was stationed at Ft.. Riley, arranged to visit the friend's husband. While the friend and her husband were visiting in the Post public reception area, CC became bored and stepped outside to sightsee a bit about the Post. CC strolled past signs reading "Off Limits to Civilians" but, never having encountered such signs in civilian life, the signs had little or no meaning to her.

She continued her stroll and was shortly in one of the Post's barracks areas. And, shortly thereafter, a near riot developed. The troops began yelling and whistling. Drilling formations fell apart. Troops were hanging out barrack windows, in all manner of undress, also yelling and whistling. Shortly, the Military Police arrived in a squadron of siren squealing jeeps. CC was surrounded immediately by the MPs demanding to know why she was in an "Off Limits" area. CC explained that she had indeed seen the signs but didn't really understand their meaning.

After further conversation, the MPs assured her they could certainly understand her confusion and they would escort her, in a jeep, back to the public area. Unfortunately, each of the MP Patrols wanted to handle the escort in his own jeep. There followed a vociferous argument among the MPs for the escort honor. Finally, an MP second lieutenant arrived and solved the Patrol's problem; he would escort CC back to the public area himself.

(I'm not sure that every word in this story is true but apparently CC made no more visits or else she now understood "Off Limits.")

Looking through the pilots side window at another 468th Bomb Group Superfortress *en route* to Anshan, Manchuria, northeastern China, on 8 September 1944. The APQ-13 30-inch radome is extended from the bottom of the fuselage. (Dave Lucabaugh)

LeMay Takes Charge

In September 1944 General Curtis LeMay arrived to take command of the 20th Bomber Command. LeMay was a veteran of the 8th Air Force in Europe. He was a leader! He instituted training and maintenance procedures which immediately began to improve efficiency and operations. He may not have been well-liked but he did gain the respect, and thanks of virtually every member of the 20th Bomber Command. Against express Air Force command tenets, he even flew some of the bombing missions. One of the results of his leadership was ordering the B-29s, on bombing missions, to fly in 12-plane formations rather than four-plane formations as in the past. The reason: better protection of the B-29s against Japanese fighter attack.

Imagine the feeling of a Japanese fighter pilot attacking a 12-plane formation, each B-29 with twelve .50 caliber machine guns and one 20mm cannon firing at him simultaneously – a total of 144 machine guns and 12 cannons each firing at the rate of 500 rounds per minute. (That would discourage the heck out of me!) Our loss rate to Japanese fighter aircraft was reduced to virtually zero. To me, inside the B-29 when the guns were firing, the sound was as I imagine it would be in a hollow metal drum with someone beating on the outside with a trip hammer – or a dozen trip hammers. The cannon had a distinct wonk, wonk, wonk sound.

As efficiency improved and operations stabilized, the 40th's missions ranged from India down to Rangoon, Burma; Bangkok, Thailand; Singapore – all up and down Indochina (including Saigon) and Palembang in Sumatra. From China, missions ranged from Shenyang ("Mukden") and Anshan in Manchuria, Nanjing ("Nanking"), and Hankou ("Hankow") in China, to all of southern Japan and Taiwan. From Tinian, as indicated previously, the entire Japanese home islands became targets. There were many people, including General LeMay, who believed the war could have been won, in a relatively short time, without the use of the "A" bomb. Initially, much of our recon was done in conjunction with bombing missions but became more and more strictly recon missions as operations and aircraft availability improved. Recons also became wider ranging than bombing operations.

Without the weight of bombs we could take on greater amounts of fuel and, without the bomb weight, use less fuel. Okinawa and the Philippines were within our recon range and, as a matter of fact, much of the mapping and recon work in support of the invasions of those islands was done by us. One of the unanticipated uses of recon was for radar mapping. Each B-29 was equipped with state of the art radar (by today's standards it would be primitive) and it was anticipated that radar might be used for bombing when a target was not visual. Trouble was no radar maps existed for targets. It fell to us to develop a system for radar target mapping, which we did, using

41

Forty-three China-based Superfortresses blast the aircraft plant and Heito airfield in Okayama, Japan, on 16 October 1944. (40th Bomb Group Collection)

an auxiliary radar scope and a 35mm camera.

The Japanese, as you might expect, took great exception to the B-29s intrusion into their plans for the future of Japan and all of Asia. They were a determined, well-equipped adversary. On almost every mission you could count on a Japanese fighter plane flying alongside us at the same altitude but outside the range of the B-29's guns. The Japanese fighter pilot was radioing altitude, speed, and direction to the anti-aircraft batteries on the ground. Normally, if we were on a single-plane recon mission, the Japanese paid little attention to us. We were high enough to be beyond anti-aircraft batteries and fast enough to be in and out before they could react.

Bombing missions were another story. They were low enough to be within range of the anti-aircraft (which we called ack-ack). The ack-ack fire directed by the tag-a-long Japanese fighter was dangerous. There was no sound, within the plane from the exploding ack-ack shells. But, I can assure you, the black puff balls of the ack-ack were not an attractive sight. We were issued flak vests and steel helmets which we were to wear in target areas – and we did. In my simple minded way; however, I would see the ack-ack exploding below us, as it usually did, and I usually placed the flak vest underneath me rather than wearing it! (I felt the "private area" was much safer with the protection underneath me.) Only one plane in which I was

flying was ever hit by ack-ack and it was a very minor shrapnel hole through a wing section.

There is the story of one much disliked colonel, an observer, on another mission which encountered ack-ack. Suddenly the colonel screamed "I'm hit, I'm hit" and threw himself on the floor of the plane. The radio operator, who was trained to administer first aid, grabbed a first aid kit and rushed over to the colonel. He couldn't find any blood or wound on the colonel.

The colonel kept screaming and pointing to his leg which appeared to be soaked with water. Turned out the colonel's canteen had indeed been hit and it was water streaming down his leg.

The colonel was quite chagrined, but the crew was somewhat disappointed that it wasn't another liquid, caused by fear, streaming down his leg. I don't mean to belittle the Japanese ack-ack. It was extremely dangerous and accounted for the loss of many B-29s.

Another incident in which I was a personal participant occurred on a Taiwan mission. A Japanese fighter came in from a high 12:00 o'clock position firing his wing mounted guns and it appeared for all the world that his intent was to ram us if his guns didn't succeed. Our Central Fire Control (CFC) gunner was countering with the four top front turret guns and suddenly the Japanese simply exploded, parts and smoke from his aircraft showered all around us,

A reconnaissance photograph of Okayama following the 16 October 1944 raid clearly shows extensive damage to the air field and surrounding area. (40th Bomb Group Collection)

but we flew through totally unscathed. (There might possibly have been some liquid in the pants of some of us that was not canteen water).

Later in the war, the Japanese fighter bombers would climb above the B-29s and drop phosphorous bombs timed to explode within the B-29's formation. The phosphorous, of course, would set fire to anything it touched. And that fact brings to mind another story.

En route to Japan the B-29s would fly singly and then rendezvous to form up at a point prior to the target. The designated formation leader had two methods by which he would identify himself to the other aircraft to form up with him. The first method was to fire a colored smoke bomb (signal). The second, then, was to lower his nose wheel until the formation was complete then he would retract the wheel and they would fly on to the target in formation. The radio operator was the person who was to drop the signal bomb through the port. The signal bomb contained phosphorous to create the smoke.

On one particular occasion, however, the procedure went horribly wrong. It was 12 April 1945 and the *City of Los Angeles* was leading the 52nd Bombardment Squadron in an attack on Koriyama, Japan. Radio operator Sgt. Henry "Red" Erwin fired the smoke bomb flare out through the port as usual, but this time, for some reason – a faulty flare or sudden air currents perhaps – the phosphorous smoke bomb popped back thorugh the port and into the plane, just a few feet from three tons of incendiary bombs. Obviously, a phosphorous bomb loose in the aircraft spelled imminent disaster.

Though blinded by the heat and smoke, "Red" Erwin, the radio operator, groped for the blazing flare and threw himself on the bomb. The cabin filled with choking, burning smoke and the aircraft began an uncontrolled plunge to earth. Erwin, his entire upper body aflame, worked the flare foward in the aircraft towards the only available opening – a cockpit window. After getting the burning canister out the window, Erwin collapsed in flames. Other crewmen put out the blaze with fire extinguishers and he was given morphine to relieve the pain. Meanwhile, the pilot, Capt. Anthony Simeral, managed to regain control of the aircraft just 300 feet from the ground, and set a course for Iwo Jima – the nearest base where Erwin could receive medical attention.

Horribly burned, Erwin was transferred to a hospital in Guam, where, completely wrapped in bandages, he was visited by General Curtis LeMay on 19 April, just one week after his ordeal. General LeMay awarded him the Congressional Medal of Honor, telling the 22-year-old sergeant: "Your effort to save the lives of your fellow airmen is the most extraordinary kind of heroism I know."

The 40th Bomb Group struck Omura repeatedly in October, November, and December 1944 and again in January 1945. (40th Bomb Group Collection)

Discharged from the Army in 1947 after enduring 43 surgical operations, Erwin went on to serve 37 years as a benefits counselor at the veterans' hospital in Birmingham, Alabama. He passed away in January 2002.

At the very end of the war, the Japanese were using what are known as "Baka bombs" to attack the B-29 formations. The Baka bomb was nothing more than a piloted, flying bomb designed to ram into the B-29 destroying both the B-29 and the Japanese pilot. The Baka was also used against Navy vessels and ground installations. A more conventional aircraft was also used for the same purpose as the Baka. The Japanese pilots of both types were called *kamikaze*. *Kamikaze,* which literally means "divine wind," apparently was the Japanese idea of an honorable suicide.

Some last stories of bravery – in India, more aircraft would be loaded with armament, including the bomb load, actually scheduled for the mission. The purpose being to have backup aircraft if, for some reason, one of the scheduled aircraft had to abort the mission. On one such mission, the bomb load included fragmentation bombs for use against Japanese ground personnel. These bombs actually consisted of a large number of very small anti-personnel bombs clustered together. There were made to spring apart before impact and spread the smaller bombs over a larger area. The spring

mechanism on the bomb was very delicate. In this incident, one of the backup aircraft not needed on the mission was being unloaded when one of the bombs sprang apart and exploded when it hit the concrete underneath the plane. That exploding bomb set up a chain reaction, exploding the other bombs and setting the plane on fire. There were six or seven crewmen killed and a very large number injured. Three other B-29s parked nearby were also destroyed or severely damaged. The base fire and medical people immediately responded as did our Group Chaplain Father Bartholomew Adler. At the scene, Father Adler immediately plunged into the maelstrom pulling out a great number of the injured, He was later awarded the Bronze Star for bravery.

In China at the time of the recon plane crash, killing photo crewman, Jake Bruzos and injuring Bob Dickens, the Acting CO was Chester A. "Red" Woolsey. Red was a pilot as well as acting Base CO. Red was in the tower when the recon plane took off. When it crashed in the nearby village, Red immediately jumped into his jeep and raced to the scene. The aircraft was on fire, but Red was able to pull Bob Dickens and a number of the crew members out. One crew member was trapped, was still alive, but Red couldn't pull him out. The trauma of that event brought tears to Red's eyes for the remainder of his life.

B-29 Superfortresses slam Omura on 25 October 1944. Badly damaged during the raid, *The Heavenly Body,* captained by Jack Ledford, goes down behind enemy lines in China. The survivors eventually make it out of Japanese-occupied territory and back to their base thanks to the help they receive from Chinese guerrilla fighters and soldiers. (40th Bomb Group Collection)

The Yawata Mission
20 August 1944

This is the story of the B-29 mission from Xinjin, a U.S. Army Air Force base near Chengdu, China, to Yawata, Japan, on 20 August 1944. The author had the privilege of making a presentation at the Nimitz Museum about the actions of the 20th Bomber Command AAF in the CBI and subsequently in the Mariana Islands. It happened that a representative of the Sino-American Heritage Foundation was in attendance and later I was asked to do a write up of one of our missions out of China so that it could be incorporated in a book being prepared by the Chinese government in celebration of the 60th anniversary of the end of the war. The book, *Fei hu de paoxiao – When tigers roared,* by Jeffery B. Greene and Xu Fan, contained similar articles by 49 other individuals, from all the countries and armed services that had participated in any action in or out of China during the war. Since its publication, that book has been available in museums in China to be used as education/research material by Chinese students. The following is an edited version of the story.

The target at Yawata was the Imperial Iron and Steel Works, which was responsible for approximately one quarter of Japan's steel production. A previous mission to the same target, the first to Japan proper since the Doolittle led mission in April 1942, had little effect on steel production. This was to be a daylight, maximum-effort mission by the 20th Bomber Command to eliminate or substantially curtail future production.

The author was a camera technician/aerial photographer attached to the 40th Bombardment Group and took part in this raid. Initial B-29 production was focused on bomber type aircraft. Consequently, aerial photographers initially utilized bomber type aircraft and, quite often, would actually participate in bombing operations. Later, some B-29 aircraft were specifically modified for recon and were designated F-13s.

The aircraft to which the writer was assigned for this mission was a bomber type B-29 named *Sir Trofrepus* commanded by Major Garth Doyle. The name *Sir Trofrepus* was a spin off of Superfortress spelled backward. "Nose art" on the aircraft showed a hairy, prehistoric type man standing upright with arms stretched overhead, holding a huge rock, which he was going to smash down on his victim. We were to be the last aircraft in a four plane diamond formation [number 4 position] which was also to be the last formation over the target area. The purpose of being last over the target was to obtain photographs of damage done to the target by preceding aircraft.

Our aircraft, including the writer, arrived at the A-1 base in Xinjin, near Chengdu, from our India base on 18 August 1944. The aircraft was fueled and prepared for the mission on the 20th. Bombs

A reconnaissance photo of Omura taken on 28 October 1944 reveals the damage inflicted by the air raid three days before. (40th Bomb Group Collection)

for the mission had been placed in the bomb bays at our primary base in India. Briefing of the crew members for the mission was held on the evening of 19 August. At the briefing we are advised the target to be bombed and other mission details such as engine start, taxi and departure times, route and altitude to be flown, time in route, bombing altitude, formation leaders, pre-bomb rendezvous point, expected weather *en route* and over the target, as well as expected fighter aircraft and anti-aircraft (AA or flak) defenses. Aircraft were to depart at 20-second intervals following departure of the initial aircraft. In this sequence, we were to be the last aircraft scheduled to take off.

Crews were awakened for breakfast at 2:30 a.m. China time, briefed for any mission changes (there were none) then transported to the assigned aircraft for aircraft and equipment checks, propeller pull through (to place oil in the engine cylinders prior to starting) and final crew inspection by the aircraft commander (didn't want anyone to be left behind, of course). After boarding the aircraft the "put-put" (internal auxiliary power unit) was started approximately 20 minutes prior to take off time, aircraft engines started and the aircraft taxied to the line-up of aircraft awaiting take off, engines are run up and a final equipment check made.

After take off, always critical for a heavily-weighted aircraft, and reaching *en route* altitude, the crew settles down for an uneventful

(hopefully) seven hours or so to the rendezvous point. Chatter on the intercom between crew members is rare during this part of the mission and is limited to necessary comments relative to aircraft/ mission operation. Smoking is heavy and residual smoke is thick. No one wants to use the "potty" because the first user, be it the commander or lowest rated crewman aboard, has responsibility to clean it after the return to base. (Nervousness can create substantial discomfort while awaiting the "first use" crew member.)

During this part of the *en route* flight, the radar operator and the navigator coordinate their talents to set our arrival at the exact location for the formation rendezvous. After takeoff, each aircraft proceeds individually to the rendezvous point. Gun turrets are exercised, guns elevated and, for me, camera ports are opened, camera operation tested, then leveled or turned to the exact angle for intended use. One of the gunners has entered the rear bomb bay and removed the bomb safety pins: in the forward compartment, the bombardier has performed the same exercise. The bombs are now armed and ready for dropping. Each of the crew members receives one of the safety pins for a souvenir. The flight engineer continues to transfer fuel between fuselage and wing tanks to maintain proper balance of the aircraft after bombs away.

Thirty minutes from the rendezvous point, located on the China coastline, the crew begins donning combat gear; i.e., strap on canteen,

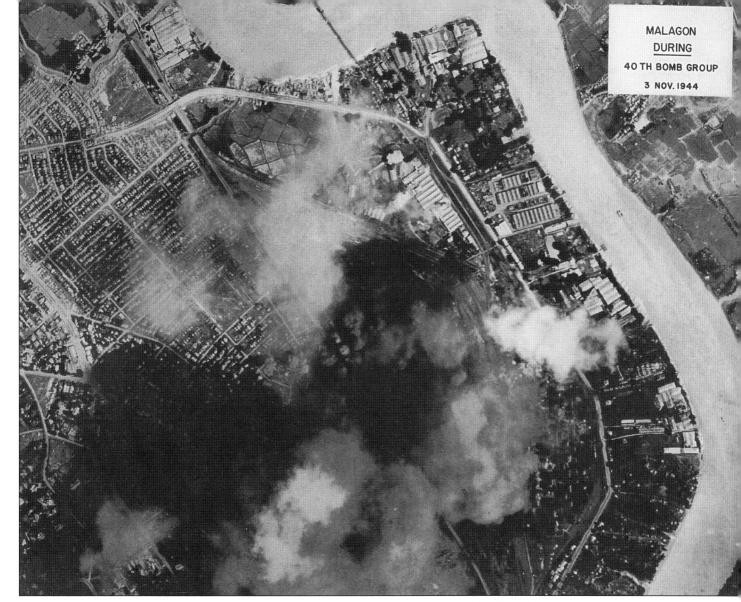

MALAGON DURING 40TH BOMB GROUP 3 NOV. 1944

Flying from its bases in Chakulia, India, the 40th Bomb Group strikes the Malagon Rail Yards and Shops in Rangoon, Burma, on 3 November 1944. Thirteen B-29s set out and 10 successfully struck the target. (40th Bomb Group Collection)

pistol, and other personal items. Then comes the parachute, which is a backpack with emergency supplies in a seat pack cushion. Lastly, the flak jacket is fitted over everything else and all capped by a metal helmet. If he hasn't previously gone back to his position, the tail gunner will make his way back to his compartment. Pressure doors are closed and the aircraft is ready for pressurization during the climb to bombing altitude – today, 25,000 feet. Radio frequencies are set for inter-aircraft communication and for the Navy's air/sea submarines operating in the Yellow Sea or Sea of Japan. Radio silence is maintained except for emergency use.

Approaching the rendezvous point, we see the formation leader, identified by his lowered nose landing gear, has been joined by the wing aircraft, numbers 2 and 3 in the formation. We will be the number 4 aircraft. As we approach, however, the formation leader breaks radio silence to advise his radar unit has become inoperative. An operating radar is necessary in event the bombing can't be done visually and the radar must be used to determine the bomb release point. Our briefing has provided for this potential by designating which aircraft is to assume the lead in such and event. Today we are the designated replacement and we assume the lead position. Precious time and fuel are used while this exercise takes place.

With the formation completed we leave the coast line and start our climb to reach the IP at bombing altitude. The IP, the point at which the bomb run is commenced, is some 10 minutes away from the "bombs away" point and is a small island just off the Japanese coastline. Guns have been test fired during the climb to altitude.

We have been briefed the target will be heavily defended. We can expect Japanese fighter aircraft to pick us up approaching, the IP, anti-aircraft fire [AA] to be heavy in the target area and the fighters to return after we leave the immediate target area. We are not to be disappointed. We are first attacked as we approach the IP by the latest Japanese fighter aircraft, twin-engine fighters code named "Tojo." Tojo's, we have been told, were designed especially for high altitude operation. When the fighters break off, we know we are entering the AA fire zone. But, so far, none of our aircraft are reporting damage. A bad harbinger; however, is that we have sighted one of the fighters just beyond range of our guns at our same altitude, same speed and direction. We know he is radioing this information to the AA gunners on the ground.

I am in the radar compartment working my cameras and can't see much that is happening outside; but, through my earphones, I can hear the gunners calling fighter passes and reporting black puffs from exploding AA shells. Black puffs won't hurt you, it's the bright red ones that are close enough to do damage. I see an unused flak

47

MALAGON
AFTER
5 Nov 1944

In all, 391 500-pound bombs were unleashed on the Malagon Rail Yards during the raid on 3 November 1944. The aiming point of the attack, the large railroad roundhouse, was totally obliterated. (40th Bomb Group Collection)

jacket, or part of one, on the floor of the aircraft, quickly grab it and insert it under the 'chute cushion' on which I'm sitting.

By now the bombardier has the specific aiming point of the target in his bombsight, opens the bomb bay doors and shortly calls "bombs away," not exactly necessary, the jolt to the plane can be felt when the bombs fall away and the bomb bay doors close. Major Doyle immediately recovers control of the aircraft from the bomb sight's automatic control and begins AA evasive action. The AA soon stops as we move outbound from the target, BUT, here come the fighters again. Fighter activity does-drop off as we get further away from the target area. Doyle asks each crew member to report in on the intercom – all do so and no damage is reported to our aircraft. The number 2 aircraft in the formation has the same response to Doyle's inquiry. All is not well; however, with aircraft numbers 3 and 4. Both have been hit and report engine loss and/or severe structural damage. Both are assessing the extent of the damage. Shortly, both report they will be unable to overfly Japanese controlled areas of China and reach our base.

Two alternatives exist for them: 1) attempt to contact the Navy subs, followed by an attempt to ditch near one of them, or, 2) attempt to reach Vladivostok in Russia. After some review, both elect to try to reach Vladivostok. After our return to A-1, we learned

they did indeed reach Russia.

As we get further away from Yawata, we descend to a lower flight altitude for our return to A-1. The tail gunner returns to the central compartment. K rations and fruit juice are broken out. The radio operator tunes to Tokyo Rose and we listen to her music while we snack. The intercom is filled with crew chatter.

By now darkness has fallen and Doyle is becoming concerned that time and fuel consumed during the change in formation leadership may have left us short of fuel. Doyle is requesting frequent location reports from our navigator – either rattling him or he is in fact unsure of our position. Shortly, Doyle directs our radar operator to restart his equipment and attempt to determine our exact position via the terrain reflected on his scope. The radar, as well as other unnecessary power equipment, had been shut down in order to conserve fuel. Radar quickly determines our position and we are able to take a direct course to base. Soon thereafter, we pick up the direction finding radio signals [ADF] from our base.

Some 16 hours after take off, we are back on the ground. My exposed film is handed off to photo lab technicians to develop and print. Next we are off to crew debriefing, following which we were treated to the usual two shots of mission whisky (medicinal purposes, or course.) Then we are whisked off to the hostel for sleep,

Taking off from their bases in Chakulia, India, 40th Bomb Group B-29s flew one of their longest missions – 4,200 miles – to strike the docks in Japanese-occupied Singapore on 5 November 1944. (40th Bomb Group Collection)

sleep, sleep.

And, I hadn't been the first user of the potty!

Subsequently, the pictures I had taken reflected heavy damage to the target, with 75% to 80% of the bombs within the target area. The mission was determined to have been successful. Cost: 75 aircraft departed the China bases, four aborted for mechanical reasons, 71 aircraft bombed the target, 14 failed to return with the loss of 155 crewmen.

Bailout, Survival and Rescue in Siberia

In 1991, Harry Changnon drew from diaries kept by Richard McGlinn, William Stocks, Lyle Turner, Melvin Webb, and Ernest Caudie with additional material from the memoir of Aleksandr Pobozhy to write his account of the harrowing ordeal of B-29 fliers downed in Siberia.

"As noted previously, two B-29s in the author's formation suffered damage during the Yawata raid and decided to attempt to reach Vladivostok in the Soviet Far East. Although both planes turned toward Vladivostok, one successfully landed there, but the other became lost in the Khabarovsk area where the crew bailed out in the darkness and was lost for a time. Both crews lived, but both were months and months being repatriated by the Soviets. Although the Soviet Union, like the United States, was at war with Nazi Germany and Fascist Italy, it maintained a precarious neutrality with Japan in order to avoid a disastrous two-front war. The rules of neutrality demanded that flyers from belligerent countries be interned, rather than repatriated and returned to the ranks in their armies. The interned B-29 crewmen spent several months in the Soviet Union in a kind of political limbo as the Soviets worked out ways to spirit them out of the USSR without sparking a crisis and possible war with Japan. During that period, the interned Americans traveled westward across Siberia and eventually surfaced in Iran. They were then repatriated to the United States and never returned to the Group. Not long thereafter, the Russians developed and built a plane very similar to the B-29s that they had impounded when the U.S. landed in their country. It is generally understood that the Soviet Tupolev Tu-4 was copied from the B-29.

In the following pages surviving B-29 crewmen who had a taste of Soviet life in World War II recall their experiences after the passage of nearly 50 years.

B-29s of the 40th Bomb Group blasted the Singapore dry docks on 5 November 1944. The long distance to the target left the aircraft limited to two 1,000-pound demolition bombs each. Yet the docks were extensively destroyed. (40th Bomb Group Collection)

The 20-21 August 1944 raid on Yawata was the seventh B-29 mission and was made in daylight. This is a condensed account of the hazardous journey made by Major Richard McGinn's crew, beginning on 20 August 1944. They had been on the mission to Yawata and had lost an engine.

All 11 men bailed out over mountainous Russian territory, north of Vladivostok and east of Khabarovsk in darkness into the forest below. They made notes or kept small diaries of their struggles to survive, their rescue and internment in the USSR. These notes and diaries were later written up for the Air Force archives. The members of McGlinn's crew and 280 others were sworn to secrecy to protect wartime U.S.-USSR relations.

Gradually, classified papers about their experiences were released. Occasional articles were printed after 1946 in newspapers and magazines, but little was known until the government removed the materials from Top Secret classification. This was not done on some papers until as late as 1986. A book, *Home From Siberia,* by Otis Hays was published in 1990 by Texas A & M University Press. Some of the Russians' "guests" agreed to talk, and Hays covers all 37 crews interned from the Doolittle mission members to Navy men in 1945.

All of the McGlinn crew's diaries were retyped years ago from little notes and papers they had hidden away during their stay with the Russians. For instance, Dick McGlinn's original diary was written on strips of paper. It was furnished by his widow, Mrs. Catherine McGlinn. Ernie Caudle supplies his and Lyle Turner's diary based on notes on calendar pages. Bill Stocks' recollections came from interrogation reports. There are other such reports in the archives.

The first B-29 mission to Japan was a night raid on 15 June 1944 – to hit the Imperial Iron and Steel Works at Yawata, on Kyushu. It didn't do much damage. It did alert the Japanese; however, that this industrial target, which produced a quarter of Japan's steel, would continue to be hit until destroyed or badly damaged. Thus the enemy concentrated defensive anti-aircraft batteries and fighters around the area.

This maximum effort daylight raid had 98 B-29s in China. Only 75, however, were airborne. A crash on the runway at the 462nd base prevented planes from taking off. A second flight took off later in the day to hit Yawata at night. A total of 71 planes bombed the primary target. They encountered heavy AA fire and rugged fighter attacks. Fourteen planes were lost on this raid, if we include 40th's No. 425 "B-Sweet." Capt. William Schaal (with Lt. Col. H. R. Sullivan aboard) bailed out over the Hump *en route* to A-1.

Several planes went down over Yawata when rammed by Japanese fighters or hit by heavy AA. Capt. James Slattery and crew were missing. Their crashed plane was found later west of A-1. Capt. Boyd Grubaugh and crew bailed out near Laohekou ("Laohokow") with three men killed. Major Richard McGlinn's crew, which is the subject of this chapter, locked their radio key down as they bailed out near Vladivostok.

There had been a mystery for years about the McGlinn crew. Secrecy had been imposed upon their story by the U.S. and the Soviet Union. It was learned in October, 1944 that they were in a neutral country, but even today most 40th Group members do not know what happened to the members of this crew or even if they are alive. In fact, all 11 members of the crew survived the bailout and the privations that followed, their internment in the USSR and their ultimate release.

Members of the crew were:

Aircraft Commander: Major Richard M. McGlinn*
Pilot: 1St Lieutenant Ernest E. Caudle
Navigator: 2nd Lieutenant Lyle C. Turner
Bombardier: 1st Lieutenant Eugene C. Murphy
Flight Engineer: 1st Lieutenant Miman W. Conrath
Radio Operator (V?): Sergeant Otis Childs*
Radar Operator: Staff Sergeant Melvin O. Webb
CFC Staff Sergeant William T. Stocks
Tail Gunner: Staff Sergeant Charles H. Robson
Right Gunner: Sergeant John G. Beckley*
Left Gunner: Sergeant Louis M. Mannatt
* Deceased

The crew had flown B-29 No. 291 from Pratt to Chakulia in April 1944. They had flown it over the Hump a few times and on two combat missions. The plane was lost in late July in a crash shortly after take-off from Chakulia when Capt. Alvin Hills had two engines fail. A replacement plant, No. 42-93829, was assigned to Maj. McGlinn in early August. Diary accounts tell the crew's story beginning with takeoff from A-1.

Richard McGlinn's Diary, 20 August 1944. "We shook hands all around before climbing to stations in No. 829, *Cait Paomat II,* (Gaelic for St. Catherine) and were in the air before dawn. We enjoyed good weather all along the route: in fact, it was excellent bombing weather over our target in Japan. Just before the IP, radar operator Childs informed me that his set was inoperative. I gave the signal for an echelon to the right, and Captain Woolsey (No. 466) took the lead, but it changed quickly as Captain Doyle (No. 237) took over. Flak bursts were really intense and coming right at us. We had dropped our bombs and started a right turn when, Bingo, No. 2 was hit, and it didn't keep its oil very long, so we feathered it. We again took the lead, being a cripple, and Mr. Nip was waiting for just such a setup. We waded through the fighters, but this did not end our troubles in going such a distance to our destination.

"We soon concluded that if we could get to Vladivostok, a good airplane could be delivered to our friends, the Russians even though they are not at war with the Japanese. *En route* we could dispose of the airplane in the sea, if necessary, rather than let our enemy get its hands on it. We bid goodbye to members of our formation , ducked under No. 2, and headed north. We had good cloud coverage as far as protection from fighter opposition, but this later worked towards our disadvantage up the Korean Coast. While on instruments, we saw that we were flying a difference of some 50 degrees between

Ding How, a 444th Bomb Group B-29, rests on ground at the Army Air Base known as A-3 in Guanghan, Sichuan Province, China, on 25 October 1944. The aircraft's nickname is derived from the Chinese expression formally spelled *dǐng hǎo* and meaning "the very best." Camels on the fuselage record the number of times it had crossed the "Hump." (Dave Lucabaugh)

Flux Gate and Magnetic, which threw us off course and our DR to Vladivostok. Now we didn't know exactly where we were.

"Darkness had set in and when we altered course and came upon lights, we were not certain if they were our friends or Japanese. We flew over a lighted area on one occasion and there were search lights playing, but we could not prove it wasn't some Japanese ruse. We, therefore, flew a course of 360 degrees for 40 minutes, hoping we would be near a railroad spur running northeast from the Trans Siberian Railroad. Plans for abandoning were carried out, and our base at A-1 was so informed even though it was giving QDMs back to A-1. I went aft and explained the situation to all the men. They were in excellent spirits. We were pretty well equipped for a bailout in a temperate climate.

"Cloud coverage below gave us no hint of lights, which wasn't very hospitable. Lt. Turner, our Nav, went to the rear, and we were on the intercom with him giving an account of the men leaving. Those in the front dropped through the nose wheel door before I went down the hatch after cutting the master switch. The 'Cait' was left on AFCE with nose turned down in hopes she might land somewhat intact, and we could get equipment such as radios, life rafts, additional food and water, plus 101 other items that would aid us in keeping alive until we could be rescued.

"After we entered the overcast, it was raining and it was not too pleasant. I hit the trees, crashing through branches and coming to a sudden stop. My body was OK. I grabbed the tree: rough bark, trunk 36" in circumference, branches small; some broke and I tossed them to the ground. But, there was no sound of them hitting. What a predicament, being hung up on the forest of Siberia with nothing to do but sit in the rain and sweat out daylight. The ground was hardly visible because of the density of the trees. Off to the west I could make out a canyon running northward. I dropped my jungle kit to the ground and cut shrouds to start the silk canopy on its way down, with help of wind and rain. The ordeal of my extraction from the tree was very tiring, a matter of six hours' work to go down 60 feet. Finally, about eight feet from the ground I became hung up and was actually choking when I managed to hack the shroud belt

A lineup of Tu-4 bombers, code named BULL by NATO, is seen at an airfield outside of Moscow in the mid-1950s. Tupolev built over 1200 Tu-4s, the first long range bomber aircraft in the Soviet Air Force. (Hans-Heiri Stapfer)

The Soviet Tu-70 commercial transport is based on the Tu-4 bomber. It has B-29 wings and tail assembly, and the glass nose cone gave it the more ominous look of a bomber rather than a transport. (Hans-Heiri Stapfer)

and drop to the ground.

"I made a temporary camp of my chute, but it was soaking wet as were my clothes, and it seemed impossible to get a fire going to dry out. I did a bit of scouting by blazing a rough trail, but did not go very far as my body was tired and weak from lack of sleep, so I made a rough lean-to and tried to get some rest.

"The first night was very uncomfortable, and much time was spent exercising to keep up my circulation. At dawn, I ate the last half of my K-ration from the day before and started out blazing as I went along. Late in the morning I noted a birch tree and, using the fire starter in the jungle kit, got a fire started. Shortly, the rain let up and I stripped to the nude. I began to dry my equipment, but it wasn't much fun gathering more wood in the cold, damp, quiet and dreary forest without wearing anything more than a set of dog tags.

"I hit a small river sometime later, but there was no trail. I shot at two grouse and a luxurious squirrel, but I missed each time. I found a bend up in the river to make a campsite where I put nicks in my machete making camp. Made a good fire and brewed a tea of grass leaves and black ants, which were numerous. Tried to use my fish line in the river, but no luck. Had a good night's sleep. I started out early to climb up over the mountain to look for the airplane. I was carrying canteen, pistol, and machete, and one K-ration. The woods were very rough, but I managed to climb the mountain with the aid of my compass. I thought I might gain a vista and spot the wreckage, but the dense woods permitted visibility of only a few hundred yards, and there was no clear path. I decided to abandon the search as it would be very easy to pass within a few feet of the wreckage and miss it. Better travel downstream for aid rather than lose valuable energy seeking an unknown. When I went back to my camp, Staff Sergeant Charles Robson, my tail gunner was there. We had a very happy reunion, and we talked until late about the rest of the men and wondered how they were doing. We ate more ants and found a dead stump with boring grubs in the bark. These were soaked and were very good. This was Wednesday, 23 August.

"William Stocks' Diary: When bailout was made on Sunday evening, 20 August from the rear of B-29 No. 829 into the sky over unknown Siberian territory, it was in order: Sergeant Otis Childs, V; Sergeant Jhn Beckley, RG; Sergeant Louis Mannatt, LG; Staff Sergeant William Stocks, CFD; Staff Sergeant Charles Robson, TG; and Second Lieutenant Lyle Turner, Navigator.

"After parachutes had opened, several men noticed the exhausts and lights of the ship as it pulled away and also saw other party members blinking flashlights as they descended through cloud layers. They alighted in a heavily wooded and hilly terrain, varying in distances apart from a half mile to two miles. All men were wearing Mae-West life jackets under their parachute harnesses as they were uncertain about being over land or water. It was raining when they bailed out and the rain continued for the next few days.

"Sgt. Webb alighted in a tree about six feet above the ground, and it was necessary for him to cut his parachute shrouds to drop to the ground, suffering no injury. He left his chute hanging in the tree.

"Lt. Conrath had filled his pockets with as many K-rations as he could handle and had difficulty getting out of the plane. After his chute opened, he blinked his flashlight around until an answer was seen from someone floating between himself and the plane. When he noticed a tree going by, he drew up his legs to break the fall, but his chute caught in the branches, and he barely touched ground. He gathered his equipment together the next morning to head north as he planned. After walking a half hour, he fired two shots and heard response from both south and southeast. When he didn't hear anymore from the others in the next half hour, he moved north another half hour before firing another shot. The answer came from the southeast, and he began walking in that direction to meet Sgts. Webb & Stocks and Lt. Murphy.

"When Lt. Murphy jumped he did not delay long enough in pulling his rip cord which caused him to black out momentarily when the chute opened. He was not prepared in the dark rainy clouds for reaching the ground and was knocked out as he went down through the tree branches. When he came to, he threw up as his back and ribs had received painful blows.

"Sergeant Childs, who was the first to leave the plane from the rear section, counted to 10 before pulling the rip cord, and he felt only a slight shock when the chute opened. He felt tree branches just before he hit the ground, slightly spraining his knees and ankles, which were to bother him for several days. Soon after daylight he started walking north and within two hours meet Sgt. Beckley.

"Beckley had no trouble with his chute opening and saw several flashlights blinking on the way down. After passing through the cloud layer, he landed in a treetop. The branches gave way, and he fell to the ground hurting his ribs and making a deep cut on his nose as he was knocked out. Most of his underclothes were torn off. He

The pilot of B-29-10-BA 42-63395 of the 468th Bomb Group, 792nd Bomb Squadron, landed hard due to an ice-covered canopy upon return to a base in China from a raid in Manchuria on 7 December 1944. The impact severed the midsection of the fuselage, and the aircraft was scrapped. The diagonal rudder stripes were white with black borders. (National Archives)

Aerial mines are loaded aboard a B-29 of the 468th Bomb group based in Chengdu, Sichuan Province, China, on 24 January 1945. (USAF)

An explosion ripped through a dispersal area while bombs were being unloaded from *Little Clambert*, B-29-40-BW 42-24582, of the 40th Bomb Group in Chakulia, India, on 14 January 1945. The remains of that B-29 litter the foreground. Damaged beyond repair in the background is the ironically nicknamed *Last Resort*, B-29-10-BA 42-63394. (National Museum of the United States Air Force)

covered himself with his chute and jungle kit blanket, remaining on the hillside until daybreak before going down to meet Childs.

"While the crew was preparing to jump, Sgt. Mannatt's rip cord handle was caught on Stocks' pack and the chute popped out onto the floor. Sgt. Robson quickly repacked the chute which soon opened to perfection. Mannatt didn't feel the jar of landing as much as others; perhaps because he was lighter. After landing, he was able to build a small lean-to, wrapped himself in chute and jungle kit blanket, and fell asleep. Mannatt had fastened a carbine to his chute harness.

"After Robson and Stocks had pushed Mannatt out the door, S/ Sgt. Stocks quickly followed him and then blacked out when the chute opened. He came to after landing in some trees, some 40 feet above the ground and was able to bring his chute down with him. He erected a crude lean- to to get out of the weather, but he could not sleep. After daylight, he was happy to see Webb show up.

"Lt. Turner remained in the spot in which he landed, until morning. His chute was caught in a tree, and he could only cut a part of it away. Shortly after he woke up in the morning, he met Lt. Caudle, and they started moving north. Both heard a few shots to the southeast and after a half day of walking north in difficult brush and terrain, they changed directions and headed south.

"Lt. Caudle, before jumping, had put three K-rations in his pockets together with halazone tablets, tourniquet and morphine. After his chute opened, the canopy split from center to rim and several shroud lines broke; probably because of his weight. This caused him to spin all the way down, but he was lucky to land atop a large fir tree with branches breaking his fall all the way to the ground where he went up to his knees in a leafy mold. He was able to pull his chute down and rolled up in it, but could not sleep. At daybreak, he cut his chute in two, made a pack of the chute straps and jungle kit and started up the mountainside where he found Turner only a couple hundred yards away. Both men must have jumped at about the same time from front and aft of the ship to land so close.

"S/Sgt. Robson's chute opened without much of a jar and he saw a light flashing before entering the clouds, but none after that. He was able to see treetops with his own light before crashing through them to almost the ground. A branch which held him soon gave way and he landed on his back, but without injury. Despite a steady rain, he was able to get under a cover of his chute and jungle kit blanket. He was awakened by sounds of shots which he answered, but was unable to see anyone in any direction. He found a stream to follow in a northwesterly direction. During his second day of travel he came upon Maj. McGlinn's camp and waited for him to return. It was odd that he would float far enough to land near McGlinn.

"Thus on Monday, 21 August, crew members gradually started

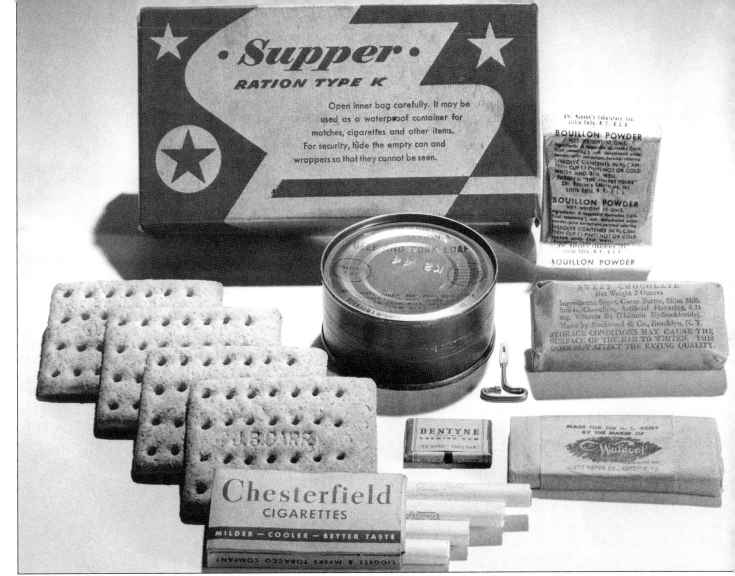

The K ration was intended as a portable individual ration for use only during assault and combat. An inner carton was slid inside a second carton, which indicated whether its content was breakfast, dinner, or supper. The supper K ration included: canned meat, biscuits, bouillon powder, confections and gum, soluble coffee, granulated sugar, cigarettes, can opener, and spoon. As with the other Ks, the biscuits, beverages, sugar, fruit bar, confections, gum, and spoon were packaged in a laminated cellophane bag, while the canned meat and cheese were in a chipboard sleeve-type box. (U.S. Army Quartermaster Museum, Ft.. Lee, Virginia)

getting together in the dense forest, but not all were following streams in the same direction. McGlinn and Robson went north, whereas Caudle and Turner circled. Beckley, Childs and Mannatt had a fire built within a couple hours to dry clothes. Murphy started north and found an insurmountable cliff, so he turned south to run into Webb and Stocks. Shortly afterwards, Lt. Conrath appeared and joined them. By the end of the day, this foursome came across the camp of Beckley, Childs and Mannatt, making a party of seven. They were trying to use a small map of Soviet Siberia that Murphy had which didn't show enough detail to locate themselves, but did show railroads running parallel to the Amur River and another running to the coast. They walked until 1700 to make a new camp with parachutes, jungle kits, pine boughs and firewood cut with the machetes. It was decided to make K-rations last as long as possible by only eating one meal per day. Anyone who woke during the night kept the fire going by adding wood.

"Tuesday, 22 August. The seven-man party arose before daylight, ate meagerly from the K- rations, broke camp and followed the stream southwesterly. Childs had wrenched knees and ankles, Beckley had rib pains and Murphy's back gave him trouble so progress was slow – estimated at four to five miles per day. Walking was extremely difficult due to the constant swamps the spreading stream caused. The heavy rains made the stream grow rapidly and every canyon added more water. At times it was necessary to walk along the sides of steep hills where water falls and the tangled vines became so bad that walking became more difficult than wading through the swampy areas. A sharp lookout was kept for game; Mannatt shot a black squirrel that was divided seven ways and was boiled in small frying pans that evening. At 1600 camp was made. Due to constant rain and walking through swamps, the entire party was soaked and several hours were spent Wing to dry shoes and clothing.

"Wednesday, 23 August. The day's travel along the stream, through brush, swamp and edge of hills was similar to previous one; but more frequent stops were made to help Murphy, Beckley and Childs with their injuries. In addition, Mannatt needed first aid when he cut his fingers while chopping firewood with a machete. Webb had been trained to use the first-aid kit. Webb also gave Murphy a morphine shot the night before to help him sleep. It was the best day for hunting as Mannatt shot four grouse and a squirrel.

"Thursday-Friday, 24-25 August – Days 4-5. Some sunshine cheered the travelers. A squirrel and a fish were cooked for the evening meal with bullion powder added to make it more tasty. No

The remains of the U.S. Army Air Force personnel buried in Chakulia during the war were later disinterred and relocated to cemeteries in the United States after the war. (40th Bomb Group Collection)

For a time, this U.S. Military Cemetery in Chengdu, China, provided a resting place for airmen who paid the ultimate price. (NEAM, Norm Olson)

noon meals were ever eaten during the long ordeal. Drinking water presented no problem as it was abundant, but halazone tables were used as a precaution. An old lean-to shelter, rotted rope and an old blazed trail along the stream, were the first signs seen of previous men in the rugged country. This cheered everyone up with the hope that rescue might be made. The stream had by now grown so large that the party was no longer able to cross it and it remained on their right side the rest of their journey. That night they ate two squirrels amongst them.

"Saturday and Sunday, 26-27 August. Each day the men struggled along the indistinct trail with Webb leading the way, breaking a new path through the rugged undergrowth. Time and again, the old occasional hatchet marks on tree trunks would disappear and then be found again. Once it led them up a steep mountain where they found thick second growth of timber, many vines and waterfalls slowing them down. They were able to find a few wild grapes to eat. Childs had a "Survival" pamphlet which was helpful. They learned "rock moss" was edible and contained large amounts of starch, so they started to boil that to supplement the occasional fish/game.

"Monday and Tuesday, 28-29 August – Days 8-9: They started wading through a swamp when they suddenly spotted the river flowing quietly and smoothly along. What had originally been a stream only a foot wide was now a river, which constantly broke down into branches and log jams. Moss, a few mushrooms and frogs added to the meager grouse and squirrels for dinner. The men had long since eaten the last of their K-rations and parachute tin rations.

The rain reduced visibility and Tuesday was almost lost when they neglected to use the compass and found they traveled in a circle in the swamp. They never failed to use it after that. Small bottles of insect repellent in the jungle kits were used to good advantage as mosquitoes were often present in the thousands and large enough to draw blood. Even more troublesome were jiggers, a short stubby fly, which were in great numbers and were constantly getting in their eyes where the repellent couldn't be used. Head nets were worn in evenings and at night, but not during the day because of snags with trees and brush. At night, the smoke under the parachute kept the insects away and made sleeping easier. In making their camp, various tasks were handled by two to three men erecting the parachute, two cutting pine boughs, one cleaning game and all cutting firewood to burn through the night. This usually took an hour and a half and consumed a considerable amount of their remaining strength.

"30-31 August – Days 10-11. Sgt. Childs had a cold which worsened, making him even weaker. Packs became lighter as rations were used and other items deemed unnecessary were abandoned. One machete was lost. Blankets were in waterproof bags, and men consolidated their packs into one so they could take turns carrying them. Sometimes swamps were avoided by trying to walk along rugged hillsides which sapped their strength and also took them away from the river. Scratches, bruises, torn clothing and insects made them grouchy as they became weaker in the wet weather. When camp was made, some of the men kept a fire going so they could thaw out and dry their clothes.

RAMA VI BRIDGE
DURING 2ND ATTACK

444 TH BOMB GROUP
2 JAN. 1945

On 2 January 1945, the 444th Bomb Group blasted the Rama VI railroad bridge over the Chao Phraya River in Bangkok, Thailand. Wartime air raids left the bridge out of commission until late 1953. (40th Bomb Group Collection)

"Friday and Saturday, 1-2 September – Days 12-13. It was decided that they would have to build rafts and float down the river, as progress was so slow. Cutting logs was done in shifts. No dry logs were available – so fallen, half-green ones were used to build a raft. Four main logs about a foot thick were used to support some 30 smaller ones. Two end and center cross members were notched to match notches in main timbers. All the rest were notched and held in place by the parachute cords. The biggest job was carrying the heavy main members to the lagoon before assembly was started. Only seven frogs and some moss made up the evening meal, so everyone went to bed tired and hungry.

"It soon became apparent that only one raft could be completed in a short time, as the light machetes were not made for log cutting. When the raft was launched, it was found only three men could ride on it and even then it was partly submerged. It was decided that the three strongest men, Lt. Murphy, Sgts. Webb and Beckley, would go ahead to seek help on the raft. Before parting, the seven men said prayers and a grouse was eaten for lunch. At about 1400, the advance party got on the raft and floated downstream. The remaining foursome sat around feeling sick and blue, dreading eventual deaths, if no help was received."

Lyle C. Turner's Diary: "I was in the rear of aircraft 42-93829 with others when abandon ship order was given by Maj. McGlinn. When we jumped we were flying at 11,000 feet on a heading of due north.

"After landing we were to go north in hope of finding the crashed plane and to assemble. I was not scared to jump. The chute opened and after several minutes, I hit the ground with a terrific wallop. I sat there in the rain, slightly dazed, for a few minutes. It was very dark and I could barely see five feet, but I could see that I was in tall trees on a steep hill. I stood up to make sure I was OK and took a step, falling into a hole. So, I decided it would be best to stay fight there until daylight. I could not pull my parachute down from the broken tree, so I laid down in the cold and tried to sleep.

"By daylight I was so wet and cold I could hardly stand up and when I did I could only see about 20-30 yards. I took inventory of my equipment: jungle pack, knife, cigarette lighter, belt, canteen and first-aid kit. I was wearing a summer flying suit, leather jacket, socks, G. I. shoes and flight cap. I carried a .45 in a shoulder holster. Around 0700 I saw Lt. Caudle coming from the south up the hill which was hard climbing. I took my parachute harness straps and tied them to my jungle pack after cutting all the chute I could reach off the tree before we started down the hill. We followed a stream to the north, but ran into trees that were very tall or fallen rotten ones

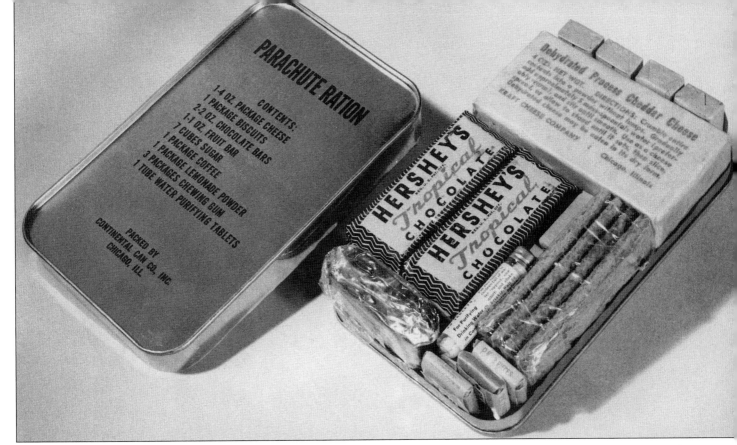

The "Ration, Parachute, Emergency," was designed to fit the pocket of the Air Force emergency vest. Weighing 11½ ounces, the 1,062-calorie ration included sweet chocolate, hard candy, dehydrated cheese and crackers, bouillon cubes, sugar, cigarettes, water-purification tablets, soluble coffee, chewing gum, and a small cellophane bag to contain the uneaten food after the can had been opened. This ration was largely unchanged throughout the war and remained in official standing until February of 1952. (U.S. Army Quartermaster Museum, Ft.. Lee, Virginia)

which we had to climb over by the hundreds in very bad footing. Sometimes we had to almost climb straight up cliffs. Caudle decided his flying boots were too heavy and discarded them.

"Early in the day, we had heard seven shots to the southeast, but never heard anything more. After changing directions, we followed a stream which became wider as we crossed two creeks flowing into it in the heavily forested mountains. We saw several waterfalls, one about 25 feet high, at the stream

"Tuesday-Wednesday, 22-23 August. Up at 0600; both of us ate one K-ration breakfast prior to walking downstream, crossing from one side to another on fallen trees, or wading the stream itself. We took approximately ten minutes of each hour to rest. Fog and trees kept us from seeing tops of the steep mountains (5-6,000'). We were a little discouraged by evening as it was still raining. We ran onto no trails of any kind, never even saw an animal of any description all day. We built a fire in the opening of our tent, but our firewood was all gone by midnight. I slept poorly, even though I was worn out. It was too cold to sleep most of the night.

"We ate the last K-rations for breakfast before going downstream on a cold, foggy, rainy day. Our stream had turned and now ran south-southwest which is better as civilization would be to the west. When we crossed another stream of equal size to ours at 1600, we camped on a flat spot in tall, wet grass. We were sore and tired with blistered feet. Again, poor sleeping after the fire went out.

"24-25 August – Days 3-4. Ate parachute rations (4-oz. chocolate bar, dehydrated bar of cheese, three sugar cubes, stick of gum and four crackers) each day (all meals). We wore head nets as mosquitoes and gnats were terrible. Still saw no game or trails, but mountains looked lower. My feet were so sore and swollen that it was difficult

to get shoes on and my socks were still wet. Caudle's feet were badly blistered and the ends of his toes were raw. We ate nothing for breakfast and finished parachute rations by the end of the day. Our jungle kits contained the following articles: pair of sunglasses, head net, machete, small blanket, fishing gear, small frying pan, first-aid kit, pocket knife and compass. We also carried the E-3 kit containing: five iodine ampoules, two tubes halazone tablets, box Benzedrine tablets, eight salt tablets, eight tea tables, three Band-Aids, small roll adhesive tape and 4-oz. chocolate bar. We found an old blazed trail which was several years old along the river. It was hard to follow, but easier than no trail at all. We also found a few game trails and saw claw marks made by bears on some trees. Caudle missed twice at the first bird seen worth shooting at; we were disappointed as we certainly needed food. We now only had 40 rounds of .45 ammunition, plus eight rounds for Caudle's .38 gun. When the sun came out for the first time, we took our jackets off and laid around in it for an hour. Caudle lost his canteen in the river while trying to fill it.

"Saturday, 26 August – Day 5. Cloudy again. Water drips off trees, grass and underbrush. We had nothing to eat except 4-oz. chocolate bar which lasted the whole day. We are weaker, feet are very sore as are our backs and shoulders from carrying equipment packs. For the first time we came upon a flat forest. Mountains are steep on the left riverbank, whereas we were a mile away on the fight before following animal trail back to the river which is now 40-50 feet wide, still running southwest. We pitched our tent early and built a fire to dry shoes and clothing, which were wet from either falling into the river or wading in it. We went to bed cold and without food.

The hearts painted under several of the bombs indicate that some crewmember had been issued a Purple Heart due to injury from flak or enemy gunfire. In addition to aircraft nicknames, nose art, and mission symbols, B-29s often sported the names of crewmen and their wives or girlfriends painted underneath their windows. (40th Bomb Group Collection)

"Sunday, 27 August – Day 6. We arose stiff, cold, sore, hungry, in the dark, foggy weather. I wrapped my legs in parachute silk because my coveralls from the knees down had been torn off. It was uncomfortable walking on legs that were raw and a mass of bites. My wrists were nearly twice normal size from mosquito and other insect bites; my small gloves gave little protection. Caudle's head net had burned during the night by a spark from the fire; thus, he wore cumbersome goggles which steamed up in the rain and were difficult to see through. The hills, covered by dense forests, were difficult to see, but appeared to be lower each day. About noon we found a fresh trail made by human feet which we thought to be made by our crew members. We soon found a campsite with empty E&E kits, Conrath's name on a canteen belt and an empty tobacco can (which would be Webb's). We knew there was at least another in the party by small footprints which could be Sgt. Robson. This really boosted our morale, despite no food. We had a cup of hot tea. Caudle's eyes were badly swollen from the insects which were worse day by day. Walking is easier because we were following the others' trail.

"Monday-Friday, 25 August-1 September – Days 7-11. We awoke wet from rain which came through the silk of the tent. We had rough going on steep hillsides which came down to the stream; sometime we would have to climb straight up 200 feet and in a few yards be forced to go down again. Caudle shot a duck and also a grouse, which we cut into small pieces to cook in our frying pans on the hillside camp. Broth and meat tasted so good as we were getting very weak by this time. We never left the camp Tuesday as the rain came down and we only had tea to drink. Wednesday- was spent trying to follow- the river through underbrush and numerous backwater streams, but it was so slow going that we went back to the mountains, despite their steepness. Thursday we caught or found three frogs and eight snails which we ate raw, but had a squirrel that Caudle shot to boil for dinner. Friday, we had to rest in the tent all day with nothing to eat.

"Saturday-Monday, 2-4 September – Days 12-14. We decided to walk the hills after running into swamps and heavy brush along the river, even though the hills were covered with fallen trees in the thick forest. We only had three raw frogs and a few berries during the day, but Caudle shot a grouse and a squirrel to go with a few snails for dinner.

"On Sunday, we moved back to crossing a swamp and backwater areas where we had to camp with only a few snails for food. On Monday, Caudle used the last of the .45 ammunition to kill a grouse. We tried fishing, but the river was so flooded that there was plenty of fish to eat even without going for our plain hooks.

"Tuesday, 5 September – Day 15. We arose later than usual and

At a time when the draft brought men with nearly every skill into the field, nose art was sometimes the work of experienced artists. (40th Bomb Group Collection)

started fishing again when we found bait for the hooks. Caudle caught a nice 16-inch trout. About 1100 we had just gotten through some underbrush when we looked across a lagoon, and there stood Sgt. Childs. We were very surprised and glad to see him. He took us to his camp where we found the three other men cutting logs to make a raft. We cooked our fish and a grouse Mannatt had shot. They told us that they had built a raft made of heavy green logs, and only three could use it in the high, swift water. Lt. Murphy and Sgts Beckley and Webb had left on it only the day before."

Richard McGinn's Diary. [From this point on no attempt was made to make daily notations.]

"24 August. We traveled through swamp land and on the side of mountains along the river for periods of time, which seemed never-ending. Thousands of acres of decadent forest caused us to crawl under, over, and around fallen trees in various stages of decay, or there were acres of shoulder-high grass and terrible areas of yew and vines. While we were strong we could plow through, but as we lost strength, it was necessary to hack our way or bypass them. At times we climbed on ridges of mountains to avoid the 'impassable' riverbank only to find tough going and a fight to get back to the stream.

"We were taught to live off the land so our meager rations were supplemented with anything that crawled. We had several good messes of frogs which were boiled in our skillets and eaten whole; sometimes we used a head as fish bait, but it was the only part we wasted. Snails were a delicacy, and field mice, though small, were tasty as was the broth from boiling them. We were disheartened many days, but then along came a mess of frogs, a fish or similar 'delicacy,' and we would have new hope for our outcome. We also filled up with berries, leaves and moss.

"Throughout our journey we were continuously attacked by gnats, houseflies, blood-sucking flies and mosquitoes; little wonder that there is no human life and little animal life in those woods. Our jungle kits contained insect repellent, two extra pair of socks to help keep our feet warm and dry. Boric acid ointment soothed our skin and sulpha power healed our wounds. A jackknife was handy for a thousand reasons in the woods. The compass kept us from going in circles. A water bag held frogs and snails. A head net was used to carry berries, moss and leaves more often than warding of insects. A handbook on survival aided our 'comfort.' Matches and fire starter gave us fires even in heavy rain and we always added pitch when available. Fish line and hooks were helpful. We'll never know if our mirrors reflected the light to help the Russian airmen find us. Gloves kept my hands from being torn to pieces by briars and rocks.

Increasingly risqué nose art eventually led to chaplain-inspired censorship. (40th Bomb Group Collection)

A feather-filled quilt protected our bodies at night.

"About September 7th, we got a bearing on a mountain ridge with a view of the river. This saved us days of travel. However, our first real view of the country ahead was a bitter disappointment, for as far as the eye could see, there were hills covered by forests. We concluded that our only way out was on a raft, and we would have to chance it regardless of the dangers of swift water. When we got back to the river, we camped alongside a quiet stream with a good bank and sufficient timber for our boat building. Unfortunately, Sgt. Robson became very weak so we changed after three days from boat building to making a raft.

"When we did get a small raft built, despite Robson's poor shape for travel, we put it in the river, but it didn't go far – about 300 yards – around a turn was white water. We soon ran into several log jams and were upset. In the dunking we got, I lost my trusty .45 and three remaining cartridges. Robson lost his left shoe and machete. Here we were, miles from civilization, and he only had one shoe to cover the distance. At first we planned to make a permanent camp in that vicinity and hole up to wait for death by starvation and exposure or to see a hunter/trapper.

"Robson made a sandal out of his .45 holster and shroud lines. After three more days of living on wild grapes and fish, we moved downstream again with very slow going as Robson suffered with his foot. Berries became less plentiful, leaves were falling and geese flew south. Living by a babbling brook might be all right for some folks, but I heard too much of a singing, talking, mocking, tantalizing steam; it almost drove us mad. One day we found an abandoned cabin with 30 old traps, crossbow and arrows and I left a ten-rupee

note with a message in case someone would happen by. On a few occasions we yelled at squirrels who had pine nuts in their mouths; they would then drop them. These choice morsels were very tasty. The arrows were used with no success of fish.

"On September 20th, a month after we had been to Yawata, things were getting desperate. Our clothes were tatters, there was hardly any food and we were very weak. We prayed to St. Theresa (Patron Saint of aviators) for some rose petal sign. A voice came back that seemed to say, 'In two days.'"

Mel Webb's Diary: "Saturday, 2 September. Day 13. Lt. Murphy, Beckley, and I (Webb) drifted about five miles before we ran into rapids where we were tossed into a log jam and dumped into the river. We were lucky we weren't drowned, but we lost ponchos and our first-aid kit. Lt. Murphy hurt his back which hindered us from then on. We spent that night on the island where the river forked. The next day, I shot a squirrel with my .45 so we had meat for breakfast for three hungry men. We got the raft out, but soon had more episodes with log jams. We gave up the raft as it took too much of our strength, which was needed for walking along the swift river.

"3-10 September. After leaving the raft, we walked for seven more days, subsisting on a few birds I shot, some berries and moss. One day we found a hunter's shelter, which was quite snug. It has a hammock swinging from two trees and was protected by branches. We knew we were getting closer to people when a couple days later, we found a field with stacks of wild hay which had been cut. It was dry so we set one on fire to see if we could get anyone's attention but no luck.

This Superfortress had indeed made many return trips to enemy targets. (40th Bomb Group Collection)

"Finally, we saw an abandoned village or logging camp across the river. While we were resting (as Lt. Murphy's back was really bothering him) a small girl stepped out of the tall grass on the riverbank. We shouted and waved at her, but this frightened her and she disappeared back into the grass. We were sure she could not be alone, but it was an hour before the child reappeared with a woman beside her. Again we yelled to them, but they couldn't understand us or our gestures. After a while, a dugout appeared from downstream paddled by a man and a boy. They pulled onto the riverbank beside us. They could not understand us, nor we them. However, by sign language, they understood we were lost. We got into the dugout and were taken across the river where the woman gave us raw vegetables to eat.

"We then followed the woman and girl on a path downstream for about two miles to a village, a cluster of log buildings. We were greeted by others, fed and slept on blankets on the floor. I shall never forget how thankful I was to see those kind Russian people. The little children soon made friends with us and we found a soft spot in our hearts for them. They were kind and loving.

"11 September: We were able to make the villagers understand that more men were still back up the river and a search party was sent from the village, but it never went far enough to see the others. A plane was used that did locate our crewmen and dropped them supplies. They thought that Lt. Conrath was baldheaded. His hair was so blond that from the air, he looked bald. Meanwhile two boys rowed us down the Monoma River about 45 miles to another village,

"Petnatsovick, where there were two Russian officers. They couldn't speak English, but treated us very well. We had a whole roast pig for supper and another for breakfast, plus a roast goose and plates of eggs. The people in the high country eat well. We all got stomach aches because we were not used to eating such rich food.

"12 September. The Soviet officers took us on horseback for two hours to Troitskoye on the Amur River where we were turned over to the Border Patrol officers; we were still dirty and in bad physical shape. We were taken to a nearby primitive, wooden hospital building where two doctors treated us for malnutrition, cuts and bruises. They took our guns from us to clean them, but of course, we never saw them again.

"16 September. We rested and were fed enough at Troitskoye to make the 200km trip by motorboat up the Amur River to Khabarovsk where we were hospitalized for recuperation and to wait for the others. We were questioned immediately about our missing crew members and told that contact had been made with a six-men party on the river above Troitskoye. The Soviets widened their search after learning the direction of our B-29 prior to leaving the plane and of our own travels."

Lyle Turner's Diary. "Days 16-22. The six of us started walking along the river, but soon came to an enormous steep hill running into the water. It was miles long. A vote was taken at noon on whether to go back and build rafts or keep on walking – which is what we did. However, we made very slow progress on the hill. Mannatt had killed four grouse and a squirrel. These, plus six frogs and 30 snails, made up the evening meal. We went to bed early,

Somewhat more conservative than the normal airman, 40th Bomb Group Chaplain Father Bartholomew Adler convinced Col. William H. Blanchard late in 1944 that all such figures had to be clothed. (40th Bomb Group Collection)

tired and wet.

"As the hillside became tougher, we decided to build rafts at the first chance, which came on our 19th day of travel. We tried to build three two-man rafts as we teamed up. Caudle and I selected a dead pine, tall enough to make three logs and 13 feet long and 14 inches thick. It took until noon to chop it down with our machetes and another three hours to cut off the first two logs. Caudle went off hunting/fishing and I finished the third log, but the others did not get their cutting done.

"As usual lately, we shared three to four grouse for dinner and the broth was good. We ate everything; heads and feet were never wasted. We always had tea or hot water each morning and night when we said prayers and read from the Bible, ending with the Lord's Prayer.

"Firewood was scarce, and it was always dark before we had cut enough to build a fire in the center of the tent, wigwam style. We could not all get around the fire during the night to keep both heads and feet warm. We got into some good arguments when someone took more than his share of space at the fire.

"It took three days to get the logs and cross pieces to the river, notching them and tying the cross pieces with parachute cord. We were not optimistic. Rafts were sure to bump into something and maybe drown us as we were too weak to swim much in the swift river. Game became scarcer and would be less since Mannatt had used the last round for his carbine and there wasn't much .45 ammunition. Just before sunset on September 12th, we saw two planes flying up the river, but we could not signal as it was cloudy and raining.

"13 September – Day 23. We waited until the sun was well up because it was very cold on the river. The water was near freezing and we knew we would be wet when we launched the rafts. Stocks and Mannatt took the lead as their raft was farthest downstream. During the first hour we went a good distance as the river moved about five mph, but we had problems guiding our heavy rafts, even with poles. The current always carried us to the outside around bends where there were usually log piles.

"Shortly after noon we went around a sharp bend. There were Stocks and Mannatt standing on a log jam with their raft hung up. They yelled for us to stop and help them, but the swift current took us a good mile downstream before we stopped. Conrath and Childs stopped their raft close to us. We started back upstream when I said to Caudle: 'Listen.' Sure enough – in a few minutes we saw two planes coming up the river. Caudle had his signal mirror on them in no time and we could see the big red star on the tail, so we knew they were Russian. The planes made a sharp bank and then flew over us several times. They dipped their wings and shot flares, so we knew they had seen us. It was a grand feeling we had at the first sight of anything human in 23 days. We were not certain they had been searching for us; they did not drop any food or messages.

"14 September – Day 24. Since we had camped where we were, we were cramped and cold all night because of lack of firewood and the small tent. We had used the cord for the rafts. About noon, we heard planes in the distance and got out mirrors and blankets to get their attention.

"They flew over several times and dropped a bag which fell in the river. We tried to get the bag by using one of the rafts, but couldn't find it. We were really disappointed. Later on, the planes returned again and this time they dropped two bags; one contained flares and a pistol; the other had two loaves of bread, lard, sugar, flour, cookies, five cans of beef and four packs of Russian cigarettes and matches. Contents were water soaked – as both had fallen into the river, but Caudle jumped in and saved them. We dug into the wet loaves of bread; it was the most wonderful taste in the world! We didn't eat much, however, for fear of getting sick.

"The bag contained a note saying Murphy, Beckley and Webb were recovering in a village and that Russian comrades were on the

Some nose art drew inspiration from music, such as the jazz hit *Sleepy Time Gal*. (40th Bomb Group Collection)

way to get us. They asked us to fire a flare every hour. We cut wood, made a fire and fried some bread in the lard and ate a half can of meat apiece. I ate too much and had a bad stomach ache.

"15-16 September – Days 25-26. We lay around all morning drying out the bread by frying it. About noon the planes returned with more bags of food; fresh salmon, four cans of American pork sausage, and two bags of black bread along with two notes. They told us to fire one flare if Maj. McGlinn had joined us; two if not. We fired two as McGlinn had not been heard from.

"The other note was from Lt. Murphy who told us to stay where we were and that they were in a small hospital 25 air miles away. No one came to get us either day. I had miserable stomach cramps all the time.

"Sunday, 17 September – Day 27. About 1100, three long, narrow, shallow boats came with six men poling them. We shook hands with each, but could not talk except by drawing pictures and using sign language. They prepared a meal of three large pots of potatoes and beef stew which we all ate, even me, because it smelled too good to resist. We got in the canoes and left in a chilly wind that made us weak passengers really cold. We soon ran into log jams completely across the river which would have ended our raft trips, if not our lives. The boatmen let us out on the bank and pulled the boars over the jams. There were several more such jams, and we could now see why it took four days for those husky men to come up the river to us. Along the way we met more men with more canoes who took us downstream until about 1700 where we got off on a gravel bank. A doctor was among the new men there. They had a nice fire and another big pot of stew with a big chunk of butter

in it. After this delicious meal we had condensed milk with our tea before we crawled into a tent which was heated by a wood stove. We were the happiest, most contented people in the world that night.

"Monday, 18 September – Day 28. We arose on a cold, cloudy day to find breakfast ready. We left by 0900 and stopped every hour for a break and to get around more log jams. At noon another man coming upstream had lunch for us on a gravel bar. We finally arrived at the village of Manoma, on the Manoma River, at about 1700 and were taken to a log cabin. We were in the mayor's cabin where people constantly came in to look at us; none could speak English. We were given lots of bread and fresh milk to drink (the first we had tasted since leaving the States) before we were served a nice vegetable soup. There, we slept in beds on the floor, the first night's sleep under a roof in 30 days. We were disappointed to learn that we had another day's travel by boat and a 15-kilometer horseback ride before we would reach the hospital with our buddies.

"Tuesday, September 19 – Day 29. We had more soup for breakfast with fresh eggs. When we left Manoma about 1100, the whole village turned out to see us off. Although we only had one log jam to cross all day, it was after dark and in a heavy thunderstorm before we reached Petnosky and went to Lt. Vanya's home. I don't know how those boatmen were able to dodge rocks, trees and debris in the river without once tipping us over. Vanya's home was a nice log building with electric lights. Mrs. Vanya had dinner waiting, including a whole roast pig. We ate far too much for our shriveled stomachs. Then we sat around listening to Russian songs and music on a Victrola. We really slept good that night.

"Wednesday, 20 September – Day 30. Our breakfast was similar

Even when clothed, to comply with official policy and religious sensibilities, some nose art figures still leave little to the imagination. (40th Bomb Group Collection)

to the night before with a new roast pig and fried eggs. At 1000 they brought horses for us. We shook hands all around with the boatmen and villagers. The major (doctor) was still with us for a four-hour ride in bright warm sunshine to Troisk where we were taken to Army headquarters. There our names and information were taken as well as snapshots. We received copies. When we arrived at the hospital, we found that the first three men had left for Khabarovsk. We took our baths, under supervision of the women and received clean clothes. We had another interrogation between meals before we went to bed for a good sleep."

Ernest Caudle's Diary. "Thursday-Friday, 21-22 September – Days 31-32: We received our first haircuts and shaves in over a month; what a relief to get the brush off my face. A Russian major who could speak English had been met the day before and was in charge of questions. Turner and I located on a map where we had bailed out. Search was started north of there for Maj. McGlinn and Sgt. Robson. Until this time, the Russians had been searching too far south for them. We were questioned all day and into the night. I bore the brunt of the interrogations since I was in command in the absence of Maj. McGlinn. The Russians were courteous and considerate, never pressing me when I refused to answer a question or sign a document.

"We received our own laundered clothing back before we left Troisk for Khabarovsk at about 9:30. We traveled up the Amur River to the south in a government launch, accompanied by the English-speaking major and a captain. We had a very nice trip in the sunshine as the boat was a cabin job, very snug and warm. We had a noon lunch of bread and Spam. We arrived at Khabarovsk about 1900. We were taken to a hospital in a Ford Model A bus where we had a happy reunion with Murphy, Webb, and Beckley. We received a bath, ate and went to bed. We were all nine in one room on the sixth floor of the hospital. We talked far into the night before we fell asleep."

Richard McGlinn's Diary. "Friday, 22 September – Day 32. As we couldn't get back to the river by evening, we made camp out of sheer exhaustion near an old hollow stump. As usual, we built a fire first and while cutting boughs to sleep on, we heard aircraft approaching. Boughs were tossed on the fire to make a smudge, but the planes passed by rather high and to the east.

"Again our hopes were shattered, but after a while, the planes became audible and we heaped more boughs on the blaze. We used our mirrors as best we could in the trees and setting sun. The planes circled and finally buzzed as it became apparent we were the objects of a search.

"Saturday, 23 September. We moved onto the river by mid-morning to set up a spot we could tend fire, fish, wait and pray. By afternoon, clouds moved in to hide the sun. We heard the planes again. They circled our old campsite. Our fire could only turn out

Low fuel forced *The Ramp Tramp,* a 771st Bomb Squadron B-29 to land at Vladivostok in the USSR in November 1944. The Soviets later patterned their Tupolev Tu-4 on such interned Superfortresses. (Hans-Heiri Stapfer collection)

a puny smudge and we couldn't use the mirrors to attract them our way. I can't explain how lost we felt when they flew away. Much later, we heard the putt-putt of a light training plane. This time, when we heaped on grass, we got a good smudge. After a couple passes, the pilot saw us and swung around to us. He dropped a, gunny sack which fell in the river. Robson was able to retrieve it.

"We had tears in our eyes when we opened it, then really cried with happiness as we read the note: 'Good day, Comrades. You are in USSR. Raise high the left hand if you need help.'

"We waved everything, not only because we were in desperate need, but for joy. We opened the water-soaked pack (contents protected by hay) to find two loaves of bread, two-pound sack of C&H sugar, canned U.S. pork, salt pork, bag of white flour and some tobacco.

"Robson rolled us cigarettes as I threw out the skillet of moss and started cooking our new food, eating bread all the while. We ate almost continuously for eight hours before dropping off to sleep under the stars for seven hours.

"When we woke on Sunday, the 24th, we said our prayers and thanked St. Theresa, before we grabbed the bread and started another session of eating. This was for four hours and the wrong thing to do, but starving men can't be reasonable when food is given to them. My legs and feet began to swell and when I finally got my shoes on, I didn't take them off for the next three days.

"Our friendly plane returned late in the afternoon to drop two packages in the woods. We found one, but never located the other.

"In addition to the food, we received more joy from a note and map enclosed which gave us our position with instructions to go to the village of Tolomo, some eight to ten miles away. We had hoped for a guide or rescue party, but were determined to do for ourselves as best we could. We had to rest a couple more days, trying to fix

our torn clothes as we gained strength from eating again. One day a plane did go by, but did not find us. We figured it would take a week to travel to Tolomo in our weakened condition and slow going along the river. However, two planes showed up a couple days later and dropped three bags of food. Their aim was good and we only had to move a few feet to retrieve them. Each bag contained food and a note stating: 'Stay where you are – do not move – our people are coming after you. Light fires along the river if you do move. Nine men of your crew are safe and well.' That news was wonderful. What a relief to hear that.

"We had a very good supper of fish. Just before making camp we came across a salmon which had been caught by an eagle that had eaten the choice parts. The gills were still a bright red so I knew the fish was fresh. It was wonderful. It also provided us with breakfast and even a light noon lunch. Shortly after this, human voices were heard shouting downstream. Finally a canoe being poled by three men was visible. We did not think it possible to get a craft up that river and had been expecting to see a land party show up.

"How can a man write of his joy of meeting human beings who are bent on rescue, when that man had almost tasted death from want, privation, starvation, exposure and just plain loneliness? The party consisted of Alex A. Pobozhy, Russian engineer and two natives, Emil John and Kobin. What an experience – we not being able to speak Russian and they unable to converse in English, but by signs we did pretty well. We were loaded into the canoe to start on a difficult trek. The boat was about 16 feet long with a forward deck of about three to four feet.

"Robson and I reclined in the middle and it was a pleasure to watch the fallen timber, tall grass and swampland go by at five to six mph. When we came to log jams, Emil John and Kobin would keep us a steady talk as they slowed the craft, jockeyed into place

Ding How (42-6358), which made a forced landing in Vladivostok in the Soviet Union on 21 November 1944, is seen here in Soviet markings at the Tupolev factory in 1945. There it served as the pattern for the Soviet Tupolev Tu-4 bomber.

and guided it through waters that we thought were impassable. Sometimes on jams, they would have to chop and cut their way through, but never once did we have to portage. Even the rugged scenery appeared more beautiful during our ride.

"About two-thirds of the way to Tolomo, we came onto a gravel bar where a Russian named Nick Nick, was operating a radio back to his base. We continued downstream in our loaded canoe through calm water, white water and under log jams. The skill of the boatman never faltered. We rounded a bend and joined another river where we saw damaged log cabins. This was all that was left of Tolomo village. High waters had washed most of the place away. Nick Nick called out 'New York.' Even the City of New York wouldn't have looked any better to us then.

"We swung over onto a gravel bar and were met by a group of Russians and natives. The natives were living in primitive-style shacks made of skins, tree bark and grass, all supported by cut saplings. They had dogs, racks drying fish, salmon (which they had speared) and venison. Skins were being dried and tanning done. Some Russians were living there as "squaw men" in a dozen or so huts. We were taken into a hut to meet other Russian engineers and given chocolate. We rested in dog fur sleeping bags until hot water was prepared and we were given a sponge bath, which felt good. Soon a meal of pork soup, canned U.S. tomatoes and bread was ready. We ate and ate without having had to build a fire, prepare the food and do dishes. That night was the first time since we left India that we slept warm.

"Nick Nick was on the radio constantly – talk that concerned us but which we could not understand. Our boatmen visited us and Kobin brought us two pairs of fancy native moccasins for which we were most grateful. Emil John and his 16-year old son would take us down the river. Alex Pobozhy kept us out of harm's way when an aircraft flew over and dropped packages. Natives came from all around to see us in their canoes which lined the riverbanks.

"After a 24-hour stay at Tolomo, we headed down the river in boats with Pobozhy and friends giving us special care and treatment. Their vigil did not relax until we were turned over to the doctors at the Red Army Hospital in Komsomolsk, 40 days after parachuting from our plane. S/Sgt. Robsons weighed 40 kilograms (88.2 pounds, a loss of 35 pounds), and I weighted 61 kilograms (135 pounds, a loss of 25 pounds). We remained under excellent care at Komsomolsk until the 44th day. We arrived at Khabarovsk on the 45th day- thus uniting the entire crew on October 5th."

Road Through The Taiga

In 1974, Russian engineer, Aleksandr Alekseyevich Pobozhy, wrote *Dorogami Taigi* (*Roads Through the Taiga),* a reminiscence published by Molodaya Gvardiya Publishing House in Moscow. In 1944 Pobozhy headed a railroad survey team in the Sikhote-Alin mountain range where the USSR planned to build a second trans-Siberian railroad. In February 1975 excerpts from his book were published in *Soviet Life* magazine. There Pobozhy recalled his part in the 1944 rescue of Richard McGlinn and Charles Robson.

Aleksandr Pobozhy recalled: "On September 20, late in the evening, a radio operator and his guide arrived at our camp on exhausted horses. The radioman handed me a sealed packet which said, in part, 'This is a government mission to rescue two men who, along with nine men already rescued, parachuted from an allied B-29 into vicinity of the Khodzuai ridge, about 60 miles from Khabarovsk.' I was told to explore the valley of the Khoso River, a tributary of the Khungari, with selected men in a search party. Two planes were assigned to us to help in search and drop supplies.

"Today is the 20th of September, which means that the American fliers had been in the Taiga for more than a month, a long time to be lost in wild, dense forests. They could have died of starvation or been torn to pieces by wild animals. A trip was nothing for us into the Taiga as we had much equipment from which to select. We quickly put together sleeping bags, cooking utensils, saws, axes and enough rations for 10 days. We planned our search to go down the Khungari by rowboat by the village of Kun and exchange our boats for local ulmagdas [pointed, log-canoes made by the native peoples of the Amur Region, ed.] which were more suited for swift, rough rivers. We rose at dawn the next day and after preparing a first-aid kit, five of us left in two boats.

"The rumble of rapids reached us long before we saw them and as we went on, the current became stronger. We met our first severe test negotiating through timber obstructions in the rapids, but could expect at least 20 more clogged rapids on ahead. After passing some cliffs, we came upon an Oroche village which noisily greeted us strangers as the village was far from any roads. Most of the Oroche men were off at the war front or fishing salmon, stocking up on food supplies for the Army. Only old women and children remained. They told us our clumsy boats, without a guide, would never make it up the Khungari channels and tributaries, but I had a map to help us. We were able to safely pass several more rapids as we worked our oars, but with close calls. Our shoulders and hands ached.

"We almost met disaster at one rapids as we were flung against a log jam and onto it. Our radio operator was hurt quite badly in the face and arms. Luckily we did save one of the boats and could continue after bandaging the victim and leaving him at the spot. Twice later in the day, we had to lug our boat/equipment along the shore for more than two hours. We covered over 35 miles against severe headwinds before we reached the Tolomo settlement that day. Part of the town washed away earlier in the spring floods and natives were rebuilding on higher ground. Our search on September 22nd and 23rd up the left valley of the Khoso yielded nothing. The next morning when we climbed out of our sleeping bags we found cold weather had set in as our bags were covered by hoar frost. The further we went up a main Khoso channel, the harder our progress became as we ran into shoals where we had to drag our boats ourselves, sometimes waist high in the water. More and more we had to chop and clear our way through fallen timber. We only covered 12 miles that day (24 September).

"At daybreak on the 25th, Sasha, Kilya and I set out making rapid progress as we only had to clear ourselves occasionally. Often we would come out on the bank to examine it and shout. By noon I was absolutely hoarse. We had already decided to return when suddenly some weak voices nearby seemed to respond to my call. We pushed our poles eagerly and after covering another 700 feet, saw a thin column of smoke and then two men standing near a campfire on the bank. I wanted to yell 'We've come for you!' and a lot more, but I didn't know any Englilsh words. Not knowing how to greet those people from far across the ocean, I shouted 'Mister America!' In a few minutes, a most confused 'conversation' started as we tried to gesticulate with words in English, Russian and Udeghe, but none of us understood a thing. The Americans broke into tears and got on their knees to pray.

"Sasha gave the fliers a bar of chocolate each and they shared them with us even though I tried to tell them they should eat; they were so weak they had to sit down as they couldn't stand for long. I looked them over calmly: they were emaciated and bearded, wearing ragged and tattered overalls that hardly covered the knees. One wore a leather jacket and battered shoes while the other had a foot covered by rags while the other foot had a pistol holster tied to it. Their faces and bodies were so lacerated by midges that sores and contusions had formed. I jabbed my finger on my chest and said slowly, 'Engineer Alexander Pobozhy.' The tall man introduced himself, 'Dick McGlinn,' and the other said he was 'Charles Robson.' By gestures, we understood they had been in an airplane.

"Our ulmagda was a rather long one and we spread out sleeping bags on the bottom so that Dick and Charles could lie on them. We moved back downstream and arrived back at our first campsite while the sun was still high. Our radio operator used his set to report the rescue news back to base while the rest of us built some shelters out of branches. We had to find out what ailed them most.

Gradually, we found they had stomach problems when McGlinn rubbed his stomach and moaned. Medicine was given to them to help overcome disorders from acute exhaustion and the plant diet they had endured. We heated water and washed our patients, put ointment on wounds and bandaged them. We collected enough clothes from amongst us to give the Americans a complete change. I ordered the airplane for the next day to drop more underwear, warm clothes, shoes, and provisions.

"After a good night's sleep for the exhausted men, I drew a map to show Dick and Charles where we were headed and where we now were. Soon two airplanes arrived and dropped their cargo where we had built our signals along the river. After we had fitted Dick and Charles out, they gave us a Colt revolver which held only two cartridges. Dick made drawings on paper which we understood to mean that they were going to wait three more days, dig their graves and then use the pistol to kill themselves. Dick wrote his name and address on a piece of paper, but it got wet in the rain and I forgot to ask him to write them again for me. The next day we approached a settlement near the mouth of the Khungari and the radio operator called out 'New York.' Both Dick and Charles smiled, and the latter said, 'Empire Empire' as he pointed to the biggest house.

"After spending a night in the clean, pleasant house of the doctor, we went down the swift Khungari out onto the broad, placid Amur River. A big launch was only two miles away and it took us all to Komsomolsk-on-Amur at midday. Charles and Dick were driven off to the hospital, but not before asking to have their pictures taken so they would have a momento of how they looked in the Taiga. We met again one more time five days later at the hospital where they were convalescing. Dick pulled out a piece of paper from which he read slowly, in Russian: 'Alexander, we Americans will never forget the exploit of the brave and gallant Russians.' I never saw them again and we didn't write to one another. I wonder now if Dick and Charles remember our friendship on a Taiga river, the Khoso?"

In all, crews from 37 planes were interned in Russian Siberia. These included one crew of a B-25 from the Doolittle raid. Of the 16 planes on the Doolittle mission, the only one that did not crash land in China set down near Vladivostok in the Soviet Union. In fact, at the time of the Doolittle mission, Gen. Doolittle proposed that the planes fly off the carrier, bomb Japan and then fly to Vladivostok. Since we were delivering planes to Russia, via Alaska, why not deliver them to Russia while doing a little bombing along the way. But the Soviet Union, at that time, was not at war with Japan and did not wish to have to deal with an assault on Siberia by the Japanese who occupied Manchuria. The Soviets were already fighting for their survival against the Nazi invasion in the west of the country. The Japanese had launched border attacks on the Soviet Union from Manchuria in 1938 and 1939. The Soviets repulsed the Japanese and negotiations to prevent further clashes began. In April 1941 the two countries signed a neutrality agreement. When Hitler invaded the USSR two months later, neither Moscow nor Tokyo were interested in reopening hostilities in the Soviet Far East. At the Tehran and Yalta Summit Conferences in 1943 and 1945, the Soviet Union pledged to join the war against Japan within three months after the end of the war in Europe. But until V-E day, U.S. and British military personnel involved in the war against Japan could not enter Soviet territory without being interned.

It was to maintain this fragile peace that the Soviets frowned on any American planes seeking sanctuary in their Far Eastern territories. Notwithstanding this, three other B-29 crews landed in the Vladivostok area. Two were from the 468th Bomb Group and one from the 462nd Bomb Group. During the war, 21 crews from the 11th Air Force flying out of Alaska landed in Russian territory or were rescued from Northern Pacific waters. Another 11 crews from the Navy Fleet Air Wing Four were interned in the USSR.

The plane from the 462nd flew to Soviet territory on 29 July 1944, after the Anshan mission when they experienced engine trouble and figured they could not make it back to friendly Chinese territory. The two planes from the 468th came after McGlinn's crew had bailed out. These planes were on missions to Omura on 11 November and 21 November 1944. On both occasions weather was a contributing factor in their having to divert to Vladivostok. In the case of the plane having to land after the November 21 mission, they had sustained battle damage over the target as well as experiencing hazards from the weather that included headwinds of up to 120 m.p.h.

All of these B-29s landed on Russian runways without incident. Of course, once the crews were escorted from the planes, they never were allowed to go back to them. In one instance, the pilot had picked out a concrete runway on an airfield where he intended to set down. Instead, Russian fighters escorting him indicated a grass field where they wanted him to land. He obeyed, but observed that he did not see how the Russians ever could get the plane out of there again.

Information from another source underscores the difficulty attendant to attacking the Yawata steel-making complex that was the target for McGlinn's crew the day they were hit. A year later when the crew of *Bockscar* was trying to find a hole in the clouds which would allow them to bomb Nagasaki visually, they flew in the area bordering Yawata. They reported that the volume of flak being thrown up around Yawata made it a very uninviting target.

The Superfortress crewmen shared their interment with the Doolittle crew members, one of whom expressed the melancholy observation that during his time in the service, he had spent one day in combat and the rest of the war was spent in a Russian internment camp. Another melancholy note may be found in the fact that some of the prisoners were not released by the Russians until after the Japanese surrender.

Of the crewmen interned in the USSR, Alman Conrath, Ernest Caudle, William Stocks, and Melvin Webb managed to keep diaries. Harry Changnon drew from the diaries, augmented by material collected from other sources, to continue the narrative of the No. 829 fliers interned in the Soviet Union.

After rescue, the men were taken from the Village of Manoma to the hospital in Khabarovsk. The first leg of the trip was by power launch on the river. Power was derived from a six-cylinder Scripps engine made in Detroit. The river trip was about 122 miles. On arrival at Khabarovsk, the crewmen were transported to the hospital by a Model "A" Ford bus. They wrote that they were receiving the best possible treatment. They slept until 8:00 a.m., then would have breakfast, and follow that up with a walk in the hospital garden. There was nothing in English to read but they could kill time by making use of the available chess sets and dominos. On 5 October, after 44 days, the entire crew was reunited at the hospital. All of the men suffered from prolonged exposure: Caudle had lost 45 pounds, down from his usual 190. Others had suffered weight loss of about 25 percent. McGlinn had a problem with his teeth: while carrying

Robson at one point, he had fallen on slippery rocks and broken his front teeth. Others had cuts and sores that took most of October to heal.

For some, the hospital stay was monotonous, yet they were able to make a complete recovery. Caudle regained his original weight, although not his former strength. The diarists describe the people at the hospital as being very kind, doing everything in their power to make the Americans comfortable. They particularly remembered nurse Marina Rudolfovna Falikova whom they called "Momma." A sergeant in charge of hospital supplies and the boss of the other nurses, Falikova was 44 years old and the wife of a military doctor with the rank of Lieutenant Colonel. The couple had a son, aged 22, who was a battalion commander and was killed fighting the Germans. The crewmen write that Falikova adopted them and called them her "children" – except for Major McGlinn whom she addressed as "Comrade Major." She learned some English from the American fliers, who, in turn, learned some Russian from her. Conrath could speak German, and the crewmen found that many Russians were able to speak some German. In addition, some French was used. "Momma" saw to it that her "children" were supplied with tobacco, but there were no tailor-made cigarettes; the men had to roll their own.

The crewmen wrote that they could never be grateful enough to "Momma" for all she did for them. She was like a mother. On 23 October she came in with a rumor that the men would be moving in three or four days. She kept them posted on developments, but told the men to "keep it quiet."

On 28 October, the men were given word to pack up their belongings. Major McGlinn called a crew meeting and told the men to uphold the American name while travelling. The crewmen were to watch their manners, their language, and present a good appearance. They left the hospital that afternoon, again in the Model "A" bus, to a rest camp for Russian officers. There they met 15 other Americans – Army and Navy personnel – who had made their way to Russian territory while flying from the Aleutians.

At this rest camp, they were able to get out-of-doors more. Even before their move on 28 October, it was snowing. Here they received new clothes and shoes, which were a big help in the colder weather. Winter was setting in fast. It stayed below zero lots of the time and went low enough at night to freeze the Amur River even though the current is fairly fast. Food was good, the diarists wrote, noting that they even had steaks for breakfast. They were issued five pairs of skis, and some of the guys were using them until Mannatt broke a pair and hurt his knee. The doctor then ordered: "no more skiing."

The camp consisted of quite a number of wooden buildings widely scattered over about 10 acres overlooking the Amur River. "We Americans have a barracks of our own. There are four of us to a room. The rooms are small, but comfortable, with clean beds and plenty of covers. Two large rooms in the building are used for recreation. Khabarovsk is about 12 miles from the Japanese on the Manchurian border," one of the fliers recorded.

One of the Americans wrote: "We walk a half mile through the snow to the mess hall for the best food we have had yet – American cheese, tea, fresh meat, white bread, etc."

But there was frustration over the lack of English-language reading material and over the fact that there was no way of communicating with the U.S. government. The crewmen wrote that they were waiting for some other crews to arrive before they could start out for

One wing gone, a Boeing B-29 Superfortress hurtles down in flames after a direct flak hit over Japan. The aircraft's nose section and a portion of one wing are visible at the lower end of the bright fiery area.

some other place, but that they were growing impatient. Everyone seemed to have a quick temper from being together for so long with nothing to do but eat and sleep. "However, we are grateful to the Russians for the care they have given us," they noted.

The crewmen reported that Robson was improving rapidly but that Major McGlinn had chills and swollen legs and feet. He didn't eat much because of his sore mouth.

In the first week of November the internees were issued some warmer clothes: shirts, pants, jackets and gloves, but no shoes. Finally they were also issued new shoes – made in America. The 7th of November 1944 was the 27th anniversary of the Russian revolution. The celebrating didn't amount to much although some Russian girls came and danced for the Americans, who were informed that Roosevelt had been reelected by a large majority.

The men found the Russians' mess hours "really screwy": 10:00, 16:00, and 21:00.

On 9 November the men were still waiting for other Americans to arrive. The day before they had heard that they were halfway here, but then heard that they had been stalled by the weather. The winter had really set in. Snow every day. Patches of ice as big as an acre could be seen flowing down the river.

Finally, on 11 November, the other Americans arrived. It was a party of 20 – which now brought their number to 46. Of the total, only one man had been wounded; he had taken a piece of shrapnel in his hand.

The men were told that they would be leaving the camp on 15 November for Tashkent, a 12- to 14-day journey on the Trans-Siberian Railroad. When boarding time came, 39 men were loaded in their car. The seven-man crew of a B-24 was left behind.

The 39 detainees found the car of the train to which they were assigned to be a very poor Russian troop car made of wood with narrow, short benches used for sitting on in the daytime and sleeping on at night. The car was infested with bedbugs. Two cars with Russian passengers separated the Americans' troop car from the dining car where they ate. The Russian passengers carried their own food – raw fish being included in their fare. "The smell would turn your stomach," one diarist complained. Although Tashkent, their destination, was supposed to be warmer, it was 5,000 miles away and they were told that *en route* the temperature may drop as low as 70 degrees below zero.

A Russian lieutenant accompanied the Americans during their trip. Called "Steve" by the men, he could speak "pretty good English," the diarists wrote, and helped the men along the way. One of the internees wrote, "We passed some barbed wire enclosures with watchtowers that looked like prison camps. When we asked Steve what they were, he professed not to have seen anything and said he did not know what we were talking about. We passed through thickly forested country. Most of the way was double-track railroad. All the bridges were guarded with machine-gun emplacements and barbed wire. We stopped at some of the larger cities along the route Chita, Irkutsk, and Novosibirsk. At Irkutsk, the train station was as big as New York's Grand Central. Much-damaged railroad equipment was seen on sidings, probably from the Russian front. Some cars observed on sidings carried signs that said they were made in Erie, Pennsylvania."

The trip across Siberia took 10 days. The following diary notes made by some of the crew members document the misery of the trip.

"Thursday, 16 November. Some fellows slept well, but most of us were eaten up by bedbugs. We eat in an international dining car which is kept warm by a samovar.

"Friday, 17 November. Spent most of the day watching the scenery which is flat like Kansas. Luckily, we now have a few magazines with which to pass the time.

"Saturday, 18 November. Countryside has changed to stunted, timbered, mountain slopes. Lakes and rivers are frozen and snow

With its No. 3 engine crippled, this B-29 from Tinian is continuing its mission over Osaka, Japan, on 1 June 1945. Oil leaking from the stricken engine also leaves its mark on the right horizontal stabilizer. (Department of Defense)

covered.

"Sunday, 19 November. We passed Lake Baikal, maybe the deepest lake in the world, and we went through more than 40 tunnels in one two-hour period. Lots of snow along the way. Time has moved back three hours in the 1,000 miles since leaving Khabarovsk and will change five more times by the time we reach Tashkent.

"Monday, 20 November. Snowed hard most of the day. Still in timber country, but the trees are not larger. We passed through Irkutsk today. We also crossed Siberia's widest river, the Angara.

"Tuesday, 21 November. We must be getting used to the bedbugs; at least there is not so much complaining. Weather is colder: -22 degrees F this morning. We arrived at Novosibirsk about 16:00 and had lunch in the station which the Russians say is the largest in the world. We got to take showers before supper and then got new sheets and pillowcases. We slept in the car parked in the rail yards. One of the guys had an ear frozen even though he was only outside about five minutes.

"Wednesday, 22 November. This morning was the coldest yet: -40 degrees C. [which is also -40 degrees Fahrenheit. Ed.] Breakfast earlier than usual at 9:30. We all got shaves and haircuts at the station before our lunch at 13:15 whereupon we left Novosibirsk.

We had dinner on the train in our own car, but it was only dry bread, butter, salted fish and dehydrated milk.

"Thursday, 23 November. Breakfast was the same as last night's supper--only small pieces of Spam instead of the fish. We saw rolling and flat country partly irrigated. We stopped for lunch at 16:00. The train is making slow time. We saw some camels pulling sleds alongside the tracks.

"Friday, 24 November. Weather seems warmer, although it snowed most of the day and snow is still on the ground. Trees don't appear to be as frozen. We are passing through desert-like country, and we see animals. Herders use camels to herd both cattle and goats in the same bunches. We passed close to Lake Balkhash. Most men's mouths are cut from eating the dry, hard bread. During the week we passed through the Russian Republics of Mongolia, Siberia, Kazakhstan and are approaching Uzbekistan where Tashkent is the capital.

"Saturday, 25 November. Weather has moderated, and snow has disappeared. We ate lunch late at a station.

"Sunday, 26 November. Arrived at Tashkent about 13:30. It is good to see fruit trees and green grass again. We found 62 more Americans at our new quarters. Some of them had landed in Russia as far back as June. There are 101 men in camp now. They have the place fixed up with baseball diamonds, basketball and volleyball courts. They also have supplies received from the American Embassy in Moscow – reading material and a radio. It is the first tuning set we've seen in Russia. We all took baths before meeting others. Our food is wonderful although those who have been here are tired of it. We had our first taste of coffee and even apple turnovers. We get more meat with meals now.

"Monday, 27 November. We are allowed to send cablegrams home and also to send letters to our families. Rumors are strong that we will be allowed to "escape" across the border to Iran as others have done. Even the Russian commandant, Maj. Putakana added to the raising of morale by saying Soviet and U.S. officials from Moscow were coming to arrange for a transfer of some kind. He cautioned that earlier attempts to escape had almost caused fatalities.

"Thursday, 30 November. Today is Thanksgiving Day. Of course it is not observed by the Russians. Lt. Col. Robert McCabe arrived today from Moscow with good news. He gave us proof that our parents have been notified about our safety. He also brought mail sacks of letters for men who have been here prior to our arrival. Those letters helped us understand the war situation."

Mel Webb's journal picks up the story: "On 2 December, we received another bath, and we are supposed to have a party of some kind, too. An eleven-member Russian band played for us this afternoon, and a choral group of 213 sang. They were very good. We had a big meal and all the beer we could drink.

"Tuesday, 5 December. We left Tashkent about midnight on the same stinking boxcars as before, and the bedbugs were still biting. There is snow on the ground, and it is plenty cold. Lt. Col. McCabe gave us a talk about following strict orders on the trip.

"Thursday, 7 December. We are still traveling toward Tifilis where our orders read we are to help with Russian plane ferrying. Late in the afternoon, the front car started having trouble with the wheels, or so the Japanese might be told. We were disconnected from the train and put on a siding about dark. Some trucks are to come to pick us up and take us near the border for an escape. However, something was fouled up, and we didn't make connections.

"Friday, 8 December: We are still on the siding, and the officer from Moscow said orders had come through to stop us. Two more days on the siding living in the boxcar was tiresome.

"Sunday, 10 December. Finally, after dark, the officer in charge said we were returning to Tashkent. This was a blow to us."

The Soviets were evidently moving the American internees into Central Asia from where they could be spirited across the border into Iran, in an officially planned "escape," a subterfuge that would allow the USSR to avoid blame for violating its neutrality treaty with Japan. Fate intervened with one of its cruel tricks at this time, however, when U.S. newspaper columnist Drew Pearson published a story claiming that the Soviets had released at the Iranian border one of the Doolittle mission crew members who had landed in Russia. Upon publication of the Pearson article, the Soviets halted the entire operation aimed at setting the Americans free. Moscow feared that the story would draw attention to the departing U.S. personnel and could prompt Tokyo to attack the USSR over the Manchurian border on the pretext that the Soviets had violated the provisions of the neutrality pact.

Mel Webb continued: "Thirty-four out of the hundred men left the train to try to make it across the border. I gave one man my compass, bread, coat, blanket and wished him good luck. I would not try it myself. I had already had all the walking in Russia I wanted. Besides, I figured it was too cold to make it. The next morning, all of the men were back except seven.

"On Monday, 11 December, we left for Tashkent at about 09:00 with Navy Lt. Cmdr. Charles Wayne in charge of our party, He is intensely disliked. We are all happier when Maj. McGlinn took over control of the Army men. We arrived back in Tashkent for the second time alter being within 30 miles of the Iranian border. It seemed like our building was cooler than ever. The poor Russian people around Tashkent don't have a chance. They are ragged, hungry and always begging for something. We see American products like trucks, engines, guns, and food almost everywhere. In fact, about 95% of their materiel seems to have come from the United States. We steal wood whenever we can to try to keep our barracks fires going. I guess we give the Russians a bad time.

"Tuesday, 12 December. Mike Losik (from Jarrell's B-29 crew) and six Navy men were apprehended by alert Russian guards at the Iranian border. These men were the last of those who tried to escape to Iran from the railroad siding where we were being held prior to our return to Tashkent. They were half frozen, hungry, and sick. They were held in cold buildings in Ashkhabad for three days while they were quizzed by their captors. Losik said that was a real low point in his life, and even in 1992, he still did not want to talk about it. The men were returned to the camp on the 17th. Lt. Cmdr. Charles Wayne tried to enforce military discipline and have the men punished, which was almost more than they could endure. The Russians threatened everyone by saying that if anyone else tried to escape, they would be put into their POW camp.

"Mai. McGlinn's Christmas Plan: After our aborted attempt to leave Tashkent, and our return to the walled camp from which we had set out, Maj. McGlinn noted that morale of the internees had really turned sour. Complaints on living conditions multiplied. Everyone noticed how cold and miserable buildings had become. This was mainly because we were worried about ever getting out of Russia. With the approach of Christmas and New Year's, which were usually festive occasions, men became sullen and mean to each other. McGlinn suggested to the new camp commandant, Lt. Col. Ivan Siminov, that preparing for a Christmas party would give the men something to do which would lift their spirits. The Russians remembered the party on 17 October when the Russians had put on a celebration for their Red Army Day. It got out of hand because too much vodka was available. Almost every door was ripped off its hinges, and windows were knocked out. The commandant would have to give thought to the suggestion before granting approval.

"On 16 December, not only was the party approved, but Siminov said the Russians would provide special food for the occasion. Committees were formed to prepare for the party. Twenty-nine more American fliers, including the Weston Price and William Mickish B-29 crews, arrived at the Tashkent camp. They quickly joined in preparations for the Christmas party."

AI Conrath recalled in 1992: "During our sojourn in Tashkent, when time was heavy, I pulled the colored threads from several towels. I used the threads to make an embroidered 20th Air Force patch and a CBI patch in color on part of my parachute. (It is framed and hangs today on the wall in my home.) Other mementos and souvenirs I have are the clock from my engineer's panel, the ripcord handle from my chute, my A-2 jacket, the blood chit flag from my jacket, a signal mirror, a Chinese soldier's cap emblem, an Uzbek

Russian cap and the cigarette lighter given to us in Tashkent."

Jerome Zuercher and others recalled: "We realized this was going to be a Christmas party different than any we had ever had before, and for some men, it was the first away from home. We wanted to include all the religious elements possible to show the Russians that Christmas in America has a very special meaning.

"Sam Gelber, a Navy gunner from the Bronx knew all the popular Christmas carols so he organized and directed a 70-man choir that often practiced far into the night. Leonard Karkoszyneski, a Polish gunner, found a large white cloth on which he painted a beautiful Christmas scene. He used a piece of charcoal to sketch a figure of an American soldier kneeling at prayer with the Christmas star shining overhead. The rest of us got some colored paper and snipped out the usual yuletide candles, wreaths and holly.

"George Hummel, a gunner on Jarrell's crew, had been a baker in civilian life. He got a special ration of flour and beet sugar and worked a whole day mixing up a delicious batch of cookies and cake. The Russians didn't restrict our plans in any way, although they did look in on us occasionally to see that we weren't destroying anything. Several days before the party, out of courtesy, we sent an invitation to the NKVD officers, and they surprised us by readily accepting,

"Christmas Eve arrived cold and clear. Sam's choir softly sang their carols and other religious numbers by flickering candlelight with Leonard's drawing dimly showing in the light. Maj. McGlinn told us how the Bible described the first Christmas. When he finished, no one said a word. All of us had forgotten where we were, because in our minds we were back home with our families, gathered around a tree, shouting 'Merry Christmas!' and exchanging gifts. Even the Russians sat in respectful silence. The lights came on, and the choir sang 'Jingle Bells.' One of the fellows got up and read a poem poking fun at our Russian commandant. He did not understand English so he sat sternly in his seat.

"When dinner was served, we had a pleasant change from our usual diet of rice and goat meat. We eagerly devoured roast chicken, potatoes, pickles, green onions, bread, tea and Hummel's whitecake. When we had finished eating, the Commandant stood up and in marched several soldiers carrying vodka for everyone. More entertainment followed, including barbershop harmony, poetry, and amateur show jokes. Two boys put on an exhibition of jitterbug dancing which amazed the Russians who demanded several repeat performances. The Russians produced an old gramophone and played tangos and polkas. We took turns dancing with the women workers who were there.

"Some of the Russian officers wanted to know if Christmas was the birthday of one of our leaders. We tried to explain that it was the birthday of Jesus Christ and were having trouble with this explanation because of the language difficulty. However, one of the NKVD colonels surprised us by explaining to his friends our feast of Christmas, its origin, the exchange of gifts and other customs. Some older officers remembered that in their youth, they had seen such celebrations. The colonel who had explained Christmas used a phrase which was explained to us as meaning 'Merry Birthday of Christ.' And that's what it was.

"The vodka caused the party to get rather wild. Pickles started flying through the air and a Russian was hit. An officer, who was drunk, hit an enlisted man."

Mel Webb notes on the period 27-31 December. "After the Christmas party, we were all in the dumps. Loneliness set in, and we felt tired. We didn't even know if we would leave this place until the war was over. We made a trip into town for a couple of hours, but we didn't see much to buy that we wanted. There was another Russian party on December 31st, but it was not well attended even though the Russians served extra vodka. We didn't feel like celebrating New Year's Eve.

"8 January, 1945. We received American supplies from Moscow evidently as a result of our requests for things when Lt. Col. McCabe was here a month ago for our aborted escape. There are rumors we may get some mail from home real soon.

"17 January. Maj. Paul Hall arrived from Moscow with bags of mail. We were told at noon we may leave soon. They told us we had to swear to secrecy about our plans and trip. They said that we had seen how publicity could hurt us or anyone else who might be in a similar position. In a letter one of the boys received from home was a clipping of the Drew Pearson article about one of the Doolittle men having talked about his leaving Russia. That was why they returned us to Tashkent.

"24 January. We turned in extra clothes a few days ago and were supposed to leave on the 22nd, but something happened, and our trip was postponed. Today I and some other boys were brought before the Officer in Charge for throwing mud balls at some Russian officer. The Russians didn't punish us, however.

"26 January. We had to sign pledges of secrecy about our Russian story. They gave us food rations again before we left Tashkent on the train about 21:00. The bedbugs sure did bite. We may cross the border in trucks tomorrow night.

"28 January. We left the train at 20:15 and got aboard G.I. trucks to make the longest, roughest, dirtiest trip I have ever had. Through all of it, we were closed in the trucks, and the trip was along dirt roads to Teheran, Iran. We did stop long enough to eat and swim in the Caspian Sea even though it was cold. We were delayed one hour at the border. We rode all that night, stopping the next day at 13:30 to eat our second meal. We crossed some mountains during the night, and it became very cold.

"30-31 January. We traveled 900 miles in 48 hours and were very tired and dirty. At the hospital at our arrival site, they backed the trucks up to the door so we were out of sight when we unloaded."

"Another member of the party picks up the story: "Once inside the hospital, we were dusted with an insecticide. Then a hot shower, a good meal and off to bed in a warm room which was a real luxury. After a day or two, 131 of us were loaded into five C-46s and flown to Suez where we spent 10 or 12 days in a little isolated tent camp while we waited for arrangements to be made to get us home. Then we were loaded back into the C-46s and flown to Naples. There we were again, put into the back of trucks, but this time only for an hour or so. We were driven to the docks and put aboard the John Sullivan, an empty Liberty ship heading back to New York.

"On the second or third day of our sea voyage, after joining a convoy at Wahrân ('Oran' in Algeria), we passed Gibraltar. Just after that, a shipboard alarm had us all scrambling to get up on deck. A German sub was operating around a loaded convoy coming toward us. The ship's crew assured us that we were safe because we had no cargo and were not a worthwhile target. This made us feel a little better because we could see that one of the loaded ships had been hit and appeared to be sinking a few miles away. After that the trip was quite pleasant with warm sunny weather even though it was

February by now. Only the last two days of the ocean trip were cold and stormy as we neared the Atlantic Coast and got out of the Gulf Stream. Some men got seasick.

"Twenty-three days after leaving Naples, we docked in a heavy fog in Brooklyn. This was 6 March 1945. We were taken to Ft.. Hamilton, New York. Within a few days, all of the repatriated men were on their way home for 30-day leaves."

The "Dixie Mission"

The experiences of one other member of the 40th Bomb Group were also unique. Louis Jones was serving as an intelligence officer with the 45th Bombardment Squadron of the 40th Bomb Group in 1944, when he received a call from Lt. Col. Reginald E. Foss at Bomber Command headquarters informing him that he had been selected to represent the 20th Bomber Command on a fact-finding mission to the headquarters of the Chinese Communists in Yan'an in northern China's Shaanxi Province.

Writing in 1986, Jones recalled: "My primary assignment was to act as liaison between the Communists and the 20th Bomber Command. I was to determine to what extent they could be of assistance in recovering B-29 crews that might be down in areas they [the Communists] controlled."

At the time, the United States officially recognized the government of Generalissimo Chiang Kai-shek, head of the Kuomintang ("Nationalist") Party, as the legitimate government of China. During the war, the capital of Chiang Kai-shek's Kuomintang government was located in Chongqing, near the Yangtze River, in southwestern China. But Chiang's Kuomintang was not the only anti-Japanese force operating in the country. China's powerful Communist Party controlled vast territories in northern China and waged a relentless guerrilla war against Japanese occupation forces.

In the last days of 1936, Chiang Kai-shek agreed to the end of the nearly 10 years of civil war against the Communists and to form, jointly with them, a united front for resistance to the Japanese occupation. Although nominally united in one army under one command, the Kuomintang army and the Communist armed forces operated against the Japanese independently of each other. Serious armed clashes between Communist and Kuomintang forces in 1940 and 1941 brought the united front to near rupture and the threat of a total breakup of the united front continued to loom over the anti-Japanese effort. In Chiang Kai-shek's presence at the Cairo Conference in December 1943, U.S. President Franklin Roosevelt stressed the need for continued unity and preventing armed clashes between the Kuomintang and the Communists. Nevertheless, until the end of the war, relations between the two Chinese power centers were tense.

Because of those strained relations, U.S. representatives in Chongqing had only limited and unreliable information regarding the Communists and their role in the war. The air war being waged by the U.S. Army Air Force over Chinese territory, including areas in which Communist guerrillas operated, necessitated some sort of direct contact with them. In addition, the Communist forces were waging an effective campaign against the Japanese and the U.S. sought better coordination with the Communists in the prosecution of the war in China, particularly in the event of the launch of a major Allied counteroffensive. For their part, the Communists, who unlike the Kuomintang received no aid or materiel from the

Chinese Communist Party Chairman Mao Zedong confers with U.S. emissary Patrick J. Hurley in Yan'an. Attending the meeting are (left to right) Chinese Communist military commander Zhu De, Mao Zedong, Col. Ivan D. Yeaton, Patrick Hurley, Kuomintang General Zhang Zhizhong, and senior Chinese Communist negotiator Zhou Enlai.

U.S., were very much interested in receiving American weapons and military supplies for use against the Japanese occupation forces.

Chiang Kai-shek opposed and rebuffed persistent U.S. pressure for the establishment of direct American contact with Communist forces, including requests coming from the White House itself. But after holding talks with visiting U.S. Vice President Henry Wallace in Chongqing in the summer of 1944, the Chinese Generalissimo finally relented and a United States Army Observation Group in Yan'an, code named "Dixie," was launched on 22 July 1944.

In 1986, Jones wrote that he joined up with the other members of the Group in Chongqing and there learned that their effort had been code named "Dixie Mission."

"The mission was composed of approximately 20 people, both officers and enlisted men, under Colonel David D. Barrett, an old China hand. We had signal corps personnel, infantry officers, Navy officers, medical personnel, weather observers, two O.S.S. officers, two California Nisei who acted as interpreters of the Japanese prisoners, as well as two high ranking State Department men, and, of course, me," Jones recalled.

"At Yan'an we lived in a walled compound area guarded by the Chinese and butressed by a hill approximately 1,500 feet high. Our rooms were actually caves in the hillside. We bunked two to a cave. A wooden frame doorway covered the entrance to the cave. The doorway openings were covered with rice paper. There was a four-foot overhanging rof that sheltered the entrance to all caves.

In a meeting with Communist leaders, I emphasized that we were going to bomb Japan from bases in Nationalist China and there was a probability that American flyers might come down in areas they controlled. They were eager to help.

"Col. Barrett ordered eight of us to make field trips to evaluate the Communist military forces. Of course I spread the word that (1) all downed American flyers were to be harbored and kept safely together and (2) that Yan'an was to be notified and everyone – crew members and rescuers – were then to wait for instructions.

"The State Department delegates and the Mission Commander remained behind in Yan'an and carried on discussions with the

Communist leadership.

"On these evaluation trips, usually we travelled in pairs. My fellow officer was Johnny Colling, a captain in the infantry who spoke fluent Chinese. His specialty was demolition.

"We rode horseback and each had a pack animal for belongings. Two Chinese attendants were assigned to each of us. One was actually a valet and the other tended to the horses. We wore American uniforms unless we were crossing Japanese controlled territory and then we dressed in Chinese Communist uniforms.

"Due to the nature of the countryside and condition of the trails, we did quite a bit of hiking. On those occasions, we led the horses. On the flat lands we rode. We would be mixed in with approximately 15 other riders. We crossed flat areas at a trot and would have approximately a company of infantry surrounding us, moving at double time.

"In the mountainous regions we traveled single file and led our horses. The company of Chinese troops would be spread out about a mile in front and behind us. Immediately in front of me – running ahead on the trail – was a German shepherd dog that hated Japanese. He would never let us out of his sight. When the trail curved, he would sit and wait until we caught up to him before running ahead again. I was impressed by this dog and the Chinese let me keep him when we completed our travels. He usually slept at the foot of my bed. We knew that if we got in a firefight with a Japanese unit and the Chinese were unable to protect us, we would no doubt be killed as spies since we were out of uniform. Nevertheless, both Colling and I thought we would be killed, if captured, whether we were in or out of uniform. So we had no hesitancy or misgivings about wearing Chinsee Communist uniforms.

"In fact we did lose one officer to the Japanese. He was captured, his hands were tied behind his back and his legs were tied at the ankles. He was made to kneel and was shot in the back of the head. A sword was also used. We later recovered his body.

"The Pointee-Talkee Chinese pamphlet in the survival kits was not as useful as was anticipated because so many Chinese peasants could not read their own language. After a flyer was down it might take him a couple of days to find someone who could read.

"Further, when we were out on tours, we would have to change our Chinese attendants every couple of days because they could not communicate with their own countrymen when they were over 50 miles from home because of the difference in dialects and inability to read.

"Other rescue materials, other than medicines, in the survival kits were of little use if you were downed. Once you were in Communist hands, you would be fed and clothed and you followed their instructions. Usually, it wouldn't be too many days before word got to Yan'an and we would begin arranging a pickup.

"The method of rescuing downed B-29 crews was to move them to an area where there was an air strip. The instructions were to stay concealed near the strip and to *wait*. We came as soon as we thought the conditions were right. We had to consider many things besides the weather – Japanese troop movements, Japanese fighters, etc.

"We used a stripped down B-25, which was actually General LeMay's personal plane, to attempt pickups.

"Ten days to two weeks might go by without a pickup attempt. The crews would get 'itchy' and would begin to lose confidence in the Communists and look for other activities.

"The rescue of George Varoff's crew is an example of how painfully boring it was to remain concealed near an air strip for 10 days to two weeks.

"When the first rescue attempt was made, Varoff's crew was not there. They had gone to a neighboring village to be wined and dined as guests of the Communists. Once it was determined the crew was not at the strip, the rescue plane took off immediately. They could not afford to stay on the ground any length of time because the Japanese fighter bases were too close.

"There were nothing but pleas over the Communist network to come again. The second attempt went smoothly. The entire crew of 11 got out safely.

"Varoff's crew was the only one I knew personally since I was in Yan'an and the rescue plane went directly back to A-1 (the base at Xinjin). By the time I got back to A-1 on a training mission, rescued personnel were already back in the States on R & R."

Not all of Jones's activities in Yan'an were related to rescuing downed flyers. He recalled that the Communists, who were anxious to get U.S. military aid, were eager to meet with General Patrick Hurley, U.S. President Roosevelt's personal emissary to Chiang Kai-shek. In September 1944, Hurley came to Yan'an to meet with the Communist leaders.

"An appropriate billet had to be prepared for General Hurley," Jones recalled. "My cave was selected since I had rigged up the only bed in the American compound. It consisted of three two-inch by 12-inch boards across two saw horses. I had an inflatable rubber mattress. I slept on this improvised bed in a sleeping bag, which I got from Red Woolsey. Everyone else slept on a Chinese 'bunk,' (called a *kàng*), which consisted of a hollow clay-based rectangular platform across the rear of the cave, about two feet high and four feet wide. Underneath one corner of the kàng bunk was a fireplace. Each night the Chinese would build a fire and this would heat the bunk. I found out the hard way that it also awakened all the hibernating vermin.

"For General Hurley, the Chinese made up my bed with a pillow, sheets, and blankets. It was very 'stateside.' They also put new rice paper over the doorway. I moved down about eight caves and stayed with the weather officer.

"In the middle of the night a problem developed and one of the guards stationed at General Hurley's cave entrance came to get me. It seems I forgot to tell my German shepherd, who always slept at the foot of my bed, that I wasn't there. Before they sent for me, the General had kicked my trusty dog out of his bed twice. The last time the dog growled at the General. That was when they sent for me.

"The next day I apologized to the General, who was really a good sport. In fact, he insisted I bring the dog around so he could see him in the daylight.

"In January 1945, when the Joint Chiefs of Staff decided that they would not land American troops on the China mainland but would island-hop to Japan, the Communists were notified that they would not receive any military aid from the United States. This put a chill on our otherwise friendly relationship. All the top military personnel and State Department representatives departed Yan'an. There remained only two officers of the original contingent – myself and the weather officer. As a result, I became the mission commander.

"Once a week Chairman Mao Zedong would invite the American Mission Commander to have dinner with him and other political and military leaders. During one of those meals I was sitting next to Chairman Mao. I reached over toward the center of the table with my chopsticks to try a succulent-looking meat dish. Mao put his chopsticks on top of mine and spoke to me in Chinese. Since I did not understand him, I turned to my interpretere who told me that Mao realized that in my country the dog was a pet, but that in China the dog was a meat animal and that I did not have to eat it if I did not want to. I started to pull back, but when I looked up I saw that everyone had stopped eating to see what my reaction would be; therefore I went ahead and ate the dog meat and everyone went back to eating and appeared satisfied with my reaction. Nevertheless, for the rest of the meal I dodged this local delicacy."

Towards the end of Jones's work with the Dixie Mission in the spring of 1945, General LeMay authorized delivery of a planeload of medical supplies to the Chinese Communists as a sign of U.S. appreciation for the rescue help they had given to the 20th Bomber Command. Jones took part in the delivery of those supplies, flying with an ATC crew in a C-46 from Kharagpur, India, to Yan'an.

The Saga of Ledford's Crew

The 13th combat mission in which the 40th participated on 25 October 1944 remains one of the most dramatic of the war. First, though, we must straighten out some confusion regarding the name of Ledford's aircraft. Prior to being assigned to Captain Jack C. Ledford's crew, the plane (No. 281) carried the name *20th Century Unlimited*. This name had been painted on the plane, and Ledford's crew were photographed beside the plane under this name.

The Ledford crew changed the name of the plane to *The Heavenly Body*. Ledford recounted later that they had a beautiful nude airbrushed on the plane by a former Vargas (*Esquire* Magazine) artist who worked in the Service Group. I think we paid him ten bucks, reports Ledford, and it was a beautiful sight to behold! The name change and the paint job took place only a day or two before we deployed to A-1 for the Omura mission. Ledford added: "Father Adler, the chaplain of the 40th Bomb Group, gave me hell about the paint job and was always convinced that it had something to do with our misfortune over Omura. He may have been right. Shortly after that, Father Adler persuaded (then) Col. William H. Blanchard (at the time, Commander of the 40th Bomb Group) to require that all nose art figures be clothed."

Another event involving Jack Halpern occurred in Chakulia before the mission that had a bearing on what happened later. Halpern later recalled: "I used to be an aerial (flight) engineer on B-18A, LB-30, B-26, and B-17 aircraft. I was briefly shown the B-29 flight engineer panel, but I never received training as a B-29 flight engineer. At Chakulia one day after our second or third mission, I passed by some flight engineers on the line. One of them was Louie Grace. They were talking to a Tech. Rep. from Curtis or Boeing and I overheard the Tech. Rep. say, 'There is another position for the fuel mixture controls that does not have a detent on the fuel mixture control panel. A move to this position will give the engines a 10% leaner fuel mixture – that is, 10% more than the normal lean detent position. In order to obtain this 10% extra lean mixture,' the Tech. Rep. said, 'move the mixture controls out of the full lean detent and move them aft towards the closed or fuel cut-off position about one quarter to three-eighths of an inch. Do not move them beyond that point or you may cut off the fuel entirely, due to cable rigging. A

A 444th BG B-29 flies over the cloud-covered Himalayan Mountains (The Hump) on 21 November 1944. The many different 'tones' of natural metal can be seen. (Jeff Ethell)

leaner fuel mixture is a means of conserving fuel. This procedure – a 10% leaner fuel mixture – has not been approved by the Air Corps but we're working on getting official approval."

The primary target of the 13th combat mission was to be the Omura aircraft plant, which manufactured engines and airframes for "Petes," "Zekes," and the new carrier plane nicknamed "Grace." The plant also served as a repair center for engines. At this stage of the war, aircraft plants were now being targeted in what was a shift from the focus on coke and steel manufacturing plants that had been the original targets for the China-based B-29s. The Omura plant was the most important aircraft manufacturing plant within range of the China bases and it had been little damaged in the attack of 9 July 1944, and so the target needed to be revisited.

As Ledford recalled later: "The field order directed that each plane carry a minimum of ten 500-lb. bombs. Average takeoff weight was 133,000 lbs. Planes were to carry 8,200 gallons of gas. Three auxiliary bomb bay tanks were to be carried to provide a 500-gallon reserve for the flight home. For this daylight raid, it was necessary to take off from A-1 at Xinjin in darkness, a hazard because the China bases were provided with few field lights, the runways were muddy, and there was the possibility of rain at takeoff. Actually, on takeoff there was a 5,000-foot ceiling and three-mile visibility in light rain and fog. Bomber Command delayed takeoff for 30 minutes, hoping for improved weather that never came. Launching all the 40th planes took an hour and 42 minutes."

"This mission represented a change over to large formations," Ledford went on. "There was confusion at the assembly points in part because Groups had different radio frequencies. High tailwinds caused the majority of the planes to drift north of their rendezvous points making it difficult to join formations.

"Forming up for this mission was a real 'camel stampede.' The planes formed seven formations to attack the target. *The Heavenly Body* (No. 281) joined a 21-plane formation led by a plane from the 444th. We were positioned as No. 3 aircraft in the left element. I traded seats with pilot 1st Lt. James DeCoster so I could get a better view the rest of the formation.

"Despite the mixed formations, post-strike photos later showed excellent results. Of the 78 planes launched, 59 reached and bombed the target from 23,000 to 25,000 feet at an Indicated Air Speed (IAS) of 195. Weather was 'ceiling and visibility unlimited' (CAVU) which was unusual."

Ledford summed up the raid as a whole: "AA was meager to moderate. Fighter action was rated as moderate, with 102 attacks by approximately 50 'Tojos,' 'Tonys,' and 'Oscars.' A new Japanese twin-engine fighter was observed. Fighter strategy seemed to be to

Lucky Lady, B-29-50-BW serial number 42-24863, was based on Tinian with the 313th Bomb Wing, 504th Bomb Group, 398th Bomb Squadron. (Stan Piet collection)

attack the B-29s after bombs away. Attacks came from the nose, and focus was on the high plane or the No. 4 plane in the formations. Twelve B-29s were damaged in addition to *The Heavenly Body* (No. 281). Planes on the mission claimed seven enemy aircraft destroyed, five probably and 18 damaged. Planes counted 14 cases of aerial phosphorus bombings."

But although the bombing mission as a whole was successful, events were not working out so well for the crew of *The Heavenly Body.*

"After bombs away, the formation turned to the right, away from the target. We were under fairly heavy fighter attack at this time since Thomas Clark, our CFC gunner, was calling out targets and allotting gun control. As we turned right away from our target, our aircraft was hit. As soon as I realized we had been hit, I pulled away from the formation in order to minimize the possibility for a collision. I also yelled at DeCoster to take the controls. The next few minutes were hectic. My legs were paralyzed, and M/Sgt Harry Miller, our flight engineer, was unconscious from a severe head wound. We had cabin explosive decompression, and everyone was busy with oxygen masks and trying to take care of Miller and me. Since we were already out of formation with No. 3 engine useless, DeCoster and I decided to take our aircraft down and ask other aircraft to drop down with us for cover. A couple did for a short time but they had to climb back up to a higher altitude to save their own fuel. Our No. 3 engine was windmilling, but we didn't feather it right away so we wouldn't attract any more enemy fighters.

"Radarman Sgt. Gilbert Rodencal, who was also our first-aid man, treated Miller and bandaged his head wounds. He then treated my side wound, poured sulfa powder in it and used a huge body bandage to wrap up my side. I learned later that shrapnel had cut away a 17x6cm. gap in flesh and muscle from my right side. Pieces grazed my spinal column (hence the paralysis of my legs, especially the right one) chipped my right hip bone and just grazed my kidney. Later, the doctor who sewed me together again in the big hospital in Chengdu said this was the biggest wound I could have sustained and not destroyed a vital organ or bone. I still have three shell fragments in my back muscles.

"I refused Rodencal's offer of morphine at the time because we had some big decisions to make. (I really wasn't hurting much at this point because I was partially paralyzed.) I asked some of the crew to carry me back to the engineer's panel so we could get the engines and fuel tanks configured for best range. I found that there was no fuel in the No. 3 tank. McCullough informed me that some of our radio equipment and navaids had been destroyed."

Ledford later wrote: "Because of the damage to the plane and the loss of fuel, we knew we couldn't make it back to A-1. We had to decide to either go to Vladivostok or try for somewhere on the mainland. I had discussed the Vladivostok option one time in a bull session with Lou Scherck. Based on what Lou had learned from other flights that had diverted there, he did not recommend any diversions there except as a last resort. I felt the same way. I didn't trust the Russians and any way, I didn't want to fly up the west side of the Japanese islands to get there and possibly expose us to further fighter attack. We decided to try to make Liangshan, a Chinese-American Composite Wing (CACW) base near Chongqing."

"About what hit us, CFC Clark and Bombardier 2nd. Lt.

William Gardner later said they thought we had been hit by a rather new Japanese aircraft nicknamed 'Jack.' Could we have been hit by our own aircraft in the formation as some have speculated? We agreed it could have happened. Damage to the plane was severe. In general, the whole right side of the aircraft was a mess. We were lucky we didn't explode when hit.

In a letter to his wife, Gardner wrote that bullets were flying around inside the cabin. One came close enough to cut his throat mike two inches from his neck.

First-aid man Rodencal later recounted: "The fact that Ledford had his back pack chute on had helped to prevent more damage. The whole bottom corner of the chute was blown to shreds. Miller was unconscious. Sgt Duoyne McCullough and 1st Lt. Howard Oblender had laid him on top of the wheel-well hatch. The only visible injuries were three very deep scalp wounds over the right ear where shrapnel had penetrated his skull. He was wearing his flak helmet, and the wounds were away from the explosion. I could not figure how he got hit on his right side."

McCullough recalled these minutes: "Shortly after bombs away, there was a loud 'ping' sound, and someone on the intercom said, 'We have been hit; put on your oxygen mask.' At that moment I looked over at Oblender and noticed that he had pieces of dried prunes all over his face that had come from a box of prunes that was apparently blown away. I asked if he was OK, and he said he was. He pointed to Miller. I leaned over to check on Miller and found him slumped forward with mucus running from his nose. I immediately put a small oxygen tank on an started to get Miller out of his seat and on the floor over the wheel well hatch, but because he was much larger than I, I had some difficulty getting him laid down properly and an oxygen mask put on him. I went back to my position, and Ledford instructed me to contact the lead plane to request two planes be assigned to fly protective formation with us. I'm not sure how long the other planes stayed with us."

S/Sgt. Russell Elwell, right gunner and electrical specialist, was called to come forward and take over the flight engineer's position. At the engineer's panel, having no hands-on experience, Elwell recalled: "I realized I didn't know enough to be helpful so Halpern was called to come up front."

At just about this time, T/Sgt. Jack Halpern, tail gunner, reported seeing fighters in the area. "They were doing 'rollover' maneuvers," he said, but noted that "they were far out of range of my guns."

"Soon after bombs away," Halpern went on, "I saw those same fighters. This time I noticed small flashes of light coming from the underside of their wings. At that moment, the inside cabin pressure of 8,000 feet immediately went to our bombing altitude pressure of 20-22,000 feet. My tail gunner's compartment fogged up. My ears popped like they were going to burst.

"DeCoster called for me to come up and man the flight engineer's position. I could not leave the tail gunner's position right then because a number of enemy fighters were now coming in around the tail.

"I fired my guns in a scatter fashion to ward off any penetrating attack. I admit firing guns in this matter could be ineffective in downing any enemy aircraft, but it had the effect of dispersing the Japanese fighters.

"As a tail gunner, I was issued a chest-type parachute that detached from my parachute harness. I left the chute detached during missions. I kept the harness on, but left my chute in the gunner's compartment when I crawled through the tunnel to the front. As I started to crawl through the tunnel I caught sight of an extra back-pack chute leaning against the left side of the fuselage in the radar compartment. It apparently had been left by the passenger we ferried from India to China. When I took over the flight engineer's position, I saw the fuel mixture control levers in 'full lean' I remembered what the Tech. Rep. had said, 'Move the mixture controls about a quarter to three-eighths inches toward the OFF position.' I did that, thinking it would give us more range from the depleted fuel supply. We were approaching the China mainland at about this time.

"I remember clearly seeing Ledford's parachute torn to shreds from enemy fire. When Ledford moved out of the flight engineer's seat, I could see the bones of his hip socket. He was obviously gravely injured. I felt air coming from the right side below the flight engineer's panel—the effect of battle damage.

"After I transferred all the fuel from the bomb bay tanks, I gave a sign to Gardner to let him know it was OK to salvo the two bomb bay tanks. Due to battle damage, Gardner could not salvo them electrically. The two bomb bay fuel tanks had to be released to relieve the plane of their dead weight.

"After failing to salvo the tanks Gardner told me to go into the bomb bay and salvo them manually.

"Without my parachute I crawled out into the forward bomb bay. Gardner had already opened the bomb bay doors.

"The wind turbulence added to the 'fright factor' of going out into the bomb bay at 10,000 feet with the doors open. I struggled across the narrow metal structure and pulled the emergency release lever. Down dropped both fuel tanks. The resulting vacuum made me feel like I was being sucked out of the bomb bay and I hung on to a stanchion with all the muscle I could muster. I then crawled back into the cockpit and resumed my seat at the engineer's panel.

"*En route* to the target I had eaten a full box of prunes from my flight lunch. Now I began to experience horrible gas pains, and I had to get to the portable john. When I left the engineer's panel, I remember seeing 40 gallons of fuel TOTAL remaining in the wing tanks. I did not want to crawl back to the portable john and then return to the forward cockpit. I thought, what if the engines quit, and I was stuck in the tunnel? I knew that bailing out was inevitable, but my parachute was in the rear." Halpern therefore opted to remain in the rear of the airplane, preparing to bail out from the rear with the other men in that part of the plane.

Halpern recalled watching Gardner who was wearing his headset. He thought he heard Gardner say "Roger" which he interpreted to be an acknowledgement of an order to bail out. Halpern later remembered his hair-raising exit from the aircraft: "I was clutching my rip cord as I pushed my way through the opened door into the 200-m.p.h. slip stream. The wind immediately yanked my right arm, pulling my rip cord and opening my parachute before I was completely out the door. My right foot caught underneath the rear entrance door jam and the wind began bashing me against the right side of the fuselage. My opened chute dragged across the right horizontal stabilizer and elevator. Gardner leaned down and untwisted my right foot, allowing me to fall free of the plane. Luckily, my chute did not become entangled with the stabilizer," Halpern said.

"I was the first to bail out from the rear of the plane. Gardner, Rodencal, Elwell, Paslay and Clark followed," Halpern continued.

Burr Bennett, Robert Dickens, and (the author) Robert Hilton receive their first decorations in Chakulia, India, around September 1944. (40th Bomb Group Collection)

"I saw the five chutes open. We all landed in the same twisting canyon 10,000 feet below but miles apart."

Elwell had these memories of the bailout: "The crew in the back of the plane bailed out a little sooner than the crew in front; thus, when they got on the ground the two segments of the crew were separated by a mountain. I remember Clark stepping into the door opening and having the slip stream pin the door jamb between his body and backpack chute and not allowing him to jump or move back. Since I was behind him, and anxious to jump, I gave him a push and then dove out myself. As I rolled face up and saw the tail assembly pass over, I pulled the rip cord. Still in the slip stream, the chute opened with a hard impact, straps slamming against the back of my head. I believe I was knocked unconscious, because there was a period of time I don't remember. I also had cuts on my neck and head. The next moment I remember floating down not far from Clark and trying to make conversation but not saying much."

Rodencal also remembered: "When the time came to jump, Halpern was the first to go. Gardner, Elwell, Paslay, Clark, and I followed. Clark had a little problem with the idea of jumping, but a stiff push helped in a hurry. My first attempt wasn't too good. I stuck my head out, lost my glasses, and got slammed against the door frame. The second time I made it. I could see the plane leaving

with puffs of smoke coming from the engines. I was now alone, flat on my back at 10,000 feet, and I open my chute. What a jolt! It was very quiet, just the swish of air from the chute. Sounds from very far away could be heard. I heard Halpern hollering way up the valley that he was in a thermal and going up. First to jump, last to get down."

Ledford and those in the front of the aircraft bailed out somewhat later. Ledford recalled: "McCullough was able to transmit a couple of messages. He received some Japanese messages trying to persuade us to turn on some bogus heading." Oblender explained: "At the navigators' briefing we were told this was not a friendly airfield, and Ledford told DeCoster to continue to fly the heading I had given him."

McCullough said of the return trip: "After flying for several hours, Ledford requested that I make a voice transmission 'May Day' distress call in an effort to locate a base for possible emergency landing. After making contact with a station, I explained our problems and requested a QDM (Direction to the base). We were asked to fly a certain pattern while I made a long count so that our position could be determined. The station then gave us a bearing, but Oblender said that the bearing was not right."

Oblender recalled: "We were on course when we crossed the

China coast on the way back. We were flying over an undercast, and the only navigational aid we had was the sun. I used the heading and wind that I received at our briefing before the mission. The sun did help us with ground speed."

McCullough continued: "I remained in radio contact with the base while bailout preparations were being made. I put the transmitter on CW and screwed the key down so that it might be possible to locate the crash site and see that the plane was destroyed to prevent anything useful from falling into the hands of the enemy. I followed Ledford out of the plane. I was a little too quick pulling my rip cord, and this caused me to black out for a short time. It also resulted in my harness separating from a section of my evasion and escape kit, and I lost some items in it."

Ledford recalled: "As we approached the Chinese mainland, there was solid cloud formation beneath us at about 12-14,000 feet. Oblender had a good sun line, but there was no way to fix our position along that line except for dead reckoning. (We found out later that we had bailed out within 10 miles of Obie's estimated position.) It soon became evident that we weren't going to locate any possible landing area before our fuel ran out, and I certainly wasn't about to let down blind through that overcast because we were in very rough mountainous country. So we prepared to bail out.

"By a stroke of great good fortune, we had a spare chute. Our guys put this chute on me and then used the shroud lines of my damaged chute to make a static line so that we could open Miller's chute after dropping him. By this time DeCoster was down to two engines and nervously encouraging us to get out. The guys dropped Miller and then carried me over to the nose wheel well and dropped me. I was still paralyzed in my legs. As I fell, I delayed opening my chute in order to slow down my forward speed and have as gentle an opening shock as possible. I also hoped I could get on the ground before Harry and see where he landed."

McCullough recalled what happened: "We bailed out at about 10,500 feet and on my way down, I noticed two other chutes. My chute caught the edge of a tree causing me to hit the ground horizontally. This made me somewhat nauseated for a little while. After my stomach settled down, I got my chute rolled up around my escape kit. I sat down on the edge of a rice paddy to gather my thoughts and look around. We had landed in a narrow valley between two mountain ranges. While sitting there, I noticed a figure in the distance coming toward me. When he got a little closer, I was relieved to see that he was a Chinese soldier. I got my translation booklet and pointed to the phrase, "Take me to your garrison." The soldier then pointed to the phrase, "You stay here," so that's what I did.

"Shortly after that, another Chinese soldier and Oblender joined us. The two soldiers then escorted us into a small village where we joined up with Ledford. About an hour or two later, DeCoster was led into the village. We had no contact with the six men who bailed out from the back of the plane."

Ledford had this to say about his landing: "I landed in a muddy rice paddy and for a few minutes, I sat there somewhat dazed by my landing in addition to being quite apprehensive about where we were in relation to the Japanese forces known to be nearby. In a few minutes, several Chinese farmers lined the banks of the rice paddy, and we traded stares for a while until suddenly two Chinese soldiers appeared on the bank. I was relieved to see the white-on-blue star of the Chinese Nationalist Army on their caps. They came

down and carried me to a small village. One by one, they brought in the rest of the crew from the forward flight deck. The Chinese had found Miller and carried him to a nearby Norwegian mission clinic. We found out the next morning that Miller had died shortly after landing. DeCoster and McCullough went to the mission. With the care of the missionaries, Miller had been given a Christian burial. (Military Graves Registration units removed the body after the war.)

"The Chinese were wonderful to us. Aided by the Norwegian missionary who had helped Miller, they built a sedan chair to carry me out. We also had a Chinese doctor who had studied Western medicine in Europe, to accompany us for the five days it took to reach Laohekou (in Hubei Province). I don't remember much about the five-day trip out. By this time I was hurting pretty bad. I had recovered most of the feeling in my left leg. My right leg was still paralyzed. My wound was beginning to throb and, in spite of the wonderful care, the doctor the Chinese and the crew gave me, I was pretty uncomfortable.

"I remember several incidents that were funny or interesting. On about the third day of our trek, we arrived at a Chinese Nationalist Army Headquarters commanded by a General Li. General Li asked me if I knew a Captain Grubaugh. Somewhat astonished I informed him that Capt. Dan Grubaugh was my best friend and my roommate at our base back in India. (Dan and his crew had bailed out in the same area several months before, and his rescue had also been aided by General Li.) The General then said to me, 'Please ask Captain Grubaugh where the hell are my tennis balls?' It turned out that Li loved to play tennis, but had run out of tennis balls and had no way to getting any. I promised General Li that I would try to get some sent to him after I got back to our base. Later at the American-Chinese Hospital in Chengdu, I arranged for some tennis balls to be sent to General Li.

"The next day General Li put us on one of his wood burning trucks on the road to Laohekou. We were all pretty much hung over from the wine we had at the dinner the might before and on the bus I kept smelling this wine, which is very potent. I noticed McCullough was several shades of green. Mac was not a drinker, but he joined in the festivities the night before. At that point our Chinese doctor informed us that, in addition to the wood, the truck also used this wine for fuel. All of us were pretty sick for several hours.

"When we arrived at Laohekou, we were to be picked up by a CACW C-47. It was escorted by two CACW P-40s. They were to fly cover for the C-47, but for some reason, one of the P-40s had to land and when it did, it ground looped on the runway. I thought, oh boy, we are in trouble because the Japanese fighters strafe the field a couple times a day and were probably on their way. Fortunately, the C-47 had enough room to land. We were quickly loaded on and roared out for the main CACW base (can't recall name). From there the others were evacuated to A-1. I was taken to the hospital in Chengdu.

"After a week of gaining control of the infection in my side wound, the doctors at Chengdu operated to close the wound. After three more weeks in the hospital, I returned to Chakulia. I was still grounded.

"My crew was permanently assigned to another Aircraft Commander. While I was awaiting for my side to completely heal, I was appointed Assistant Group Operations Officer. I was notified

Flying the "Hump" was so dangerous that air crews were eventually given combat credit for the trip.

that I had been appointed to the Army Command and General Staff School at Ft.. Leavenworth. I was on my way back to Tinian from the school when the war ended."

McCullough remembered: "Most of the communicating between us and the Chinese was handled by a Chinese civilian official (who I believe was in the mail service) and a Norwegian woman missionary who had lived in this village for 20 years. Both of them spoke very limited English. They informed us that Miller had died about 10 minutes after the parachute landing and that his body had been taken to the Chinese garrison just outside the village. Since it was dark by then, it was suggested that we go to view his body in the morning.

"Shortly after awakening, DeCoster and I were escorted by a soldier to their garrison for the purpose of obtaining one of Miller's dog tags. It took us about 30 minutes to get there. They had Miller lying on boards supported by two sawhorses and covered with some kind of material resembling cheesecloth.

"We removed the dog tag, and I suggested we have a short silent prayer before heading back to the village. The Norwegian missionary assured us that Miller would have a Christian burial the following day. We could not stay for the burial because of the need to get Ledford to a hospital.

"Before leaving the village, the civilian officials honored us by providing a very elaborate mid-morning meal. We then left the village, each of us being carried on a stretcher-like pallet. At the end of the village, there was a group of Chinese children waving at us with crudely made little U.S. flags. We acknowledged them by waving back. We were on the trail until well after dark at which time we stopped at what appeared to be a cluster of farmhouses. We slept the night on boards covered with straw.

"The next morning we immediately got back on the trail with the Chinese again carrying us. After being on the trail for a while, I decided it would be much safer walking on the uneven surface than being carried. The Chinese official escorting us was concerned that I would not be able to keep up, but I had no problem. I believe Oblender also decided to walk from that point on. After walking the mountain ridge for a lengthy time, we came to a fortress-type structure that had two very large doors and a courtyard. As I recall, we resumed our trek after a short stop there. The next thing I remember was that then we started down the mountain range. As we did so, a large city could be seen in the distance. We spent the night in a large garrison there where we were treated to a fine Chinese dinner with high-ranking officers.

"The morning after breakfast, we were loaded into an old school bus in which all the seats had been removed. The bus was fueled by a charcoal burner. A Chinese solder ran alongside and stoked the burner occasionally when we would go up a steep incline.

"After traveling in the bus all day, we arrived at an advance fighter base. Shortly after arriving at the field, a C-47 landed. We immediately loaded onto the plane and took off. This was just at dusk.

"After about an hour of flying, we arrived at a medium bomber base, but we could not land because the based was on blackout. There was an air raid alert. The tower requested that we circle the field with our lights on so that we would not be mistaken for a Jap bomber. After about 30 minutes of this, the field lights were turned on, and we were given clearance to land. We spent the night at this field and enjoyed our first good American meal. Next morning we continued our trip to A-1 in the C-47."

The men who had jumped from the rear of *The Heavenly Body*

B-29s of the 468th Bomb Group, Twentieth Air Force, bomb a Japanese airfield near Rangoon, Burma. To the left is B-29-25-BA 42-63529, assigned to the 795th Bomb Squadron, which was redesignated the 794th Bomb Squadron after an October 1944 reorganization. This aircraft was listed as missing in action on 26 May 1945. (National Museum of the United States Air Force)

had a different route home.

Rodencal recalled: "I came down near the top of the mountains, but I could see a village down in the valley. A straight line is not a good way to go down a mountain. After a few falls, I came to a trail, and some Chinese appeared and motioned me to follow. I was worried because I did not know if they were friend or foe, but I followed them. After a while we came to a house in the mountains which seemed to have several generations living in it. The first thing they did was to make tea. I tried to use my pointy-talky, but none of them could read. After a while a boy came in who could read, and I got the message across that I wanted to get to the village. He and an adult took me down the mountain to the village. The rest of the crew from the back of the plane had already arrived.

"We spent the night in the village. During the night, a runner had gone down to the next village and came back with some police/ soldiers to guide us out. The next day we arrived at a village where we met Mr. B.T. Chang who spoke English. We talked him into staying with us as an interpreter. We spent one whole day on a riverboat drifting down into the valley where we ended up at a grass landing strip. It took us several days to get to the strip because we were on the other side of the mountain, and we had no roads, just trails.

"While at the village near the airstrip, we stayed with some missionaries who fed us. There was also a small unit of GIs (maybe four or five) who took care of the strip. They had a radio and some 55-gallon drums of fuel–that was the total of the equipment at the "air base." We were at this strip for several days because every time

they would try to get a C-47 in to rescue us, the Japanese would send fighters to strafe the place. One day I got so damn mad lying on my back in a ditch that I opened fired on the Japanese planes with my .45."

Elwell gave his version of the rescue and walk out: "Clark landed safety on the tile roof of a peasant house with his feet going through the roof. He wound up straddling a rafter. I landed some distance away in a garden. I will never forget the old, bent-over Chinese farmer with a white goatee and clay pipe appearing from around the corner of the house, looking up to see what was on his roof. He disappeared only to return with a bamboo ladder and again disappeared, unconcerned, as though this happened every day.

"Gardner landed in a small rocky river bed and injured his knee. Halpern hung up in trees on a rock cliff.

"Within a short time, all six of us from the back of the plane got together and arranged to spend the night in the shed of a house nearby. During the night, one of the Chinese people secretly took one of our jungle packs as proof we were there. He traveled about 20 miles to a village for help. The next morning we heard a commotion outside. When we looked out we found about 15 Chinese soldiers with guns drawn. After some pointy-talky conversations with their leader, the Chinese set about cutting bamboo plants and building litters. Because Gardner was limping, they wanted to carry him.

"The rest of us were to be carried, too. There were no roads in this area, only foot trails. For extra manpower, the soldiers drafted the peasants from their gardens and homes as bearers. If they refused, they got a rifle butt in the back. About halfway through this first day, as we went over a steep rise in the trail, a bearer put down his end of the litter and took off up the mountain. Two soldiers took off in pursuit. A little later, we heard a gun shot.

"Towards the end of the day, as we approached a walled village the path leading to it was lined on both sides with villagers, boy scouts, girl scouts, and a band. They were all waving flags and clapping for the great "American heroes." A delegation of village elders approached. A young Chinese put out his hand and said. 'Hiya Joe, am I glad to see you.' This fellow, Chan Ching Yang (Mr. Chang) stayed with us for the next several days as an interpreter. He apparently learned English at one of our air bases. He was also traveling behind Japanese lines to Shanghai. He said the inside lining of his jacket was stuffed with bribe money with which to get through the lines.

"We spent the night in a schoolhouse, and there had our first meals. The next morning, so the village people could see how we came down from the sky, I put on my open parachute and paraded in a gathering area. It was at this village, I believe, that Gardner was able to communicate by telephone with someone about our destination. On this day we also started walking to our next destination. Our entourage was complete with live chickens in a crate, donkeys, and several soldiers. That destination was a small village on a steep bank next to a river. We spent the night there. Next day we boarded a sampan and drifted with the current most of the day before arriving at a sizable town. Here, we rode rickshaws into the town's main street and paraded on foot through crowds of people celebrating in our honor. The street echoed with exploding firecrackers. The smoke from them was knee deep.

Flags were waving in celebration. That night at a tin roof theater, a special show took place in our honor complete with knife twirling, fiery baton twirling, singing and all the rest. The scouts sang an American patriotic song. It was a hot night. Notwithstanding, by tradition, they supplied steaming hot towels for us to freshen ourselves.

"Next morning we posed for pictures with a large group of VIPs and then rode rickshaws to a house outside of town where we jammed into a small car, traveled to another town, boarded an old school bus, drove on to a ferry to cross a river (the raft almost submerged) and on to the village and a Norwegian mission near the field being used as a landing strip. We spent about three days waiting here for the C-47 to evade the Japanese fighters and get in. When it arrived, we jumped in and were on our way back to A-1."

Halpern had his own stories about the experience: "All six of us landed in the same twisting canyon, though miles apart. I crashed through a tree on the side of the mountain. My chute caught the branches and there I was, dangling from my shroud lines, unable to touch the side of the mountain. I looked down to the valley below and saw several Chinese men looking up to where I was perched. I kept hollering 'MEG-Wah-Fiji' which I remembered to be Chinese for 'I am an American airman.' I really needed help to get out of the tree and down the mountain to the river below.

"About 10 minutes later, I saw two men climb the side of the mountain and move towards me. They both climbed a little above my level. I noticed then that they were carrying a rope that had been made by twisting vines together. There was lots of sign language, pointing here and there, hollering and listening. They spoke Chinese, which, of course I did not understand. They threw the 'rope' down to me. I caught it and tied it around my waist. They then pulled me up a bit to relieve the tension from the parachute shroud lines. Next, I took my GI knife and cut the shroud lines. The Chinese then slowly lowered me to the valley floor below. I had forgotten to take my .45 with me when we left India and now I felt defenseless when surrounded by seven or eight muscular mountain men – all waving and pointing and urging me to move on.

"I removed my Escape and Evasion (E&E) kit and took out the Pointy-Talky. I turned to the page with the question, 'Where are the Japanese?' They pointed while turning around 360 degrees. I understood. The Japanese were nearby and all around looking for me. In those days I smoked two packs of cigarettes on a mission, one pack going to the target and the other on the flight home. I had one full pack left. I opened the pack and offered the cigarettes all around. The whole pack was gone within seconds.

"The E&E kit contained $50,000 American money. I saved the money for other payments.

"I wanted to recover my parachute and take it with me, but the Chinese men motioned that I could not go back. My plan of escape was to head down the river and, as I was always taught in those Evasion and Escape classes, follow trails downstream to get to civilization. But the Chinese who surrounded me, forbid me to go downstream. I was beginning to fear the worst – that these Chinese were really bandits who would turn me over to the Japanese. In some manner, I got the message from the Chinese that the Japs were still looking for me and the others and that there were Chinese soldiers who would fight the Japanese to prevent them from getting us. Against my better judgment, this being a matter of survival vs. judgment, I continued to follow the two Chinese men up the river. The other 'mountain men' who initially surrounded me after I was lowered to the ground, had disappeared. I asked my guides. 'Where did they go?' Answer: 'Go fight Japanese.'

"Just before dark, on the other side of the river, I saw something white moving down the trail. I stopped out of fear and could barely make out the figures with white objects in their arms. They were the five other crew members who had bailed out from the back of the ship who were carrying their parachutes. The five other crew members did what we were trained to do, 'walk downstream.' The six of us all got together and, that night, the two Chinese that led me upstream, hid us in a loft of a farmhouse.

"The Chinese rescuers, it turned out, wanted our parachutes to show a Chinese general that there were others bedsides me, who bailed out and needed help in escaping and evading the Japs.

"Around 10:00 the next morning, about 15 Chinese scout troops with their general, came to the farmhouse. All were carrying their live chickens in wicker baskets and all of their cooking gear in addition to machine guns and other war-fighting equipment. After the usual Chinese greetings and exchanges using the Pointy-Talky books, the message conveyed was: Some of the Chinese troops went downriver and killed the Japanese to clear the way for our escape. They also returned Gardner's parachute. A young Chinese boy returned my parachute after recovering it from the tree where I left it.

"With the general and half his troops up front, the six of us following and then the other half of the Chinese armed party bringing up the rear, we started out. The general ordered some of the troops to cross the river and the others to remain with us. They were to clear the way of Japanese. I could hear the sound of gunfire.

"Gardner was having much difficulty walking because of his bad knee. The general noticed his limping and ordered us to stop.

He motioned to the scout troops to assemble in front of him and within 45 minutes they had fashioned six stretchers. The rope they used was made from vines, and the canvas for the stretchers came from the covering of their cooking utensils, chicken baskets, etc. Thin trees were used for the twin poles that formed each stretcher. The general ordered us each into a stretcher and then motioned for the scout troops to do something. About 10 minutes later, the soldiers returned with 11 farmers. We were later told that they were conscripted right off their farms to act as our stretcher bearers. I walked next to the general. Within minutes we were ordered to stop. The general began to talk to a farmer next to the trail, pointing for him to come with us. The farmer hesitated and instead started to run away. The general took his pistol and fired at the farmer while, at the same time, all 15 of his soldiers let loose a rifle barrage at the farmer. The poor guy never had a chance. Again we started walking and again we stopped. The general started to talk to another farmer, but this time the farmer joined the group.

"We started off again, this time all six of us sitting on our stretchers. It was an uncomfortable means of transportation traveling up and over mountain ridges. After a couple of hours being carried on a stretcher, we rifled through our Pointy-Talky booklets to find an appropriate English to Chinese translation of what we wanted to say, which was: 'Dear General, we know you mean well, and we wouldn't want to hurt your feelings for anything, but you're wearing us out. We are not making much progress, so let us walk and let Gardner stay on his stretcher.' Of course, we could not find any such translation, but after a lot of arm movement, pointing, and talking off the top of our heads, the general got the word and ordered stretcher bearers to stop and put us down.

"There were frequent skirmishes between our soldiers and the Japanese and we all saw three or four dead Japanese floating down the river. We made frequent stops while the Chinese troops cleared the way for us.

"We finally came out of the mountain area and onto a huge meadow. Standing almost in the middle of that clearing and off to the side of the trail was a Chinese man. He was dressed in usual garb – a long robe with a shawl-like collar. As we got closer, to the surprise of all of us, he said, 'Hiya! Any way I can help you?' It was spoken in perfect English, but with a New York accent. We all shouted, 'Do you speak Chinese?' He answered, 'Why, sure, I am Chinese.' We asked him if he would be our guide and speak to the general for us. He answered, 'Why certainly. I'll help you get out and back to your base.' His name was Mr. Chang.

"Around the third week of our trek, I had worn through the sole and toe of my GI boots. It was continuous hiking, hiding from the Japanese, climbing mountains and hiking down them, fording streams. Each day the general and his troops outfoxed the Japanese.

"Now with Mr. Chang up front with the general, communication was easy. Mr. Chang would tell us every move the general was about to make and where we were heading. Around the end of the third week, we finally hiked out of the mountains and away from the Japanese. I got to know the general well. I did some cigarette tricks and Chinese coin-disappearing tricks for him. I even showed him how I did them. He liked this more than anything else. I showed a few magic tricks to the soldiers from time to time. A day or so after we met Mr. Chang, the general said we still had a long way to go, but it would be a safe passage from here on. We bid farewell to

the general and his troops. We tried as best we could to express our thanks to them. As he was leaving, the general walked up to me, took his dagger and sheath from his belt and gave it to me. I still have that dagger.

"We were now getting into Chinese civilization which was indicated by ancient Chinese cities and villages all located along rivers. Mr. Chang told us from where we bailed out, we had covered approximately 300 miles. We still had about 300 miles more to go.

"By now we had come to know Mr. Chang very well. He gave us a world of information, but we never did find out how and where he learned to speak English with a New York accent. By this time I had replaced my GI boots with a pair of Chinese sandals. Walking on the trail adjacent to the river, I saw a walled city in the distance. We were heading for the entrance to the city. The entrance was two huge gates of carved wood. The two gates opened slowly, and both sides of the street were lined with hundreds of city officials. Men, women, and children were all waiting for our arrival. Mr. Chang told us this was a 3,000-year-old city, and these people had never seen a white person. There were banners all over the city. We learned the school-children had used English language dictionaries to make up the signs, one of which read, 'Welcome Back American Airmen.'

"Some of our crew played basketball with the upper-grade school children. I put on a magic show for a group of them. As we traveled through other towns, when we entered the town, they would declare a holiday for the school children. As we were leaving one of these towns, a general surprised us with a ride in his 1927-1929 Dodge, four-door, touring sedan. It was hard to understand how that car stayed together taking into account the dirt roads it traveled over, dropping into deep, wide holes at 35-40 m.p.h.

"By now the stretcher-bearer farmers had left us. We had accumulated loads of gifts from each village – bolts of colored silk, ceramic pieces, metal and wooden ornaments and several sets of sandals.

"We finally got to the Chinese P-40 fighter strip. Adjacent to the field was a Norwegian mission. We stayed at the mission for about two weeks. Every day the six of us would go out to the strip and wait for a C-46 to come in and fly us out. Field operations consisted of a shelter with a flat roof covered by a bush. It was supported by four poles at each corner. Inside was a stand with a small aircraft radio.

"The radio was salvaged from a P-40 on the field that was out of action. There was no such thing as scheduled arrivals and departures. Jap fighter planes strafed the field almost every day. Finally, a C-46 did arrive and landed. Both its engines remained running while we were ordered to get aboard fast. The C-46 had no extra chutes, so I chickened out. I was afraid to fly without a chute.

"Standing next to us on the ground beside the small ladder into the plane was a Chinese P-40 pilot. He immediately took his own parachute off and gave it to me. The C-46 crew told him that the next time they came back they would return the chute to him. Incidentally, the parachute the Chinese pilot gave me was made of silk instead of nylon.

"We landed at A-1 and stayed there for two days. We visited Ledford who was still in the hospital in Chengdu. The second day we got word that a B-29 that had brought gasoline up was on its way back to Chakulia. We caught a ride on it. The night before we left, while we were asleep in the barracks at A-1, someone stole all the gifts we had received. I did have my parachute and the dagger the general gave me."

Four B-29s from the 40th Bomb Group head for Japan on a mission in summer 1945. In the foreground is *Eddy Allen II,* serial number 44-70151. (58th BW Memorial)

On 26 January 1945 the author's very good friend, Art Jordan, was killed on a mission to Southeast Asia. The author recalls Art as the "best" buddy, one who had been through photo school with him, was at Pratt, and was the one who was home with him at Christmas time 1943. Notwithstanding, or because of, the traumatic shock of his death, the author forced it into the depths of his mind for the balance of the war. He was successful in keeping it there for years, until one night he awoke from a sound sleep in a cold sweat asking the questions: "Why Art? Why not me? Why was I spared?" No answer! The author had not dwelled on his death yet it still haunts him.

That tragic loss occurred shortly before the whole unit was moved from its bases near Calcutta to the newly liberated Mariana Islands in the Western Pacific. The new location would facilitate the launch of devastating air strikes on the strongholds of the Japanese home islands.

In the fall of 1944 the U.S. Marines and U.S. Army units invaded and recaptured Guam and also captured the Japanese-held islands of Saipan and Tinian in the Mariana Islands. These islands, as well as numerous other smaller islands, lay in a chain approximately 100 miles long and were situated about 1,500 miles almost directly south of Tokyo. All the Japanese home islands were well within the range of the B-29s operating from the Marianas. Almost before the fighting had ended the Navy construction battalions (CBs or Seabees) were at work building runways for the B-29. In fact, Saipan was the first island captured and runway construction began there before Guam and Tinian had been captured.

In the winter of 1944 a B-29 Wing moved to Saipan from the States and began combat operations to Japan.

It was obvious that 20th Bomber Command operations could be conducted much more efficiently from the Marianas than from either China or India. Accordingly, in the early spring of 1945, we were given orders to move to the Marianas. The first of the support people departed in February. General LeMay and many of his staff also departed and LeMay became commander of the 20th Air Force with headquarters on Guam. What had been the 20th Bomber Command in the CBI, now became the 58th Bomb wing of the 20th Air Force. Our Base was to be on the island of Tinian. Aircraft and flight personnel departed India in March and early April. The route required one last crossing of the Hump, refueling at a 14th Air Force Base in Luliang, China, and then nonstop to Tinian. The route from Luliang was almost directly over Hong Kong, just north of the Philippines and on into Tinian. The last of the support personnel then departed India for Tinian from Calcutta.

B-29-35-BN *Miss Judy,* **serial number 44-61555, served with the 58th Bomb Wing, 462nd Bomb Group, 770th Bomb Squadron, of the Twentieth Air Force. The art shows a girl hammering a Tojo-esque head with a rising sun in the background. (Stan Piet collection)**

When we first arrived at Tinian, only the runways had been completed for us. Housing had not been started although the area in which it was to be located had been selected. Latrines and a mess hall had been quickly thrown together. We were supplied with tents sleeping six men to a tent. The first night on Tinian I slept on the concrete floor of the newly completed, but still unusable, latrine. Our housing area was situated on a cliff with the Pacific on one side and sugar cane fields on the other side. In the cliffs were numerous caves. We were warned that not all the Japanese soldiers had been captured and that many remained hidden in the caves. We were also warned to stay out of the cane fields; the Japanese soldiers would come out of the caves to seek food and water and would make their way through the cane fields to do so. We learned quickly this was more than a rumor; Japanese soldiers continued to be captured throughout our time in Tinian, including some following the end of the war.

Tinian was basically a coral formed island. It was roughly the size and shape of New York's Manhattan Island so it was only natural that roads followed the names of New York streets. Broadway was our main thoroughfare running the length of the island. Tinian Town, the only village on the island, also served as its harbor. The history of Tinian runs back into the mists of antiquity as can be gleaned from the stone monoliths erected there at some time in the past. More modern construction included all the roads and runways that had to be bulldozed from the coral base underlying the entire island. The island was longer north to south than the east-west width. The prevailing wind in that part of the Pacific was east to west and the width of the island was sufficient to construct the 8,000-foot runways required for B-29 operations. Tinian simply became one large air base. The 40th was based at what was termed West Field as were the other, 58th Wing Bomb Groups that had

been with us in India. Adjacent to our runways, on the south, was a third, shorter runway which served as a Naval Air Base and also, for a short period of time, home to a P-51 AAF Fighter Group.

On arrival at Tinian each of the Group photo laboratories was combined into a single 58th Wing photo lab. Those of us involved with flying and camera work remained with each of our original Groups and were headquartered in the areas where the B-29s roosted and were maintained. We not only had to construct our own personal housing, we also had to construct our own Quonset hut (building) out of which we operated.

At North Field four runways were constructed and, I believe, became the home to two B-29 Wings. When the 509th Composite Bomb Group, the Atomic Bomb Group, came to the Marianas, it too was based at North Field. It was from this location at North Field that the Hiroshima and Nagasaki missions were flown. Further north, with two to three miles of the Pacific between the islands, lay Saipan. Saipan's south shore was the location of a B-29 Base with two runways and one Bomb Wing. In other words, on Tinian and Saipan combined there were eight runways, four Bomb Wings, 13 Bomb Groups and some 600 or more B-29s. Later in the war, when some all-out combined missions were flown, all runways would be simultaneously active with a B-29 departing each of the runways at 30-second to one-minute intervals – a fantastic sight, particularly if a nighttime departure was involved.

The Seabees also constructed an outdoor theater for us on the cliff overlooking the Pacific. The seating area was not covered and it was necessary to carry a poncho or raincoat for protection from evening rain showers. The movie screen was housed in the stage where the USO shows also performed. Audience seating facing the screen also overlooked the ocean. It was from this location early one evening, after the arrival of the 509th Bomb Group, that we saw a very beautiful Navy heavy cruiser, the *Indianapolis,* glide along in the ocean not far offshore. We learned later it had transported the nuclear materials for two atom bombs from the States to Tinian and had just off-loaded them at Tinian Town. Two or three days later we learned that the Indianapolis had been sunk by a Japanese submarine with the loss of most of its crew. The Indianapolis was then on its way to join the U.S. fleet at Okinawa. I was touched by the loss and felt it very personally after having seen it up close so recently.

I mentioned previously the arrival of the atomic 509th Bomb Group and its location at North Field. We all knew the 509th was designated for a special mission but what that might be, we didn't know. Our curiosity was rampant, however, and with our security clearance we could go anywhere on the island. Nothing would do but that two or three of us would go to visit the 509th. The first thing we noticed was that all armament had been removed from their B-29s.

We also noticed that underneath the parked aircraft was a large, long pit quite similar to an automobile oil change/grease pit. Very odd we thought, and no one could, or would, explain its purpose to us. After the two missions we could only speculate that it was necessary for special loading procedures related to the Bombs. Near the hardstand area were two Quonset Huts, both air conditioned, which was something totally unheard of anywhere I had been in the Air Force. The bombs were in these buildings for final assembly. Each was totally different from the other. One was shaped very similar to a standard bomb and about the size of a 2,000-pound bomb. The other was ball shaped and appeared to be six feet in diameter. Neither meant anything to us. Only later did we learn they were the atomic bombs and that the smaller, more normally shaped bomb was the 'Little Boy' dropped on Hiroshima. The large round one was 'Fat Boy' dropped at Nagasaki. I do not remember seeing a B-29 named the *Enola Gay* but I assume it was one of the aircraft on one of the hardstands we visited.

Fast forward to 1994:

Some years previously the Air Force had given the Smithsonian Air and Space Museum the *Enola Gay* but it had never been displayed. As a matter of fact, the *Enola Gay* had been dismantled and lay in pieces on the floor of the warehouse in Maryland. In 1994, however, the Museum was preparing an exhibit commemorating the 50th anniversary of use of the Bomb. Two guys, Bill Rooney and Burr Bennett, who had been in the 40th Bomb Group learned that the Exhibit was going to focus on the terrible results of using the Bombs rather than the fact that the Bombs had ended the war and had prevented not only the loss of lives of thousands and thousands of service people of both the U.S. and its Allies but also Japanese civilians and armed services. Not only was much loss of life prevented but also prevented was very, very widespread damage to cities and countryside in Japan. Bill and Burr organized a national crusade, of which I was privileged to play a part, and succeeded in changing the Exhibit plans of the Smithsonian. Rather than focusing on the negative aspect of the Bomb's use (and everybody is aware of the terrible things that did result from its use) the Exhibit would focus on the positive aspects of its use and would include a section of the *Enola Gay* (it was much too large to display in the whole in the museum) as well as a mock up of Little Boy.

When the Exhibit opened a number of us who had participated in the crusade attended a reception hosted by the Museum which also included a private opening of the Exhibit for us. One of the attendees was Col. (later General, Retired) Tibbets who flew the *Enola Gay* on its Hiroshima mission and commanded the 509th Group. It was my honor to meet the General and have the opportunity to visit with him. The *Enola Gay,* by the way, was named for General Tibbet's mother.

Resuming our account of the 40th Bomb Group in the Marianas, the general hospital for Saipan/Tinian was located on Saipan. As with all other facilities, the shower rooms, latrines, etc., at the hospital were afforded privacy from ground level, however, all were roofless and subject to the fresh, balmy ocean breezes. Also on Saipan was the major aircraft parts depot for repair and maintenance of the B-29s. The Air Force operated daily air taxi type service between Saipan and Tinian to pick up parts and provide whatever other inter-island services were required. One pilot soon picked up the idea that some of the troops would be happy to barter goods or money for an island tour which, of course, included the hospital area as one of the main points of interest. (The area where the nurses showered and sunbathed was purely coincidental), Somehow, word of the tourist operator's business reached higher command and the pilot was then provided a specific approach chart for his flights from which he wasn't allowed to deviate – his tour business dropped off dramatically.

Late in the summer we were visited by General Hap Arnold, the Air Force Chief of Staff, and he presented the Group with its third Presidential Citation.

Tokyo Rose was always along for the ride home. She did have good Stateside music. At Tinian, however, she was supplemented by the Saipan Armed Forces Radio Service. The currency of Rose's record library also deteriorated noticeably.

The various air crews occasionally encountered an unexplained phenomenon at high altitudes over Japan. Although airspeed showed 200 m.p.h. or more, they found that at ground speed they were barely moving. The problem could be remedied by a change of altitude. We had discovered the jetstream, unknown at that time.

Tokyo Firebombing

Two of the largest air raids of World War II were the night fire-bombing missions against Tokyo in the early morning hours of 24 and 25 May 1945. Over 500 B-29s (including about 30 from the 40th Group) bombed Tokyo, dropping about 3,500 to 4,000 tons of incendiaries on each of the two missions, and starting a major fire storm that burned out 22 square miles of Tokyo. The B-29's faced intense opposition, including over 100 searchlights, heavy flak and automatic weapons fire, night fighters, and rocket-propelled Bakas. On those two nights, 43 B-29s were lost, and 169 were damaged. The 40th Group lost 3 planes, with some others damaged so severely that they never flew again. Here are presented the memories of several participants from the 40th Bomb Group, including one (Dale Johnson) who bailed out over Tokyo on May 26 and was the sole survivor of Ronald Harte's crew in No. 269.

In 1985, J. E. ("Dusty") Child, Pilot of No. 233, *Tabooma II* recalled the event:

"The years have dimmed details, but the two raids were very similar overall. Flight out past Iwo Jima and in to the IP (Initial Point) was quite routine. On the 24 May mission we did have one troubling experience while we were still some distance south of the

58th BOMB WING MISSION #325
14 AUGUST 1945
HIKARI NAVAL ARSENAL

On the last day of combat in the war, 14 August 1945, 157 Superfortresses strike the Japanese naval arsenal at Hikari. As they returned from the mission, aircrews learned of President Harry S. Truman's announcement that the war had ended. No aircraft or crewmen were lost.(40th Bomb Group Collection)

IP, which was west of Tokyo. A shape crossed our path from left to right or west to east. It was night and dark, of course, but there was enough light to see this definite shadow, in a few seconds, we hit several sharp, rather violent bumps-the telltale turbulence of an aircraft crossing our path, as opposed to the rolling motion of propwash from an aircraft ahead of us. I have no idea, really, how close we came. There was speculation that it might have been a fighter, but I was and am convinced that it was a B-29. Where it was going and where it came from, I don1 know. But the air in our cockpit was blue with a few thousand well-chosen words.

"From the IP in to the target, again, the missions were similar. Batteries of searchlights picked us up shortly after we started our run. Each battery of lights would 'walk' us into the next battery as we proceeded on course. We could see other B-29s in the lights off to our right and left. And from time to time B-29's would be silhouetted against the background of fire. Based on ground flashes and occasional tracers the flak seemed to be light to moderate. I had

reports of some fighters in the area but saw none myself.

"By the time we reached the immediate target area fires were building up rapidly. There were patches of fire on the eastern outskirts of Tokyo and larger areas of fire in the center of the city. There was enough light to see certain key portions of the city. On the whole it was one horrendous area of fire.

"The smoke billowed up thousands of feet. We had released our bombs shortly before we hit the smoke cloud. Naturally there was extreme turbulence and the thermals caused the aircraft to rise several thousands of feet. We were like a cork on the ocean, bouncing in every direction. We entered the cloud at the prescribed bombing altitude, which was 10 or 11,000 feet, as I recall. We came out of the smoke a few minutes later at 16,000 or 17,000 feet. At our speed that meant the smoke cloud was some 10-15 miles in diameter. The odor of smoke was very evident inside the aircraft.

"We left the target and proceeded home to Tinian. After flashlight checks at night and further checks after daybreak we could

O SHIMA NAVAL
OIL STORAGE
BEFORE

Target - 1884

The Amami Oshima naval oil storage facilities were targeted in the Twentieth Air Force's Mission No. 166 on 10 May 1945. (40th Bomb Group Collection)

see some flak damage. But all engines were turning. Ground checks confirmed minor damage on both missions. Strangely enough, we logged the same time, to the minute, on both missions-14 hours, 50 minutes.

"The Tokyo raids were significant and memorable. However, as I was to learn later (in mid-June), the most significant event for me had to be my wife giving birth, in California, to my son, John, at about the same time I was over Tokyo on 26 May 1945."

In February 1985, the right gunner on Ronald Harte's crew in the 44th Bomb Squadron, Dale Johnson, remembered how he was taken into captivity.

"Everything was going fine till we got near Tokyo and made our turn toward the target. Our altitude was pretty low, we all thought. The searchlights started to pick us up. I think we could have read a newspaper in the gunners' compartment.

"We had not dropped our bombs before we were hit. I think we were hit by anti-aircraft guns from the ground, There was no communication from any crew members after we were hit. The plane had a big hole near my position (Right Gunner), and I felt it was falling, so I rolled out the hole, waited a few seconds, and pulled the ripcord on my chute. That was the last I saw any members of my crew.

"I landed on the edge of a bay or lake. Needless to say, I was scared to death. An anti-aircraft Gun Camp was about a half-mile from where I landed. I watched them shoot down two planes, plus it looked like they hit some. I never did see any night fighters from the ground where I was. I hid out the rest of the night, and the next morning I walked to the Gun-Camp MP booth and gave myself up. I thought that was better than the civilians catching me. I caused a lot of excitement. I should mention I had only a few cuts and bruises from the hit and bailing out. I believe the good Lord must have been watching over me.

"The Japanese took me to an office and took my watch, pens, jacket, rings, knife, and anything they thought they could use. They then took me in a truck to an interrogation center. I was always blindfolded, so I really didn't know for sure where I went. Some English speaking Japanese asked me a lot of questions about family, where home was, where I was stationed, and if I was in a B-29. My answers were pretty vague, so he made me stand on my head with my feet on the wall, then beat my back and rear. After I collapsed on the floor, they finally quit asking questions and let me be.

"Next they took me to where I spent most of my POW time-a building with about six rooms where they put 12 to 14 men in about a 10 by 12 foot space. Food was rice balls and water with a little fish once in awhile. I went from 150 lbs. down to 100 lbs. in the 100 days I was there. Most of the other men in my room were from other island invasions; some were Navy men. Once they brought in two Navy pilots who were injured badly (plus a broken leg), and

POST STRIKE
TARGET 1884
XXI BC MISSION 166
10 MAY 1945

On 10 May 1945, 80 Superfortresses took off from Tinian and bombed the Amami Oshima naval oil storage facilities. (40th Bomb Group Collection)

they got no medical attention. They got so sick they took them out, but I'm sure they died they were so bad. We would get some news through the knot holes from room to room when somebody new was brought in. We were not supposed to talk at all. It was hard for that many men in one room to get along with a shortage of food. Some would get greedy and want more than their share. The guards would take one or two men out each day to clean the toilet boxes, which was the only exercise we got. I got out twice in the time I was there.

"After the U.S. dropped the A-Bomb and they declared the truce, we were moved to a regular POW Camp (Omori). Conditions were much better there. We even got to wash and take baths, which was the first time since I bailed out. After a few days the American planes were flying over dropping clothes and food. What a beautiful sight!

"A Navy small boat came in and took us to a Hospital ship in Tokyo Bay area. That was a great day in my life. We got good food for a change, but we couldn't eat too much as we were not used to it. I got to send a telegram home through the Red Cross. This was the first I could let my parents know I was still alive.

"Next, we were put on an LSV navy boat and sent to Guam, where we were put in the Base Hospital for a few days for a check up. Most of us just needed time to get our strength back and gain some weight. I guess they didn't have enough planes to airlift us back to the States, so they put us back on the same ship, and we

headed to San Francisco with a stop at Honolulu. It took us about a week until I was in Letterman General Hospital in San Francisco. This was about the last week of September.

"I had more check-ups and recuperation. They took us to Berkeley, California, to a college football game, over the Golden Gate Bridge, and on tours of the city. From there, I took the train back home to Rio, Illinois, and a thirty-day leave. I was real happy to be home after three years! I was an outpatient at Mayo General Hospital, Galesburg, Illinois, until March, 1946. It was April, 1946 before I was discharged from the service."

Late in 1985, Fountain L. Brown, a pilot with the 44th Bomb Squadron committed his memories of the raid to paper.

"I've flown through a few violent cumulonimbus (thunderstorm) clouds in my day, but none of them were as violent as the thermal smoke cloud we flew through on one of the Tokyo missions," Brown wrote. "Our assigned time to make our bomb drop was such that we arrived over the city long after many other B-29s had started a fire storm below. It was impossible to avoid the massive cloud of smoke-laden, turbulent updrafts. A B-29 always popped up a few feet at bomb release due to the sudden decrease in gross weight, and over Tokyo we not only had that sudden gain in altitude, but at the same time we flew into the cloud's violent updrafts which took control of the aircraft.

"Our crew Copilot was O. Wade Burchett, a big, strong, young

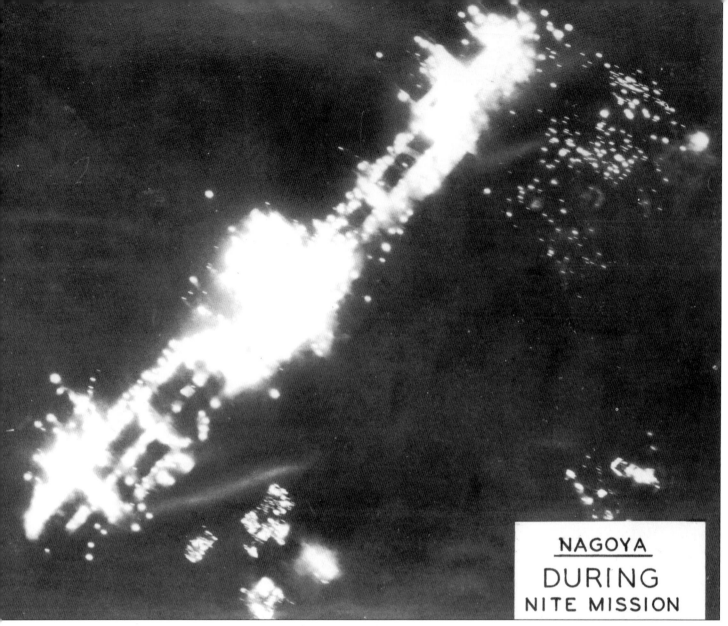

NAGOYA
DURING
NITE MISSION

Between 0300 and 0600 hours local time on 17 May 1945, 457 Superfortresses attacked the urban area of Nagoya, Japan, in the last major raid on the city. The southern part of Nagoya, the Mitsubishi Aircraft Works, the Aichi Aircraft Company's Atsuta plant, the Atsuta branch of the Nagoya Arsenal, and the Nippon Vehicle Company were among the targets in the low-level attack. (40th Bomb Group Collection)

fella fresh off an Iowa cattle ranch. When the turbulence started, Wade joined me on the flight controls to try to keep the wings straight and level. We lost the battle. In less than the minute it took to fly completely through the smoke cloud, our aircraft was lifted more than 3,000 feet and the aircraft heading was turned about 90 degrees. The additional altitude was appreciated because it helped Flight Engineer Leonard Morris use less fuel on the way home. However, the crew would have gladly given back the 3000 feet if it could have been spared the wild ride in the smoke cloud."

In December 1985, Robert L. Hall of 44th Bomb Squadron, the CFC gunner in Fountain Brown's crew, offered his recollection of the firebombing.

"I cannot separate the two Tokyo missions in my mind; they blur together. Over the preceding year we had flown many different kinds of missions: daylight formation, solo high-altitude precision, radar bombing through overcast, night low-altitude fire bombing, some with heavy anti-aircraft fire, some with aggressive fighters, some with little opposition. But these two Tokyo missions were unique.

"They started out like earlier night fire-bombing missions, except that we were warned that the opposition might be intense. What we found on arriving at the target was awe-inspiring – a baffling, surrealistic fireworks display. There were searchlights wandering around the sky, occasionally catching a B-29 and forming a bright cone of lights that made the plane a luminous target. There were fires already burning on the ground-large fires pouring up a huge smoke cloud over the city. There were tracer bullets from the automatic cannons forming graceful parabolic arcs in the sky around us. There were explosions of heavy-caliber anti-aircraft fire, some with streamers of hot-burning phosphorous. There were fast moving balls of fire that looked like rockets. There were slow-moving balls of fire-perhaps burning airplanes.

"There were unexplained explosions. There was billowing black smoke, silhouetted against a red glowing sky, with an occasional searchlight dancing on the surface of the smoke cloud. The whole effect was eerie and unreal: so many puzzling things were flying in all directions that I sat awe-struck, a little disoriented. I felt helpless because, though my finger was ready on the trigger, I had nothing to

This B-29 ditched 60 miles north of Saipan on 4 March 1945. A flying boat from VPB-27 picked up most of the crew from life rafts some distance from the bomber, but one of the B-29 crewmen was missing. When this photo was snapped from a rescue plane, that missing crewman was clinging for life to the No. 4 engine nacelle of the stricken Superfortress. (National Museum of the United States Air Force)

shoot at. I had to sit still, clamp my teeth together, and take it.

"There were moments of harsh reality in this surrealistic world: a plane going down in flames, the blinding light of searchlights when they caught our plane and held us helplessly lighted for a seeming eternity, the terrifying turbulence of the thermal smoke cloud when we flew into it, still carrying a full load of those treacherous "matchstick" bombs. Inside the smoke cloud we could see nothing, but we could smell the powerful odor of the burning city and feel the violent gyrations. When the bombardier finally called, "Bombs away," our 50 or 60 tons of airplane was being tossed around like a leaf, and I wondered if those firebombs would make it out of the bomb bay without hitting our plane.

"At last we emerged from the thermal cloud, a few thousand feet higher than we entered it, into a strangely peaceful quiet of the night sky, flying smoothly, with the surrealistic inferno safely behind us. Forty minutes later, over a hundred miles off the Japanese coast, we could still see the red glow of Tokyo burning. I had never heard our crew so quiet on the way back to home base.

"I have one other sharp memory – the hollow, sinking feeling I had at the briefing for the second mission. Back just over a day from the harrowing experience of May 24, we were called to a briefing and told that we were to repeat the whole exercise. I could think of no experience I was more reluctant to repeat, but repeat it we did – such a faithful repetition that I cannot separate the two in my mind. By the way, it took 25 years after the war before I could stand to watch a fireworks display."

Hibbard A. Smith also remembered the raids: "I flew both missions in No. 555 with Maj. Glen Landreth as pilot. The Tokyo missions were the 4th and 5th I flew in May, and my recollection is hazy. Because there was a shortage of Bombardiers (Plexiglas is lousy armorplate), I flew several times with Maj. Landreth as check pilot with new crews. However, on both Tokyo missions I believe it was his regular crew, but am not sure. Both missions were similar in plan. A series of four or five aiming points on a north/south line. Approach was from the southwest, with breakaway over the bay. As I recall, the aiming points were shifted to south on the second mission to take in undamaged areas.

"The sight of Tokyo in the midst of a fire raid was awesome. As a bombardier I had a view like no one else's. If I had the talent to put on canvas what I can still see in my mind's eye, and do it with extreme detail, unless you were told what it was, it would appear to be the purest of abstractions. There was fire on the ground, fire in the sky, and no line of separation. The defenses included some sort of pale green pyrotechnics on the ground to light up the sky, but they also lit up the target.

"The 40th must have been one of the last groups over the target both nights. The area was heavily involved in flames as we came in. I could see B-29's ahead and lower silhouetted against the city. I could only hope there were no stragglers under us or over us. On May 24th there were B-29's to the north and south of us caught in searchlights, and we slipped thru undetected. Aiming was visual, and I picked out an area not yet burning heavily. Later study of

Tokyo burns during the firebombing of 26 May 1945. (40th Bomb Group Collection)

detail target charts lead me to believe we had unloaded in the general vicinity of the American Embassy.

"The May 26 mission was almost a replay of May 24. Again B-29s to left and right caught in searchlights, and we tried to sneak thru again. This time they weren't fooled. A light pulled off the cones of light north and south and locked onto us. Being in searchlights is a most helpless feeling. You can not see beyond the surface of your window. I assume the pilots went to instruments. Maj. Landreth took violent evasive action, and shook off the lights. I do not recall if radar released or I saivoed to get rid of the weight, but the bombs did go out the doors they were supposed to and we broke away out over the bay. Tail gunner reported a suspected Baka Bomb behind us, but a relatively gentle turn to the right settled that problem, and we were on our way back to Tinian."

Carter McGregor, Pilot, 45th Bomb Squadron, remembered the incident in his book, *The Kasu-Tsuchi Bomb Group,* published 1981.

"At the briefing, the roll was called and all were present," McGregor wrote. "The Group Commander told us, This is a special occasion for the benefit of the Japanese. Tonight every B-29 in the Pacific that is ready to fly will take a load of fire bombs to Tokyo and we are going to bum the place to the ground. You will go in lower than we have ever done before-your bombing altitude will be between 10,000 and 11,000 feet.' When he said that, there was an audible gasp from the assembled flight crews. Ten thousand feet over Tokyo – they could throw rocks at us at that altitude-somebody had to be crazy to send us in that low!"

McGregor later recalled what came into view as they approached the Japanese capital. "As we droned on closer, we could see the city was an inferno. Mixed with the reflection from the fire was the bursting of anti-aircraft shells and the glare of countless crossing searchlight beams, trying to pin one of our bombers in a relentless ray. This was truly a scene from hell, horrible in its reality, beyond the wildest imagination, vividly etched in the minds of those who

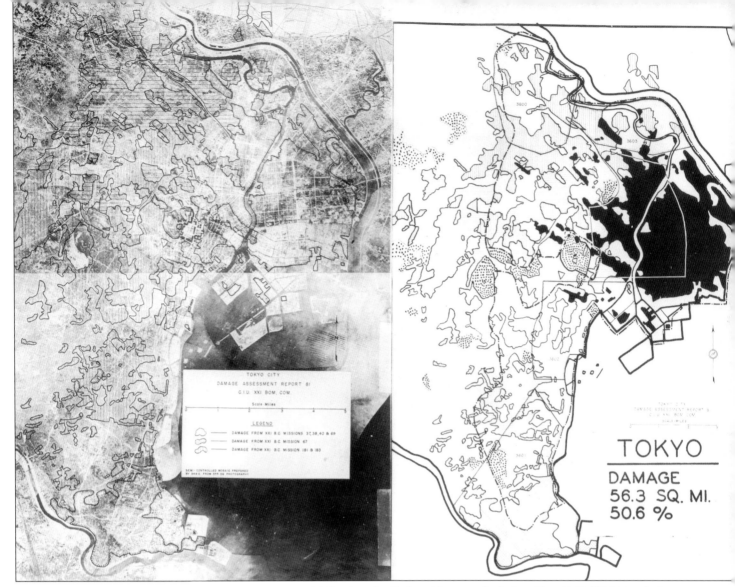

Damage inflicted on the Japanese capital was assessed following the firebombing attacks in late May 1945. (40th Bomb Group Collection)

were witness to this holocaust. Tokyo engulfed in a sea of flames was truly a modem Armageddon! . . . One of the searchlights caught us in the beam and we were momentarily blinded. At 10,400 feet, two miles above the city, the interior of the flight deck was brighter than day, as though a giant light globe had just been turned on. I could not take evasive action to try to get out of the beam, for that would have upset the bombardier's sighting, and a turn at the time of release would have thrown them to the side, just as a boat would sling water in a skid. Other searchlights saw our silhouette outlined by the first light, so they too pinned us in their beams. On all my missions I had never experienced a situation like this-a nightmare of flame, flashing lights, bursting anti-air-craft shells, and the smell of smoke and fire."

McGregor continued: "'Did any of you guys see any of our planes in trouble?' The right gunner spoke, 'I saw one 29 take a hit from flak and it looked like the wing came off. I could not see any chutes before I lost sight of him.' The tail gunner reported that he saw a plane on fire, just a ball of flames, but he couldn't tell what it was, whether it was: a -29 or one of the Nip fighters. The tone of voice of all our crewmen indicated the awesome devastation they were witnessing, a picture of horror and carnage. . . . Not until later did I think about the women, children, the old, the sick, the non-combatants trapped in the funeral pyre of the city of Tokyo. More

people died that night than in any other single incident of the war, including the dropping of either of the two cataclysmic bombs that were destined for later in the war.

"Right on our flight path was a black area. As we plunged into the stygian darkness, it was as though a giant hand had grabbed our plane and was attempting to tear it to shreds. We had entered the smoke cloud from the buming city, and I had never experienced such turbulence, not even in the most vicious thunderstorm. I yelled for the copilot to get on the controls with me, and we had no thought of trying to maintain altitude or direction. We were just struggling to keep the plane from tuming on its back. The wild gyrations continued for what seemed an eternity until we emerged from the other side, and although it had been only a few minutes, both of us were exhausted and shaken from the fight to keep our -29 in the air.

"As we passed over Tokyo Bay, we could see a rotating beacon on the surface of the water. Our radio operator called on intercom, 'There is a -29 ditching in the bay, and that signal is from an American sub so the plane can ditch close to that spot.' The nerve of that sub captain, taking his vessel right into Tokyo Bay and then surfacing, lighting his rotating beacon to guide the crippled bomber. The Navy was on the job!"

James O'Keefe, Bombardier, 25th Bomb Squadron recalled the

The total land area of the island of Tinian – viewed here from the north, looking southward – is only 39 square miles (101 square kilometers). In the foreground is North Field with its four runways, where the 509th Composite Atom-Bomb Group was based. West Field, base of the 40th Bomb Group, is visible beyond and to the right of North Field. In the top right corner of the photo is Aguijan, a small, elongated, coraline island located five miles from Tinian. A stubborn Japanese garrison kept Aguijan under its control until 4 September 1945, it when finally laid down arms – two days *after* the Japanese surrender aboard the USS *Missouri* in Tokyo Bay.

episode years later.

"'Now what?' we all wondered as we filed in to hear a special critique and briefing. A number of us were still shaking from the mission of 24 May 1945, when the antiaircraft guns and night fighters in and around Tokyo had inflicted heavy losses on the B-29s. Shaking also from what we had seen of the hell created by our incendiary bombs that night. We were to go back to that city almost immediately, and the crews who were scheduled for the mission were not envied by the others.

"Strange sightings had been reported to the intelligence officers at the interrogations following the 24 May mission. Discounting overwrought imaginations and the tricks that night shadows play on the vision, there was still evidence that something new and ominous in the way of a night fighter had been present in the skies over Tokyo in the early morning hours. We could account for many of our lost planes for they had been seen going down. But some had disappeared with no trace. Over the target several blinding explosion, many times greater than ordinary flak bursts, had been observed, and we now suspected that the planes unaccounted for had vanished in them.

"Our intelligence officers sorted through the interrogation reports, details of a crude, small aircraft captured on Okinawa, radio messages broadcast by raving Japanese military leaders, and came up with . . . the baka bomb, a suicide plane that could be launched from the belly of a bomber such as the Betty, a standard Japanese medium bomber. Aside from the demented pilot, the plane carried a warhead weighing close to a ton, rocket fuel sufficient to keep the plane airborne for half an hour, and a rising sun flag, presumably to be waved exultantly in the last few seconds before the explosion that would atomize the baka, its pilot, and its unfortunate target.

"'The baka can be aimed and released at you when you're caught in and illuminated by ground searchlight. But before you come in range of those searchlights, beware of the mother plane that we think also carries a powerful searchlight capable of picking you up at a distance. And of course if the mother plane is one of the fast Bettys, it can keep up with you, hold you in its light while its baka is released and overtakes you. And. . . uh. . .' The intelligence officer's voice trailed away. 'You're welcome to look at these diagrams and pictures of this . . . uh . . . new weapon.'

"He knew what we wanted from him – a means of dealing with a suicide attack. We knew about the appalling losses suffered by our Navy off Okinawa and that the losses were due primarily to kamikaze attacks. But there were no satisfactory tactics that he or anyone could devise for us, and we had no new, ingenious weapons that could neutralize the bakas. Like the Navy, we would have to stand up to them, fight back with our present armament, and hope that at their present stage of development, the new suicide craft would be clumsy and crude enough so that we could evade them.

"The following evening we took off, once more heading for Tokyo with the diagrams and pictures of the crude but deadly baka vivid in our mind. Hours later, in the early morning, we crossed the Japanese coastline-a landfall that always set the nerves on edge. Passing Mt. Fujiyama, easily visible at night, we picked up the IP and began the forty mile run to Tokyo. An alert, thinking enemy had seen only too well the advantages to us of this upwind approach, and had lined it with searchlights and antiaircraft weapons of all kinds. Given the rage and fury of the people below us I could even picture slingshot brigades preparing to loose rocks at us.

"One of our gunners now went to the rear hatch with sacks of 'window,' metallic strips which, when thrown out, would drift slowly downward and cloud up the radar scopes with which the searchlight crews and antiaircraft gunners would try to track us. Searchlights picked us up immediately, and out the hatch went the "window." Brick thrown at the searchlights would have been more useful. Radar was not needed to spot us on such a clear night, and once the lights caught us they clung to us tenaciously, and with maddening precision and skill each searchlight crew passed us on to the next light on the run.

"Now the guns opened up. At an altitude of 9,000 feet we were in range of medium and light antiaircraft weapons as well as the heavy guns. The plane shook from direct hits. Before we reached the city, shells took out one engine, aerated both wings, set fire to incendiary bombs in both bomb bays, and punctured and shredded so many parts that only by prayer and luck did we stay airborne. Not one of us was scratched –'a miracle,' I think. The minutes, always long on a bomb run, dragged and dragged. Finally we staggered over the city where rising smoke obscured us from the infuriating searchlights. The final seconds of the bomb run ticked off; then the bombs went away to add to the inferno and horror below us. Thermal updrafts now tossed us violently. Rod Wriston, as cool and able a pilot as ever I flew with, banked the battered plane slowly and carefully away from the burning city, the searchlights, and the antiaircraft guns. We caught our collective breaths only to gasp in sudden shock and alarm at the bright light which appeared above and in front of us. A mother plane's searchlight probing for us? And then below us a stream of tracers shot into the darkness, a B-29 gunner firing at what unknown menace?

"I swung my gunsight to cover the light and brought four calibre-50 machine guns to bear on it. We staggered on, the light neither gaining on us nor fading away. We banked again, and this brought us onto a south heading toward Tinian. The great bright light was now to the east of us, and it stayed there and was visible until the sun came up. It had been out there in space a few million years, sometimes appearing in the evening sky, sometimes in the morning sky. To us earthlings, studying the skies, Venus is far and away the brightest and most brilliant of our neighbor planets.

"There was yet another miracle that morning: our plane held together all the way home to Tinian. Rod landed it gently and with tenderness, but while taxiing to our hardstand it seemed to sigh with weariness and hurt, then it shuddered and collapsed. It never flew again.

"At interrogation we had many things to report. Our own experiences, shaking though they had been, were as nothing compared to the fates of other crews. Stricken, burning B-29s had been seen to plunge to earth all along that fearful run from the initial point to the city. Cruelest and most sickening of all sights that night: a B-29 with one engine on fire which had been turned into flaming wreckage by the guns of hysterical gunners on another B-29.

Kempei Tai Prison

Four members of the crew survived when *Winged Victory II*, B-29 No. 42-63538, crashed on a night mission to Tokyo on 25 May 1945. The crew of the aircraft consisted of:

Capt. Andrew C. Papson, Pilot
1stLt. Martin J. Long, Co-Pilot
1stLt. Joseph N. Murphy, Nay
2ndLt. Delbert Miller, Bomb -
2ndLt. Adolph C. Katzbach, F.E.
2ndLt. Patrick E. Pellecchia, Radar
Staff Sergeant John A. Yon Gonten, T.G.
Corporal Ralph Allen, L.G.
Corporal Walter W. Oestreich, R.G.
Corporal Elmer K. Bertsch, CFC
PFC Hershell Hill, Radio

Of the members of this plane's crew, only four survived the crash and were taken prisoner. They were Deibert Miller, Walter Oestreich, Elmer Bertsch and Patrick Pellecchia. Elmer Bertsch died in the Kepei Tai prison. One of the survivors, Walter Oestreich, told his story 45 years later:

"We were an hour late for takeoff because of a hydraulic leak in the landing gear. We reached the target area around 01:00 on May 26th. I was called by Capt Papson to go to the camera hatch and throw out foil to jam the Japanese radar. While throwing out the foil, I heard Ralph Allen say on intercom that we were hit and on fire. Then everything went dead.

"When standing up and looking out the top hatch, I saw No. 2 and No 3 engines on fire. We were hit before we could drop the bombs. I tried to call that I was bailing out, but received no answer. Lt. Pat Pelledcchia came out of the radar room and said, "Let's get out of here." I ripped off my flak suit and dove out; he followed. My parachute opened with a bang, everything below was on fire and I could feel the heat. I said some prayers on the way down. Soon I drifted away from the fire below. I noticed my head was bleeding. I didn't have time to think of that for I could see where I was landing., and a mob was on the ground to greet me. They piled on top of me and gave me a beating. Two Japanese MPs pullded them off. I was disarmed and handcuffed and taken to an office with another crew

B-29-26-BA serial number 42-63508, nicknamed *Peachy*, served with the 505th Bomb Group. This plane and its crew were lost on the Tokyo raid of 26 May 1945. The nose art featured a scantily clad cowgirl superimposed over a wagon wheel. (Air Force Historical Research Agency)

member and put under guard. We had to kneel and could not talk.

"At daylight I was taken by flat-bed truck to Kempei Tai headquarters. I was taken to a big room which held all the rest of the prisoners who were shot down on the night of May 26th. Everyone was blindfolded, and we all sat on the floor with our backs to the wall. At roll call, I believed I heard Corporal Elmer Bertsch's name called. My blindfold slipped, and I believe I saw him. They had trouble pronouncing his name. He did not answer at first and got a kick in the ribs. I never saw him again. In a telephone conversation with Delbert Miller, when we arrived home, we both believed it was Elmer Bertsch we saw.

"In the afternoon of May 26th we were placed in cells. There were 13 prisoners in the cell about 9 x 10. There was a hole in the floor with a cover on it. That was our latrine.

"The names of the prisoners in the cell were 1st Lt John Newcomb, 1st Lt Arthur O'Hara, 2nd Lt Delbert Miller, 2nd Lt James Marins, 2nd Lt Thodore Fox, 2nd Lt Patrick Pellecchia, Staff Sergeant Dale Johnson, Staff Sergeant Micahel J. Robertson, Technical Sergeant Harold B. Hallvarsen, Staff Sergent Sivia LaMarca, and Corporal Walter Oestreich. Lt Theodore Fox and Technical Sergeant Harold Hallvarsen died while in prison.

"About a week alter being captured, I was taken for questioning. My answers did not please the interrogator. Two guards gave me a beating with a bamboo club across my back which I will never forgeL I was kicked in the ribs and stomach and poked in the face with the jagged end of the club. They said they would poke my eyes out.

"I blacked out for a while. When I came to, the guard gave me a kick in the ribs and spit in my face. I was taken back to the cell. I was questioned by a Japanese Navy officer about 10 days later. They were nice. I received no beatings from the Navy men.

Wreckers are in the process of recovering a B-29 of the 314th Bomb Wing that suffered a crash on or around 16 May 1945. It appears that the wing has sheared from its attachments to the fuselage and has been severely twisted. More often than not, an aircraft this badly damaged would be unceremoniously dumped in the scrapyard. (Air Force Historical Research Agency)

"Our food was three balls of rice with water per day. Sometimes had seaweed, and once or twice a fish head. The cell was full of lice and fleas; we were all full of flea bites. I lost around 70 pounds. We all suffered from malnutrition, beri-beri, and infections of some kind. We received no medical treatment as we were "special prisoners" (B-29 crewmen) if the United States had not used the atomic bomb, none of us ever would have got out alive.

"On 6 August 1945, the atomic bomb was dropped on Hiroshima. We did not know about it at the time, but a lot of shouting and yelling could be heard outside the prison. We knew something was happening. On 9 August, a second bomb was dropped on Nagasaki. On 15 August, we were awakened early in the morning, blindfolded, and loaded on trucks, and taken to Omori prison camp, not far from Tokyo.

"There we were given more food and a box of vitamins. We were told we would soon be going home. Some B-29s came over and dropped clothing, food, and candy bars.

"On 29 August, the U.S. Navy came ashore in landing craft. We were taken to the hospital ship Benevolence. We had our first shave and shower and full meal since we were captured. I was on the hospital ship until 18 September, when Colonel Richard Carmichael, a Navy lieutenant, and I were flown back to the U.S.A.

in a C-54. W reached the U.S.A. on 21 September 1945. I was taken to Letterman General Hospital in San Francisco. I was processed and promoted to Sergeant. On 2 October I was taken to Vaughn V.A. Hospital in Hines, Illinois, and was there until 1 December. I was separated from the service on 3 December 1945."

The End at Last

The last bombing mission of the war was flown by the 40th on 14 August 1945. Takeoff had been delayed several hours because it was thought an announcement of the war's end would be forthcoming, but none did come and takeoff was finally ordered. President Harry Truman's announcement was broadcast as the planes were returning from a successful mission. No aircraft had been lost.

And so it ended.

During the night of 15 August 1945 we were awakened by the CQ running through our housing area shouting "the war is over, the war is over!" Sweetest music ever heard! Needless to say, there was no more sleep that night and the next day, at the opening bell of the newly completed NCO club the entire Group went on a glorious binge. (At home my father did the same thing much to the displeasure of my mother who thought they should be on their

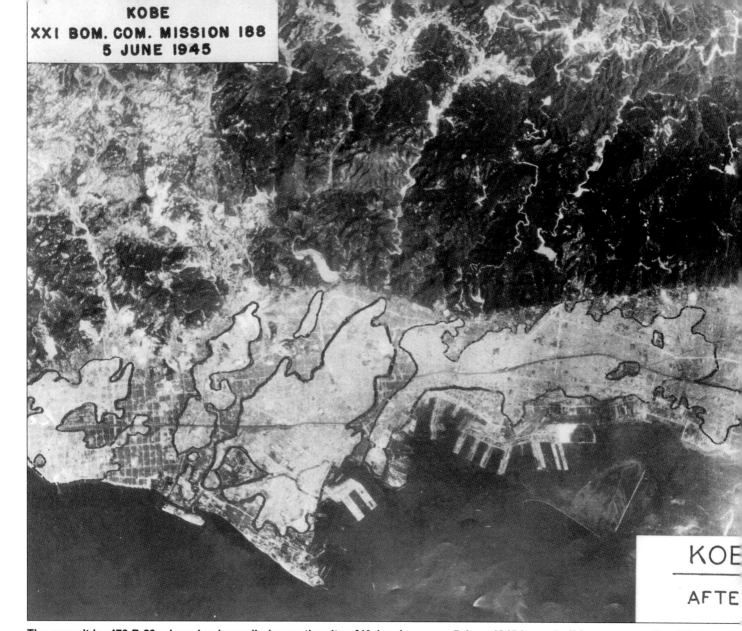

KOBE
XXI BOM. COM. MISSION 188
5 JUNE 1945

KOBE

AFTE

The assault by 473 B-29s dropping incendiaries on the city of Kobe, Japan, on 5 June 1945 burned off four square miles (10.4 square kilometers) and damaged more than half of the city. (40th Bomb Group Collection)

knees in church giving thanks. Both had their points but I was certainly simpatico with my father).

Our Group had flown a total of 144 missions including our recon missions. I had flown both recon and bombing missions plus uncounted Hump trips. We lost 79 aircraft. Fifty one crewmen were killed in action. One hundred twelve were missing and presumed dead. Thirty two were wounded.

In addition to the POW mercy missions at war's end, the 40th also flew in the huge power display over Tokyo and the battleship Missouri at the time of the signing of the Japanese surrender. There were approximately 800 B-29s in formations of twelve each in the fly by.

Years later, in 1994 or 1995, I received in the mail, from the Commanding General of the Chinese Air Force, a set of Chinese Air Force wings with a note in recognition of service in China.

One postwar mission story:

A grizzled old Air Force vet sitting on a bar stool visiting with the bartender. The vet says "yes, back in WWII I flew recon over enemy territory". Bartender says "you mean like the U2"? Vet says "no, it was more like the "why me?"

Supply Missions to POWs

At the end of the war in the Pacific, late in August of 1945, POW camps in Japan, China, and Korea contained many prisoners – American, British, Dutch, Australian, etc. – some of whom had been living under harsh prison conditions for a long time. From 27 August through 20 September, there were 1,066 B-29 take-offs on mercy missions which dropped over 4,400 tons of supplies to 154 different POW camps housing an estimated 63,400 prisoners. Tragically, though the war was over, eight B-29s and 77 crew members were lost on these missions. Here we present the stories of four members of the 40th Group who were involved in these missions.

O. W. Burchett, pilot of B-29 No. 44-70100 recalled the events of 30 August 1945:

"I will do the best I can with my recollections of this mercy mission. We had extra personnel on board, but I do not recall just who they were. I do recall they were ground personnel. One of these men was busy with the K-20 camera.

"The Japanese envoys who met with U.S. representatives to

OSAKA
XXI BOM. COM. MISSION 189
7 JUNE 1945

OSAKA
————
AFTER

Aerial reconnaissance photos allowed the Army Air Force to assess the extent of damage inflicted by B-29 assault on the Japanese city of Osaka on 7 June 1945. (40th Bomb Group Collection)

The target of Mission 215 on 22 June 1945 is the Kure Naval Arsenal in Japan. (40th Bomb Group Collection)

arrange terms of the peace agreement were asked for, and provided, longitude and latitude of the POW camps. Some aircrews in the 40th and other Groups were immediately assigned and started loading aircraft with oil drums rigged with parachutes and loaded with medical supplies, food, and clothing. This was to be our first contact with our surviving comrades in the prison situations. Both bomb bays were loaded, and we were briefed with very little information as to the identity of our drop zone and very little information on the anticipated drop trajectory. It seems to me there were four other aircraft in addition to mine. We were assigned to drop on a camp at Taihokli, Formosa. We were briefed to fly direct to Formosa, locate the target, drop one bomb bay from very low altitude of less than 500 feet. After observing the results, we then could make some calculated corrections to drop the second bomb bay of supplies.

"We arrived over Formosa in good weather, but finding and properly identifying the POW camp proved to be difficult and time consuming. We did locate the camp at the base of some hills on the edge of a small stream. We observed a sign on a roof reading, 'TWO KILLED AVOID CAMP,' and next to the camp was an open field with a sign reading, 'PW SUPPLIES DROP HERE.' We took K-20 pictures of these signs. Then we dropped the first bomb bay satisfactorily, but the prisoners rushed the field in such panic that we had to delay the second drop until they cleared the field. This was an extremely tear jerking sight. We really would have enjoyed stopping to pick up the load of POWs.

"While circling this area, we observed an adjoining airstrip that was extremely well camouflaged, it appeared to have large bomb craters, etc. However, a white, twin-engine Japanese aircraft, with a large green identity cross on the side of the fuselage, came in, refueled and left from this strip. This aircraft was carrying the Japanese envoy who had been in the Philippines discussing the peace. We also observed during our time of circling at low altitude that the civilian population were apparently informed of our arrival and seemed to completely ignore us. They were walking, riding bikes and a few vehicles on the roads in a very normal manner.

"After making our second drop, we had depleted our fuel until it was necessary for us to head for Yon Tan airstrip on Okinawa to refuel. *En route* to Okinawa I enjoyed a moment of superiority. We overtook the white envoy aircraft. We were cruising approximately 1,000 feet above it. I could not resist a shallow dive, some extra throttle and buzzing him real well, much to my pleasure as well as the crew's.

"Upon landing at Yon Tan, I lost tread from one of the tires on the right landing gear that not only ruined the tire but did skin damage to the aircraft. Because of the war's end, things were well disorganized, and repairs took two days. Upon my return to Tinian I found I had been removed from orders to fly back into the states with a composite crew of high mission and high point men. At the time this seemed like the end of the world to Vonnie (my wife) and me. However, we later flew back into the states as a group. Our crew and passengers arrived stateside on 16 October 1945, My recollections of the POWs waving and greeting us will never fade, and I will never regret that mission. I am proud that the 40th had the opportunity of sharing this mercy mission."Delmar Johnson, bombardier, had his own recollections of the mercy missions to

On 22 June 1945, Tinian-based Superfortresses blasted the Kure Arsenal. Afterward reconnaissance photos revealed the extent of the damage inflicted. (40th Bomb Group Collection)

POW camps.

"After the end of hostilities, volunteers were requested to fly POW supply missions, two of which I flew on. The second, which was to Yawata, became the eventful trip. This was also the mission on which John Comwell, our original CP, flew on another aircraft. Knowing some of each crew, I had my choice of AC and crew. Since I had flown once before with Ken Dothage as AC, I chose his crew, which was to be our good fortune. The flight was long and uneventful until we were approaching the Islands, which were completely "socked in." We stayed on top in almost clear weather, searching for openings to get down to our drop altitude of 800 feet. After a couple of hours circling the target with no such opening appearing, we decided to go out over the water to get down under the heavy clouds, head into the harbor, make our drop, and immediately climb out. If my memory serves me correctly, our maps showed hills, etc., to be not over 600-650 feet nearby in the heading we were on. There was absolutely no visibility above our approximate 600-800 feet. Our drop was made- and as we began climbing slowly, my recollection is that the radar observer screamed to "pull up and tum right," which Ken immediately did-with all throttles at limit. Evidently the radar operator saw a dark left patch on his screen and lighter on the right. Not too many seconds later-and I remember as I was looking off to the right-we were about 1,300-1,350 feet altitude-and for a brief second clouds disappeared. Off our right wing, not more than twenty or thirty feet, were the trees, just as we cleared the top. Ken Dothage, John Laxton and I saw what in all probability John Comwell and the others in the B-29 a couple of minutes behind us did not see-and they were killed in the crash of their plane.

"Several times during the flight out, we had seen their aircraft slightly higher and behind us by two or three miles. This was not, however, to be the last of our worries. Because we had been up in the air so much longer than expected, we could never make it back on our fuel supply. Our heading was changed to Okinawa, and when we landed among all the little potholes on the runway, it was on fumes and not fuel. We were told, and Ken's engineer and CP can verify, we had no more than 25 gallons of gas in each of our tanks. We slept under the plane, and through the night we heard gunfire somewhere not too far away. Next morning we were refueled, partially I'm told, because of the shorter runway, and took off, clearing the masts of ships below us in the harbor by not too many feet, and returned. I wish I could remember all of the crewmen on this flight, but to those I remember-Ken Dothage (pilot), John Laxton (CP), Pat Daily (Navigator), and Sgt. Valley (Engineer)... 'we were lucky.'"

Maudce Righetti, Copilot, recalled: "Alter V-J day, I helped load our B-29 on Saipan for a drop at a POW camp a few days later in Japan. It was the hardest work I had done in a long while. We looked forward to the low-level drop with no enemy opposition. At the last possible moment, I was scratched as second pilot, and Lt. John G. Cornwell (from Texas) went in my place. His ship never came back. The pallets did not jettison completely and banged the

The Kawanishi Aircraft factory in Takarazuka, near Osaka, is attacked on 24 July 1945. (40th Bomb Group)

plane into uncontrollability, I later learned. It was just not my time to go."

The following is the full text of a letter written by Lt. Dan Sweeney, Jr., to his parents on Sunday, 2 September 1945. Sweeney was navigator on Capt. Ralph Learn's crew. We are grateful to Sweeney's family for making the letter available to us.

"Dearest Mother and Daddy,

"I just heard the president proclaim V-J day-the day we've been waiting for so long. Now all I need to convince me that the war is over is for them to send me home. I still haven't heard much about that. There are a lot of rumors going around over here but nothing official has come out yet. A few guys that had quite a number of points have already gone home. I believe that something will turn up pretty soon now, though, since the treaty is all signed and everything seems to be going along pretty well with the occupation. I still have hopes of being home by Thanksgiving but I'm not building myself up for it because it would he a big disappointment if I didn't make it. I really took a nice tour Thursday. We flew a mission way up into northern Korea carrying 9,000 lbs. of supplies to a prisoner of war camp. We had a lot of rank aboard our ship, too-a colonel from the continental air force in Washington, and the group operations officer, a major, of the 40th Group. Dobney was the only one of the crew that didn't go. I'll just start from the first and tell you all about it. We took off from here Thursday morning about 3:00 and headed for Okinawa. We landed at Okinawa about the middle of the morning and refueled before going on into Korea. We only stayed

at Okinawa for 2 1/2 hours, so none of us got a chance to look the island over except from the air. We took off about noon for Korea. When we hit the coast of Korea, the weather began closing in on us so I 'suggested' to the colonel that we go up a few thousand more feet to be sure of clearing the mountains as it is very mountainous country and not very well charted either. I can' t see much sense in flying below the tops of the mountain, especially when you can't see the tops. We got through the weather OK, though, and broke into the clear about an hour before we got to the target. We were flying only 1,000 feet above the terrain so we could see everything, We flew right over Japanese cities and airfields, and could practically look the Japanese on the ground straight in the eye. We all "sweated it out" a little at first because we weren't too sure the Japanese in Korea knew the war was over, but we were all tickled to death to see they had heard the good news and weren't shooting at us. It would have only taken about one good burst of anti-aircraft fire to knock us down as low as we were. Well, after that we relaxed a little and finally reached the target area about 4:00 p.m. that afternoon. We found the prison camp pretty easily and incidentally, we were down to 800 ft.. above the ground by this time. We had to make one run over the camp to check the wind because the supplies had parachutes on them and they had to be dropped within the camp but still they had to miss the huts the prisoners were kept in to prevent killing some of then. Boy, you should have seen those guys down there that was probably one of the biggest moments in their lives seeing a B-29 circling around there after their being imprisoned

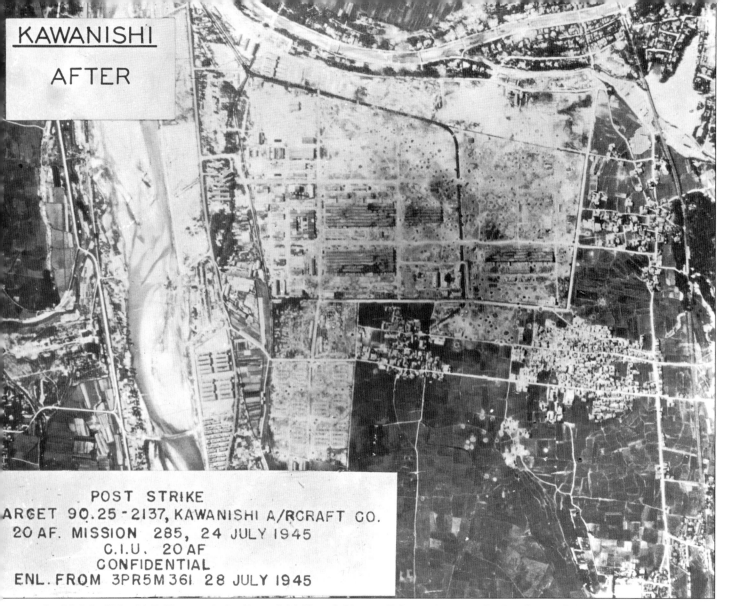

POST STRIKE
ARGET 90.25-2137, KAWANISHI A/RCRAFT CO.
20 AF. MISSION 285, 24 JULY 1945
C.I.U. 20 AF
CONFIDENTIAL
ENL. FROM 3PR5M361 28 JULY 1945

On 24 July 1945, 81 B-29s struck the Kawanishi Aircraft Plant at Takarazuka, near Osaka, Japan. Subsequent reconnaissance revealed that 77 percent of the plant was destroyed in the air raid. (40th Bomb Group Collection)

way up there in Korea for a few years or more. They started running around patting each other on the back and waving everything from sticks to handkerchiefs, we made two more runs over the camp dropping the supplies this time, and then we made one last run to check everything and see where the packages had landed. They all hit right in the camp and didn't touch the huts. Two fell outside the big wire fences but we saw some of the guys outside the fence dragging the packages in, so they got them all OK. We headed back home then, coming across the Japanese mainland at a fairly low altitude on our way back but we didn't have any trouble there either. I was very lucky in my navigation all the way and the colonel complimented us all when we got back on the ground here at Tinian. We got back Friday morning about 2:00. We flew 20 hours and 20 minutes and a total of 4,400 miles. That's the longest ride I've ever had. We all feel like we did more good on this mission than any we've ever flown-you can drop tons of bombs and never be too sure where they hit and just how much good your own bombs did, but we know those guys needed the supplies and we also know we got 'em there just right! Put yourself in one of those American prisoner's places and try to imagine how happy you would be to see an American plane for the first time in quite awhile only 800 feet overhead and carrying a big load of supplies for you. The packages

contained cartons of cigarettes, chewing gum, canned foods, and medicine and probably a lot of other things like clothing. We had no information on the location of this camp except its approximate position since nobody had ever been up that far before. We thought we were pretty lucky to find it so easily. Learn asked for one of these missions quite awhile ago when we first heard the 29s were going to fly some of them. I don't blame him a bit since his father is in Japanese hands somewhere. It would really be something if it turns out that his dad was in this particular camp we hit.

"The trip was pretty nice for sightseeing, too. As I said before, we didn't see much of Okinawa except from the air, but we could see enough from there to tell that it was pretty well torn up from the recent battles. There was absolutely nothing left of the villages there and you could see bomb craters over the island. I saw a few of those caves they had to blast the Japanese out of, and it beats me how they ever got those rascals out of there-but everything is very peaceful there now. We flew right over Ie Shima, the little island Emie Pyle was killed on and also the place the Japanese envoys landed when they went to Manila to confer with MacArthur. Korea was really beautiful-much nicer than I ever imagined. There were big rivers running all through mountains almost like you see on a golf course. Along the coast they have some of the prettiest beaches I have ever

Overlooking the Pacific Ocean on Tinian is the 40th Bomb Group's theater, used for Group personnel meetings, USO shows, and other gatherings. The author witnessed the ill-fated cruiser USS *Indianapolis* pass by this point after delivering nuclear material to the 509th Bomb Group for the attack on Hiroshima. (40th Bomb Group Collection)

On the evening of 6 August 1945, *Enola Gay* sits on North Field, Tinian, following the Hiroshima attack. A Martin-built B-29-35, *Enola Gay* was devoid of turrets and had a modified bomb bay for carriage of the atomic weapon. (Peter Bowers)

A dense column of smoke rises more than 60,000 feet into the air over the Japanese port of Nagasaki as the result of an atomic bomb, the second ever used in warfare, dropped on the industrial center on 9 August 1945, from a B-29 nicknamed *Bockscar*.

The *Enola Gay* comes in to land on Tinian's North Field, following the atomic bombing mission on Hiroshima, Japan. (U.S. Air Force)

seen. There are small cottages near the beaches and it really looked nice. We saw one big yacht along the beach, something like you would expect a millionaire or big sportsman to have back in the states. There were quite a few large cities and a lot of industry all over the place. We are all pretty well convinced that the fighting is over now after flying over that once-considered enemy territory at low altitudes.

"I got a letter from you Wednesday-the first in some time. I think the army has all the transport planes tied up with occupation business so that slows down our mail now.

Show of Strength

In addition to the POW mercy missions at war's end, the 40th also flew in the huge power display over Tokyo and the battleship Missouri at the time of the signing of the Japanese surrender. There were approximately 800 B-29s in formations of twelve each in the fly by.

Sometime after VE Day in Europe everyone began to anticipate

the war with Japan would end in the not to distant future and we began to think in terms of postwar life – career, education, marriage to sweethearts, recovery from "Dear John" letters, etc. The Army Air Force (and all services for that matter) developed a "point" system by which the order of rotation and release from Service would be based – those with the highest number of "points" would be first out. Points were developed based on months of service, service awards and decorations, and, in the Air Force, missions flown. "Old Air Force" personnel with years of service obviously banked a lot of points. Based on the other criteria, the author came up with a fairly high number – not in the highest category, but enough to earn one of the early returns.

With the end of the war all the major flying activities, except for a limited number of mercy missions to parachute food, medicines and other goodies into POW camps, came to an end. We went into a buttoning up phase, disposing of worn out and perishable materials (i.e., film) and packing the rest for storage. Before leaving, however, the Pacific Ocean had one more experience for us. In September we were treated to a full-fledged typhoon which

Four aircraft from the 468th Bomb Group fly over Japan on the day WWII ended, 15 August 1945. Most people agree that the two nuclear weapons were not the only cause of the war's end. Two other factors came into play. The fire bombing of Japan by the 20th Air Force was one factor, and the declaration of war on Japan by the USSR, and the Soviet sweep through Manchuria, neutralizing Japan's main reserve army and threatening Soviet involvement in the occupation of Japan, was the other factor. The lead B-29 with the number 55 on it is the original *Jack's Hack*. (58th BW Memorial)

The "S" inscribed within a triangle was the mark of the 40th Bomb Group of the 58th Bomb Wing, adopted in May 1945, after the unit had relocated from India to the Marianas. This aircraft is bringing supplies to POWs just after the end of hostilities. (40th Bomb Group Collection)

seemed to center on the Marianas. We had little advance warning but there was minimal damage. The ground crews on the B-29s, at least in some instances, stayed with their planes, turning them as the wind changed direction, so that they were always facing into the wind. Strangely enough, our tent remained in place – some did blow away but not all. The morning following the typhoon one of my tent mates displayed the ingenuity of his wife. She had sent him, from time to time, canned fruit juices which he seemed to savor and continually sipped. He opened one of his cans, which I distinctly remember was labeled Grapefruit Segments, and, for the first time, offered to share it with the rest of us. Strange grapefruit; it tasted something like a fine bourbon! Which, in fact, it was. That sucker had been receiving cans of whiskey, labeled as fruit juices, all through the war! He nearly didn't survive to go home when we learned his secret.

In early October the much looked forward to orders for the 40th to return to the States were received. The first B-29 of the Group would depart on 12 October 1945, would be flown by the Group CO and all aboard would have re-upped to stay in the Air Force. As anxious as I was to return, I resisted any temptation to re-up and catch that first plane. Other B-29s also left that day- the Group's B-29s were scheduled for departure over a three day period. The B-29 to which I was assigned departed on October 13. We overnighted at Kwajalein in the Marshall Islands then had two great days in Honolulu before landing at Mather Field in Sacramento, California. The sight of the Golden Gate was the goal of every returning serviceman, it truly meant HOME. I had looked forward to seeing the Golden Gate as we passed San Francisco but, as usual, it was covered with fog. We did, however, watch the Golden Gate approach on the B-29's radar, as it passed below us, but somehow it wasn't the same thing. Ironically, I arrived home before the high point "Old Air Force" guys who had started their return trip in September. They had been placed on a troopship at Saipan for their return.

For a few years immediately following the war, a few of the guys who had been together in the Photo Unit would meet at various places around the country for mini-reunions. These soon gave way to the press of forming families and careers and, except for occasional Christmas cards, contact among us was lost. Then, in 1980, several ex-40th Group people began to plan a reunion for the entire Group.

New Orleans was picked as the location and invitations were sent to all the ex-40th people whose addresses could be located. A group of some 180 ex-members along with many wives and kids attended.

Among those attending were ten or so of the Photo Unit members including our first CO whose home was in New Orleans. CC and I also attended. One of the highlights was the fly in of the only remaining flyable B-29. This last B-29 was named Fifi and was a part of the Confederate Air Force located in Harlingen, Texas. Fifi was reconstructed from the Naval Weapons storage facility in China Lake, California. The Confederate Air Force, now renamed the Commemorative Air Force, is a museum for flyable airplanes from the World War II era and is currently located in Midland, Texas. Each aircraft is flown all over the country to air shows and various other expositions. Not only were the ex-40th members beginning to show their age, but so was Fifi. In 1993, for the 50th anniversary of the first B-29 flight, Fifi was taken back to the Boeing plant in Seattle for a complete rebuilding and refurbishing. With a new crew (our ex-40th pilot has flown into the Wilde Blue), Fifi remains an active part of the CAF and continues to tour the country. She looks good for another 50 years. Would that some of the other ex-B-29 members could be so rebuilt and refurbished! Perhaps Viagra is the first step in that direction. Following that first Group reunion in 1981, the reunions have become an annual affair.

The second reunion in 1982 was held here in Arlington, Texas and the author was privileged to work with a committee of 40th exes to stage the reunion. It, too, was successful and it was decided by the Group executives to formalize the organization. The author was elected its first president and aided in formalizing the organization with the necessary legal steps and documentation.

We also planned for our third reunion at the Disneyland Hotel in Anaheim, California. We learned that General LeMay, long since retired, lived nearby in Newport Beach and we decided to invite him to attend. We were advised that the General received many, many similar invitations and, because there were so many he couldn't accept all of them, so he declined all. Nonetheless, the previously mentioned Bobby Shanks, one of our committee members who had bailed out on a Rangoon mission and became a POW, wrangled an invitation to visit General LeMay at his home. As a result, General LeMay did agree to attend the reunion.

One of the highlights of our visit to LeMay's home, perhaps the

Silver Lady, **B-29-65-BW 44-69844, rests on a hardstand in the Marianas next to a stock of bombs ready to be loaded in its bomb bays. The nickname the crew bestowed on this aircraft was a reference to its bright, bare-aluminum appearance. The first operational B-29s were delivered with camouflage paint, but the vast majority of Superfortresses were delivered unpainted. By late 1943, the USAAF had decided that the advantages unpainted aircraft offered, reduced drag and lower weight, outweighed the higher visibility created by the bare aluminum. The tail markings on** *Silver Lady* **are those standardized by the 313th Bomb Wing in early 1945: the barely visible yellow tip on the vertical fin and the letter E inside the circle on the tail signified the 504th Bomb Group. (Stan Piet collection)**

greatest personal highlight for the author, was that General LeMay, after CC had told him of my aerial photo work, was quite lavish in his comments about the work of what he termed "his photographers" and the contributions they had made to the success of the 20th Air Force over Japan.

On the night of the reunion, LeMay and the author shared the dais. We presented him with a 40th Group hat, which he promptly wore for the balance of the evening. During the war, General LeMay was a fanatic about maximizing bomb load on target. I had been primed to ask him if the story was true that he had the panel clock on the B-29's copilot panel, which General LeMay considered superfluous, removed and an additional 500-pound bomb added to the bomb load. He allowed the story wasn't true, but, he would have liked to have had me on his staff at the time and he would certainly have accepted the suggestion. CC, the ex sergeant's wife, shared her side of the dais with Mrs. LeMay, who informed her that Curtie (Mrs. LeMay's sobriquet for him) could be somewhat headstrong on occasion and needed someone to dampen his Godlike aspirations. On the whole it was a long evening for CC

who couldn't quite top Mrs. LeMay's comments about tea with the Queen when "Curtie" was Commanding General of NATO. At the conclusion of the dinner and "Curtie's" remarks to the Group, We asked him casually, thinking he'd decline, if he would like to join us in our 'war room' where we had Group memorabilia and after-dinner drinks. "Curtie" allowed he would love to join us, did so, and spent considerable time with us, much to CC's dismay, since it meant that Mrs. LeMay remained with her for more "small talk" about her experiences. Although many of LeMay's old staff officers, with their wives, were in the war room, each one managed to elude CC's plea for relief.

Mrs. LeMay was a very, very nice person, but there was no doubt that her postwar experiences, as well as those of "Curtie," were somewhat removed from the flow of budgeting household expenses to the income provided for education by the GI Bill as CC and I had done. At one of our reunions, CC was elected an honorary member of one of the crews that had been POWed at Rangoon. CC was a great listener for their experiences and shed many, many tears (and laughter too) over their stories of survival.

Salome! was B-29B-40-BA 44-83893 of the 331st Bomb Group, 355th Bomb Squadron. The airplane commander/pilot was 1st Lt. William Y. Quinn. (Stan Piet collection)

Many of the 40th Group's members remained career members of the Air Force. Many went through the B-36, B-47, and B-52 programs. Others attained command ranks, including three who became generals. One became Commanding Officer of a supersonic SR-71 reconnaissance group. Another flew the B-29 that dropped the atom bomb at the Bikini and Eniwetok nuclear tests in 1946, and one led a non-stop, round-the-world flight of three B-29s in a test of in-flight refuelling. Of course many of the 40th's veterans returned to civilian life and professional careers in many fields of endeavor. Virtually all retained a life-long interest in aviation and aircraft. A large number became airline pilots.

And only one member known to the author had to escape police in Mexico by exiting through a bathroom and racing back across the border!

Targets hit by the 40th BG

IN CHINA-BURMA-INDIA THEATER
Bangkok 5- 6-1944
Yawata 15-6-1944
Sasebo 7-7-1944
Anshan 29-7-1944

Palembang (on Sumatra, now in Indonesia) 10-8-1944
Nagasaki 10-8-1944
Yawata 20-8-1944
Anshan 8-9-1944
Anshan 26-9-1944
Taiwan ("Formosa")14-10-1944
Taiwan 17-10-1944
Omura 25-10-1944
Rangoon (modern Yangon) 3-11-1944
Singapore 5-11-1944
Nanjing (Nanking) 11-11-1944
Omura 21-11-1944
Bangkok 27-11-1944
Shenyang (Mukden) 7-12-1944
Rangoon 14-12-1944
Hankou (Hankow) 18-12-1944
Omura 19-12-1944
Shenyang (Mukden) 21-12-1944
Bangkok 2-1-1945
Omura 6-1-1945
Taiwan (Formosa) 9-1-1945
Singapore 11-1-1945

A wealth of visual details of an operational B-29 air base is present in this color view. Although the base is not identified, it is most likely North Field on Tinian: the two B-29s in the background have the "X" over a triangle unit symbols of the 9th Bomb Group of the 313th Bomb Wing, which was based at North Field. In the foreground are bombs resting on stands, awaiting loading in the adjacent B-29. In the background are assorted vehicles, including Jeeps and a fuel-tank semi-trailer and tractor. Tents and shacks dot the area, and in the background are rows of B-29s. (Stan Piet collection)

Taiwan (Formosa) 14-1-1945
Taiwan 17-1-1945
Saigon (now Ho Chi Minh City) 27-1-1945
Singapore 1-2-1945
Bangkok 7-2-1945
Rangoon 11-2-1945
Singapore 24-2-1945
Singapore 2-3-1945
Singapore 12-3-1945
Rangoon 17-3-1945
Rangoon 22-3-1945
Singapore 29-3-1945
IN PACIFIC OCEAN AREA
Nrio Naval Aircraft Factory at Kure 5-5-1945
Oshima Naval Oil Storage 10-5-1945
Nagoya Urban Area 14-5-1945
Nagoya Urban Area 16-5-1945
Hamamatsu 19-5-1945
Tokyo Urban Area 24-5-1945
Tokyo Urban Area 26-5-1945
Yokohama 29-5-1945
Osaka Urban Area 1-6-1945
Kobe Urban Area 5-6-1945
Osaka Urban Area 7-6-1945
Kasumigaura Seaplane Base 10-6-1945
Osaka Urban Area 15-6-1945
Omuta Urban Area 17-6-1945
Toyohashi Urban Area 19-6-1945
Himeji, Kawanishi Aircraft factory 22-6-1945

Kagamigahara, Kawasaki Aircraft Factory 26-6-1945
Okayama Urban Area 28-6-1945
Kure Urban Area 1-7-1945
Takematsu Urban Area 3-7-1945
Chiba Urban Area 6-7-1945
Sendai Urban Area 9-7-1945
Utsonomiya Urban Area 12-7-1945
Namazu Urban Area 16-7-1945
Fukui Urban Area 19-7-1945
Osaka, Sumitoma Metal Industry 24-7-1945
Izu Industrial Urban Area 28-7-1945
Hachioji 1-8-1945
Imabari 5-8-1945
Tokoyawa 7-8-1945
Fukuyama 9-8-1945
Hikari Naval Arsenal 14-8-1945

Records of the 40th BG

144 Missions
18,065 tons of bombs dropped
132 enemy planes destroyed
79 B-29s lost; 175 damaged
76 killed in action, 117 mission
3 Presidential Citations
7 Battle Stars
1st B-29 flight 21 September 1942
3,900 built
Average cost $639,188

A B-29 undergoes maintenance at a base in China in 1944. The mechanic at the upper right is servicing the number-one engine. Cowl panels have been removed to allow access to the cylinders and engine components, exposing the bare-metal cowl frame. The top and bottom forward turrets are not installed. The antenna just aft of the pilot's side windows is part of the identification, friend or foe (IFF), a highly classified system that used a coded radio signal, changed daily, to identify friendly versus enemy aircraft in the vicinity. (Stan Piet collection)

B-29 Specifications

Crew	Pilot, copilot, flight engineer, bombardier, navigator, radio operator, radar observer, CFC blister gunners (two), CFC upper gunner, and tail gunner.
Length	99 ft (30.2m)
Wingspan	141 feet. 3 inches (43.1m)
Height	27 feet 9 inches (8.5m)
Wing area	1,736 square feet (161.3 square meters)
Empty weight	74,500 pounds (33,800kg)
Loaded weight	120,000 pounds (54,000kg)
Maximum takeoff weight	133,500 pounds (60,560kg)
Powerplant	4 Wright R3350-23 turbosupercharged radial engines, 2,200 h.p. (1,640kW) each
Zero-lift drag coeffficient	0.0241
Drag area	41.16 square feet (3.82 square meters)
Aspect ratio	11.50
Maximum speed	357 m.p.h. (310knots, 574km/h)
Cruising speed	220 m.p.h. (190 knots, 170km/h)
Stall speed	105 m.p.h. (91 knots, 170km/hr)
Combat radius	3,250 miles (2,800 nautical miles, 5,230km)
Ferry range	5,600 miles (4,900 nautical miles, 9,000km)
Service ceiling	33,600 ft (10,200m)
Rate of climb	900 feet per minute (4.5 meters per second)
Wing loading	69.12 pounds per square foot (337kg per square meter)
Power/mass	0.073 h.p/lb. (121 W/kilogram)
Lift-to-drag ratio	16.8
Armament	12 x .50 caliber (12.7mm) M2 Browning machine guns in remote controlled turrets. 1 x 20mm M2 cannon in tail (later eliminated) Bomb capacity: 20,000 pounds (9,000kg) capacity

14 AUG. 45
HIKARI NAVAL ARSENAL

Mission No. 325, targeting the Japanese naval arsenal at Hikari, took place on the last day of combat in the war. (40th Bomb Group Collection)

Toward the end of the war we were told the nickname for the 40th was "The Kagu Tsuchi Bomb Group." Who suggested the name, dreamed it up or approved it we had no idea. Kagu Tsuchi was the name of a mythical Japanese fire god who, in antiquity, had sworn to return some day and destroy Japan by fire. Frankly, none of us were impressed. True, a very substantial part of Japan had been destroyed by fire but we felt a rather personal, proprietary interest in the deed. General LeMay, who devised and instituted the low level

massive fire bombing of Japanese cities, was the initiating party. He may have had our total respect and admiration but we didn't think anyone attributed any godlike characteristics to him – unless it was some rank-happy staff person.

After Iwo Jima was captured, it became a much used emergency stop for B-29s that had encountered problems over Japan or were running short of fuel. As a regular fueling spot for recon missions, Iwo greatly extended the time that could be spent over Japan. Iwo

113

500-pound High Explosive (HE) bombs sit ready for loading aboard a 468th BG B-29 at Pengshan, Sichuan Province, China (Base A-7). The B-29 could carry a maximum of 10,000 pounds of bombs internally. (Ernie McDowell)

also became the Base for a group of P-51 fighters which performed escort service for the B-29s and were very effective in keeping Japanese fighters at bay. The P-51s were also able to do low-level attacks on Japanese air fields, trains and other targets of opportunity. We were always delighted to see them alongside.

December 1944 was the 40th's worst day for losses. A bombing mission consisting of 35 aircraft to Rangoon, Burma lost four aircraft and crews. Seven aircraft sustained heavy damage. At least two crews were able to bail out of their damaged aircraft and became Japanese prisoners of war. The crews were imprisoned from that date until the following May when British ground troops recaptured Rangoon. One of the author's very good friends, Bobby Shanks, who was pilot of one of the lost aircraft, and later resided in the Dallas suburb of Grand Prairie, swore it was only the dream of getting home to eat homemade ice cream again that kept his hopes alive.

The cause of the mission losses was one of those stupid ideas or experiments that can only be hatched in wartime. Some armament officer, or some target analyst, thought it would be a good idea to use a mixed load of bombs for better effect on target. Rather than carrying only 500-pound bombs or only 1,000-pounders, or any bombs all of the same type, someone had the idea that a mixed load might get better results and orders to do so for the Rangoon mission were issued. There was substantial protest at all levels, but the orders stuck. Over target, on bomb release, the difference in air flow around the bombs caused one or more of the bombs to collide. The resulting explosion, not Japanese action, was the cause of the loss.

In accordance with Bobby Shanks's instructions, his crewmembers were to bail out while he and Fletcher [his copilot] attempted to continue control of the aircraft. All the crew exited per his instructions, however, as the last crewman dropped out thought the forward hatch the hatch slammed shut and tempora6_ly prevented their bailout. After they controlled their panic they were able to pry the hatch door open again and escape the aircraft. All the crew survived the bailout but were immediately captured by the Japanese and were imprisoned in Rangoon.

Each of the crewmen was individually interrogated by Japanese intelligence. One of the crewmen suffered an arm injury during the bailout requiring that his arm be surgically removed. This was promptly done – without anesthesia! Another crewman refused to turn over his wife's picture from his billfold, resulting in a severe beating and the picture was forcefully removed. Another crewman, during his interrogation, reached across his interrogator's desk, picked up the cigarette the interrogator was smoking and took several puffs before he, too, was beaten to unconsciousness. He was then sentenced to death before a firing squad. Taken out of his cell the next morning and standing before the firing squad the interrogator, for reasons unknown, relented and the crewman was returned to his cell where he remained until liberated by British forces in May 1945.

During their imprisonment, food consisted primarily of boiled rice plus such insects as they could catch and boil with the rice. In one instance they were able to construct a string loop from an item of clothing, place it on the cell's open window and catch a bird which had landed on the window. The three inmates of the cell then boiled the bird with their next rice meal – a real treat which the three of them shared.

On one early mission after our arrival in India, some B-29s were returning to base via Burma when they were jumped by a flight of British Beaufighters. We lost one B-29. Dreadfully sorry old boy! But no explanation reached us.

There were emergency air fields located around the perimeter of Japanese occupied areas where the B-29s could land if necessary. Some were so much "emergency" that a B-29 could only land. Once down it couldn't take off and had to be destroyed. We also had procedures for crews, who had to bail out, to contact Chinese personnel to assist them in returning to our bases. Some such Chinese personnel were even in Japanese occupied territory.

One unexpected and unknown benefit of our recon missions came to our attention from a POW who had been imprisoned in Japan early in the war. The ex-POW attended one of our reunions and was asked to make a few formal remarks. He did so and one of his comments was that from the first day they saw a lone, high flying B-29 recon aircraft `they (the POW's) regained their hope that some day the war would end and they would be rescued. After that first one B-29 recon the POW's saw, they began counting the increasing frequency, then the bomb formations, and finally, the use of P-51 escorts and knew that each one brought the day of freedom closer.

The longest mission that the author flew in terms of hours was unplanned. I was assigned to do a mission to cover the length of the Mekong River from northern Thailand to Saigon then north up the Indo-China coast past Cam Ranh Bay. Normal time for the mission would have been about 18 hours. Two hours into the mission the flight engineer reported he was unable to transfer fuel from the bomb bay tanks to the wing tanks. We returned to Chakulia, transferred all my camera equipment and film supplies to another aircraft and departed again. Flying time for the full mission was over 22 hours. But with briefing, reloading the substitute aircraft and debriefing, it took up almost 30 hours total. Tails were dragging that night.

Because our missions were almost never less that fifteen hours, we were supplied K-rations for snacks and cases of canned fruit juices for liquid – along with bottled water. K-rations, for the knowledge of current gourmands, came in a box about five inches wide, ten inches long and one and a half inches thick. It contained a tin of canned spam, or ham and eggs, or cheese, or some other unknown or unmentionable food product. (Ham and eggs were tolerable. Actually, when you were hungry enough, it was all tolerable). Always included was a package of biscuits or crackers, a chocolate or fruit bar (the chocolate was fortified with some grade of mortar to keep it from melting in the tropics). Also included was a four-cigarettte package with matches, chewing gum, and a mini-roll of toilet paper. There was also a package of powdered lemonade, or similar, drink mix. So few K-rations were eaten that we thought

Immediately after the end of the war, B-29s took on a new role: delivering urgently needed supplies to Allied POWs in Japan and other areas still under Japanese control.

some B-29s returned to the States at war's end carrying many of the same K-ration packages that had been stowed aboard them when they left the factory. The fruit juices were okay and, if any tomato or V8 juices were left at the end of the mission, The author took them with him for breakfast when he slept in – or for bloody marys. At Tinian, sandwiches and coffee joined the menus. One of the other mission supplies was Benzedrine tablets which were to be popped to keep us awake. (Some crewmen even returned from missions slightly wired).

Clifton Nickerson, Rolla Kehrman, and Roger Stook check out their Superfortress. (National Museum of the United States Air Force)

115

Killed In Action

James Abernathy, Jr.
Ralph W. Allen
Roy B. Allen
Byron E. Angevine
George P. Appignani
Edwin G. Baetjer, II
Cleo A. Baker
Henry B. Baker
Laverne V. Bauer
Elliott W. Beidler, Jr.
Howard A. Betz
Lawrence J. Bilon
Theodore A. Birkmaier
William T. Blank
Norman A. Brothers
Robert L. Brush
Jacob W. Bruzos, Jr.
Irving Burness
Russell A. Butterworth
Arthur A. Carnes, Jr.
Edward E. Cassidy
Mansel R. Clark
Lawrence E. Cole
Robert W. Conway
John G. Cornwell
Chester L. Cummins
Robert E. Dalton
John D. Dangerfield
Charles F. Denson
James J. Dignan
Roger G. DiLollo
George Dirkinsha
Owen P. Donehue
Ed Donnelly
William L. Douglas
Alfred F. Eiken
Ed Elefant
Sol Fishman
Robert H. Fitzpatrick
John F. Forhan
Henry W. Frees, J.
Charles C. Fulton
Elwyn C. Gardner
Irvin B Gaver
Howard L. Gerber
Edward A. Gisburne, Jr.
Edwin R. Glass
Clements E. Gorman
Elmo W. Gray
Solomon H. Groner
Robert "Tiny" Gunns
Walter R. Gustaveson
James D. Haddow
Stacey B. Hall
August A. Harmison
Ronald A. Harte
Joseph W. Harvey
Richard P. Haynes
Paul W. Heard
Vernon L. Henning

Norman E. Henninger
Hershell J. Hill
John M. Hodges, Jr.
Theodore E. Houck
William G. Houston
James R. James
Francis R. Jelacic
Norman E. Johnson
Arthur H. Jordon
Harvey L. Kantlehner
Adolph C. Katzbeck
John B. Keller
Leonard Kwiatkowski
Thomas W. Lacy
Charles L. Lancaster
Harry O. Lee, Jr.
Richard H. Lemin
Robert A. Linton
Martin J. Long
David Lustig
Clement W. Lyman
John J. Madeline
Algernon Matulis
James M. McCarthy
Leon I. McCutcheon
Lyman F. McGhee
Bob L. Miller
Harry C. Miller
Maxine B. Montgomery
Henry Morgan
William L. Mueller
Joseph N. Murphy
John A. Myers, Jr.
Charles A. Olauson
Bernard L. Page
Andrew C. Papson
Charles O. Patterson
Jess V. Pierce
William S. Plattenburg
Samuel Polensky
Clark N. Rauth
Ira B. Redmon
Allen J. Rice
Jack L. Riggs
Fred J. Riley
Edward H. Ringgold, III
Earl O. Rogers
Frank E. Rutledge
John Scharli
Al Schaumaker
Alvin R. Schwanz
Leldon Sheal
Grady W. Shiflet
Murr E. Skousen
James A. Slattery, Jr.
Fred J. Smerke
Theodore T. Smith
Vernon D. Smith
Halloran E. Soules
Leon H. South

40th Group Honor Roll

Killed In Action

Harry Spack
Robert E. Spain
Elmer E. Stilfield
Neuman H. Taylor
Dorsey B. Thomas
Wayne W. Treimer
James A. Vermillion
Richard L. Vickery
Albert Vlahovic

John A. Von Gonten
Roy E. Wagner
Paul C. Wilfinger
George H. Williamson
William D. Wilson
Wilbur J. Wortman
Alex N. Zamry
Arthur S. Zinstein

Missing In Action

Carl E. Blackwell
James Brennan
Herbert E. Bridges
John Carney
Carson E. Cole
Jesse J. Cotton
Harry V. Crawford
William P. Donelan
Richard O. Dugas
John A. Eudy
Robert J. Fancher
William R. Fesler
Alvin K. Fiedler
Martin B. Fisk
William J. Gabriel
John G. Gettler
George W. Hanger
Edward S. Hornyia
Vern H. Hunnell
Walter Ingalls
Max. S. Kendzur
Oliver M. Kidd
William Kintis
Lewis C. Landauer

Richard P. Leckliter
Douglas M. Lyon
Melvin S. March
Robert A. McCormick
Paul F. McKee
James E. Miller
James Moffit
Cecil P. Monahan
John E. Montero
Jose J. Morales
Donald L. Newhall
L.D.E. Powers
William A. Pruitt
Aubrey J. Richard
Bernard Roth
Leon Schneider
Raymond G. Schuette
Monroe Stein
Marvin Stockett
William T. Stone
Edward R. Walter
William H. Webster
Joseph R. Willis

Prisoner Of War

Arnold Basche
Cameron Benedict
Elmer H. Bertsch, Jr. Died in Tokyo Kempei Tai Headquarters
Richard Brooks
Marion B. Burke
Frederick Carlton
Julian Cochran
Lionel F. Coffin
Robert E. Derrington
Stanton L. Dow
Francis R. Edwards
Galpin Etherington
Harold Fletcher
Harlan B. Green
Richard M. Hurley – executed
Dale L. Johnson
Watson Lankford
Norman Larson
Walter Lentz
Joseph Levine

Ferrell Majors
James B. McGiven
Cornelius C. Meyer
Delbert W. Miller
Richard Montgomery
Walter W. Oestreich
Nicholas Oblesby
David Parmelee
Chester E. Paul
Patrick E. Pellecchia
Enrico Pisterzi
Carl Rieger
Elgie L. Robertson – executed
Robert Shanks
Lewis Summers
Karnik Tomasian
Edward F. Trinker, Jr.
William J. Walsh
Charles W. Whitley

The 40th Bomb Group Association reaquaints itself with the B-29, visiting *Fifi* in New Orleans in 1980. (40th Bomb Group Collection)

Fifi, the Commemorative Air Force's B-29, escaped the frustrations of the Battle of Kansas and subsequent combat.

Fifi was manufactured in 1945 at Boeing's Renton, Washington, plant. She was delivered to the AAF at the Smoky Hill Air Base in Salina, Kansas on 31 July 1945, A late bloomer, *Fifi* did not see wartime service. Following acceptance by the AAF *Fifi* became a part of the Strategic Air Command. In 1946 she was utilized as a training aircraft, then placed in storage, probably at Davis Monthan AAB in Arizona. In 1952 she was re-modified into standard bomber configuration for use in the Korean War as part of the 310th Bomb Wing at Smoky Hill AAB. In August 1953 she was returned to status as a trainer at the AAF Air Training Command at Randolph Field in San Antonio. Three years later, in 1956 she was transferred to the US Navy and placed in storage at the China Lake Weapons Center and remained there until discovered, and rescued, for the Confederate Air Force by a CAF search group headed by Col. Victor Agather.

The story of the founding of the Commemorative Air Force has been well documented. Suffice to say here is that the goal of the CAF was, and remains, to find, maintain in flyable condition and historically preserve those US, aircraft which were responsible for carrying U.S. Air Power to victory in WW II. In accordance with that goal the CAF reached a decision in 1966 to seek out and obtain a B-29 Superfortress.

Early contacts with the USAF revealed that, to its knowledge, there were no remaining B-29s. Some publicity followed which attracted the attention of an airline pilot who reported that he had flown over an installation of some type in the California desert which seemed to contain some B-29 aircraft. Further investigation by the CAF did reveal there were a number of B-29s at the China Lake Naval Storage facility and were to serve as test targets for Naval gunners. More digging determined there was a possibility one of those aircraft could be obtained by the CAF.

A group of ex-WWII CAF members then joined forces to select and obtain one of the China Lake B-29s. The search and rescue for *Fifi* [then unnamed] required months of negotiation, patience and a substantial dollar investment to obtain and deliver the B-29 to CAF headquarters then located in Harlingen, TX. A group of members headed by Mr. Agather funded and worked tirelessly to bring the B-29 to flyable condition. Mr. Agather's persistence with time and money eventually brought the B-29 to not only flyable condition but also to FAA approval to appear at public events and provide public participation via rides in the aircraft, In response, and to honor Mr. Agather's contribution to the aircraft it would carry the name *Fifi,* his wife and the original *Fifi.*

In 1980 the 40th Bomb Group Assn. held the first of many Group reunions at New Orleans. Carter McGregor, one of the original 40th Group pilots and a veteran of B-29 combat missions in China, Burma and India had also become a CAF member and was type-rated to fly *Fifi.* Carter volunteered to fly *Fifi* to New Orleans to be part of that initial reunion. The result, obviously, was a the development of a close relationship between CAF, *Fifi* and the 40th.

In 1992 Boeing volunteered to overhaul and virtually rebuild *Fifi.* At the conclusion of Boeing's rejuvenation of the aircraft, the four original units of the 20th Bomber Command held simultaneous reunions in Seattle to honor Boeing's work as well as to see *Fifi's* flybys. U.S. Defense Secretary Dick Cheney flew to Seattle to participate in the event.

Most recently, the original Wright-Cyclone engines were replaced with more newly developed engines to allow ongoing public participations by *Fifi.*

Mr. Agather's contribution to the B-29's development and success in WWII was extremely important to that program and is worthy of mention in the short biography which follows. His story of the "Battle of Kansas" is illustrative of his contribution to the development.

Victor was born in Montana but migrated to the east coast in the 1930s. He obtained an MBA in Finance and became an employee of a Wall Street investment/financial firm. During this period he also

The Commemorative Air Force's B-29, *Fifi* was manufactured at Boeing's Renton, Washington, plant in 1945. (40th Bomb Group Collection)

B-29 Superfortresses show their muscle in flight past Mt. Fujiyama, Japan, in 1945.

joined the Army Air Corps [AAC], was taught to fly and became a member of the AAC "Ready Reserve". His career developed as a talented management expert in the world of finance. In 1940 he met and married the lady known as *Fifi*.

At the beginning of WW 2, Victor was called to active duty by the AAC and, as a result of his talented management skills, was assigned by the AAC to the developing B-29 program. The B-29 program was already showing many of the problems which were to plague the program throughout early production and combat periods.

Victor's reporting of program problems, and recommendations for solving those problems, went to the highest levels of the AAC. As a result it was determined by the AAC high command that he should be detached from the AAC and assigned to the B-29 program in a civilian capacity in order to quicken bringing the program to a successful conclusion. His own story of the "Battle of Kansas" is well documented in previous pages of this book.

Following the "Battle of Kansas" Victor followed with B-29 activities as a part of the China, Burma, India Theater of Operations as well as the Mariana Is. In September 1945, with the ending of the War, Victor was returned to the US, relieved of his AAC [by then established as an independent Army Air Force] and returned to his Wall Street firm. His wartime activity in the AAF was restored as

was his rank of rank of Major. Subsequently, he remained a formal part of the AAF Reserve until normal retirement as a bird Colonel.

Within the business world Victor, and his wife *Fifi*, moved to Mexico City where they remained for the balance of his business life During that period Victor developed, for historical purposes, an interest in finding, and maintaining in flyable condition, a last remaining B-29. He had also developed a relationship with the Confederate Air Force, the forerunner of the Commemorative Air Force, and it was their combined efforts that led to the finding and resurrection of the B-29 which was to become known as *Fifi*.

Source Credits

Jeffery B. Greene and Xu Fan, *Fei hu de paoxiao – When tigers roared,* Kunming: Yunnan Jiaoyu Publishing House, 2005. (In Chinese).

Otis Hays, *Home From Siberia.* College Station, Texas: A&M Press, 1990

Aleksandr Alekseyevich Pobozhy, *Dorogami Taigi* (*Roads Through the Taiga*), Moscow: Molodaya Gvardiya Publishing House, 1974. (In Russian). Excerpted in *Soviet Life,* February 1975.

J. Ivan Potts, *Remembrance of War.* Shelbyville, Tennessee 37160: J. Ivan Potts & Associates, 1995.